Kirtley Library
Columbia College
8th and Rogers
Columbia, MO. 65201

THE INDIAN IN AMERICAN LITERATURE

BY
ALBERT KEISER

OCTAGON BOOKS

A division of Farrar, Straus and Giroux

New York   1975

Copyright, 1933 by Oxford University Press, New York, Inc.
Copyright renewed 1961 by Mrs. Albert Keiser

Reprinted 1970
by special arrangement with Oxford University Press, Inc.

Second Octagon printing 1975

OCTAGON BOOKS
A DIVISION OF FARRAR, STRAUS & GIROUX, INC.
19 Union Square West
New York, N. Y. 10003

LIBRARY OF CONGRESS CATALOG CARD NUMBER: 72-96160
ISBN 0-374-94541-1

Manufactured by Braun-Brumfield, Inc.
Ann Arbor, Michigan

Printed in the United States of America

TO
HAMLIN GARLAND
FRIEND OF THE AMERICAN INDIAN

PREFACE

From Captain John Smith's *A True Relation* in 1608 down to Edna Ferber's recent portrait of the Osage in *Cimarron* the American Indian has furnished inspiration to a multitude of writers. The English speaking settlers of the North American continent from the very beginning were confronted by natives who, alarmed by the inroads of the newcomers, began to dispute every advance of the palefaces. This westward movement of a virile race from the Atlantic seaboard to the shores of the Pacific across the hunting-grounds of the most diverse tribes has left its imprint in the records of those who by main force or superior cunning succeeded in wresting the country from the original owners of the soil. Naturally the red actors of this colorful drama play a large part in the literature that grew up around the most significant events, especially as the life and character of the natives also were a source of never-failing interest. No wonder then that the books dealing with the aborigines are legion, touching upon every conceivable phase of the subject. Much of this material the general reader may, however, safely ignore, engrossing as the study may appear to the specialist and the literary historian. For not a few of the dusky figures are very distant relatives of the red man, and bear as little resemblance to the original as the tobacco store brave to a live Indian. Time has accordingly consigned these works to a merciful oblivion, and it would be serving no useful purpose to arouse the sleepers from their well-deserved rest and parade them in public.

From out of this great mass of material, good, indifferent, and bad, the author has sifted the truly significant, guided occasionally by tribal, geographical, and historical considerations. It is with the Indian portraits painted by the major figures in American literature that this book is chiefly concerned, not with the forgotten works of minor writers. And though the Indian plays a prominent part only for comparatively short periods, it is significant and perhaps appropriate that the former owners of this country should have been immortalized in what many critics have proclaimed the most original American poem and the most vital and popular prose fiction our nation has so far produced.

It is a pleasant duty to acknowledge the help received from not a few quarters. In particular should be mentioned Prof. Raymond Adams of the University of North Carolina, Prof. Ernest E. Leisy of the Southern Methodist University, Prof. Arthur H. Quinn of the University of Pennsylvania, and the Dean of American Letters, Hamlin Garland, all of whom have read parts of the manuscript and offered valuable suggestions. The staffs of the libraries of the University of Colorado, the University of North Carolina, the University of Pennsylvania, and especially of the Pierpont Morgan Library and of the Library of Congress have been unfailing in their courtesy and assistance, all of which is hereby gratefully acknowledged.

ALBERT KEISER

HICKORY, N. C., December 7, 1932.

CONTENTS

CHAPTER		PAGE
	PREFACE	V
I.	THE POCAHONTAS LEGEND	1
II.	PURITAN WRATH AND INDIAN CAPTIVITIES	10
III.	THE INDIAN COMES INTO HIS OWN	21
IV.	FICTION DISCOVERS THE NATIVE	33
V.	FATE FROWNS UPON MISCEGENATION	38
VI.	IN PAULDING'S HUMOROUS VEIN	46
VII.	THE NATIVES THROUGH THE EYES OF AN OPTIMIST	52
VIII.	THE INDIAN DRAMA	65
IX.	JAMES FENIMORE COOPER	101
X.	STARK REALISM ON KENTUCKY'S DARK AND BLOODY GROUND	144
XI.	SIMMS' ROMANTIC NATURALISM	154
XII.	A PROMISE UNFULFILLED AND A MELANCHOLY FATE	175
XIII.	THE ATOTARHO OF THE IROQUOIS	181
XIV.	HIAWATHA — THE DAWN OF CULTURE	189
XV.	THOREAU — FRIEND OF THE NATIVE	209
XVI.	THE ROMANCE OF JOAQUIN MILLER	233
XVII.	THE MISSION INDIANS AS VIEWED BY A WOMAN	249
XVIII.	TRAGEDY STALKS AMONG THE CLIFF DWELLERS	253
XIX.	THE STRUGGLE FOR THE BISON PASTURES OF THE PLAINS	264
XX.	TRAVELLING THE WHITE MAN'S ROAD	279
XXI.	CONCLUSION	293
	SELECTED BIBLIOGRAPHY	300
	INDEX	307

CHAPTER I

THE POCAHONTAS LEGEND

It is deeply significant that the Indian should have made his appearance in American literature at the very beginning of the first permanent English settlement in the New World. Unwittingly the first " American " author originated a literary tradition both vital and far-reaching. A supposed incident during the early months of the existence of Jamestown, the famous rescue of Captain John Smith (1580?–1631) by the " Princess " Pocahontas, furnished the material out of which were later woven romantic designs, and a veritable deluge of poems and dramas descended upon the reading and play-going public. For this reason alone, if for no other, the story that made Pocahontas the most romantic character in colonial history merits detailed treatment.

Somewhat contrary to expectations, it was at least fourteen years after the supposed event that a report of it was given to the world. In the second edition of his *New England Trials,* which appeared in 1622 after the fearful massacre of the settlers of Virginia, the ambitious captain, chafing under his enforced retirement, contrasts his own energetic measures in dealing with the savages with the deplorable weakness of the officials then in charge: " For wronging a souldier but the value of a penny, I have caused *Powhatan* send his owne men to *James* Town to receive their punishment at my discretion. It is true in our greatest extremitie they shot me, slue three of my men, and by the folly of them that fled tooke me prisoner; yet God made *Pocahontas* the Kings Daughter the meanes to deliuer me: & there-by taught me to know their treacheries to preserve the rest." If we waive the authenticity of a letter Smith claims to have written to the Queen in 1616, a claim that at present rests solely upon the authority of his *Generall Historie,* this is the earliest and rather general statement of a supposed occurrence of which he was soon to give more colorful details.

Only two years later, in 1624, these details appeared in *The Generall Historie of Virginia, New England & the Summer Isles*. Already in the dedication to the Duchess of Richmond and Lennox, whose gracious hand " hath given birth to the publication of this Narration," Smith rather extravagantly remarks: " In the utmost of many extremities, the blessed Pokahontas, the great Kings daughter of Virginia, oft saved my life," an assertion hardly substantiated by the narrative itself. There he speaks in a rather detailed manner of his capture and his effort to conciliate the Indians by giving a compass to their leader, the brother of the Powhatan. " When he demonstrated by the Globelike Jewell, the roundness of the earth, and skies, the sphere of the Sunne, Moone, and Starres, and how the Sunne did chase the night round about the world continually; the greatnesse of the Land and Sea, the diversitie of Nations, varietie of complexions, and how we were to them Antipodes, and many other such like matters, they all stood as amazed with admiration. Notwithstanding, within an hour after they tyed him to a tree, and as many as could stand about him prepared to shoot him, but the King holding up the Compass in his hand, they all laid downe their bows and Arrowes, and in triumphant manner led him to Orapaks, where he was after their manner kindly feasted, and well used."

For three successive days, Indians performing symbolic rites or dressed as devils tried to frighten him. " At last they brought him to Meronocomo, where was Powhatan their Emperor. Here more than two hundred of those grim Courtiers stood wondering at him, as he had beene a monster; till Powhatan and his trayne had put themselves in their greatest braveries. Before a fire upon a seat like a bedstead, he sat covered with a great robe, made of Rarowcun skinnes, and all the tayles hanging by. On either hand did sit a young wench of 16 or 18 yeares, and along on each side of the house, two rowes of men, and behind them as many women, with all their heads and shoulders painted red; many of their heads bedecked with the white downe of Birds; but every one with something: and a great chayne of white beads about their necks."

So far Captain Smith's description of Powhatan and his court differs only in minor respects from that given in *A True Relation* of 1608. In the following passage, however, appears the much fought over rescue. " At his entrance before the King, all the people gave a great shout. The Queene of Appamatuck was appointed to bring him water to wash his hands, and another brought him a bunch of feathers, in stead of a Towell to dry them: having feasted him after their best barbarous manner they could, a long consultation was held, but the conclusion was, two great stones were brought before Powhatan: then as many as could layd hands on him, dragged him to them, and thereon laid his head, and being ready with their clubs, to beat out his braines, Pocahontas the Kings dearest daughter, when no intreaty could prevaile, got his head in her armes, and laid her owne upon his to save him from death: whereat the Emperour was contented he should live to make him hatchets, and her bells, beads, and copper; for they thought him aswel of all occupations as themselves. For the King himselfe will make his owne robes, shooes, bowes, arrowes, pots; plant, hunt, or doe any thing so well as the rest."

After several days, a ceremonial reconciliation was effected, and Smith sent home to Jamestown with twelve guides. Instead of the two great guns (demi-culverins) and the grindstone which had been promised but proved to be too heavy, the Indians, frightened by the discharge of the cannon, were content with toys and other presents. The friendship of the chief's daughter fortunately continued. For " now even once in foure or five dayes, Pocahontas with her attendants, brought him so much provision, that saved many of their lives, that els for all this had starved with hunger." According to Smith, the knowledge of abundant provisions being available and, especially, the generosity of Pocahontas, revived the dead spirits of the colonists, who in consequence abandoned all fears. Though several other references to Pocahontas during Smith's stay in Virginia are found in the *Generall Historie,* none of them is of any importance.

In *A True Relation,* written by Smith on the ground in 1608 and published in London the same year, not a word is said of Powhatan's hostile attitude during the captain's imprisonment and

Pocahontas' intervention. Otherwise, the account does not differ greatly in essentials, if we remember that Smith never was a stickler for exact details. Practically all the seeming discrepancies can be explained by the unprejudiced, except that either Smith's memory or love of exaggeration was at fault when in the earlier report he makes his escort consist of four men who in the later account increase to twelve. Pocahontas appears in the former only toward the end, with never a word about any previous service. Powhatan, learning that the English detained certain Indians, " sent his Daughter, a child of tenne yeares old, which not only for feature, countenance, & proportion, much exceedeth any of the rest of his people, but for wit, and spirit, the only Nonpareil of his Country." As an expression of the chief's sincerity and kindness, the " child, which he most esteemed," proceeded to Jamestown with a messenger, and not only was the release of the prisoners granted, but in addition Pocahontas was rewarded " with such trifles as contented her," certainly a very satisfactory conclusion of the mission for all concerned.

However, even with Smith's return to England in 1609 the relationship did not come to an end, for seven years later the " Lady Rebecca " was the God-sent means of bringing Smith back into the limelight he so much loved. In 1612 Pocahontas had been lured aboard ship and for some time held prisoner. After some hostilities between the parties, she finally succeeded in concluding a lasting peace between the colonists and her father, a peace which proved of incalculable value to the settlers, who without such respite and help probably would have been wiped out. But " long before this, Master John Rolfe, an honest Gentleman, and of good behaviour, had beene in love with Pocahontas, and she with him." Her father seems to have been well pleased with the prospective marriage, for at the wedding he was represented by deputy.

Not only did the young couple rejoice in conjugal love, but the dusky bride, after some preliminary instruction, also renounced her country's idolatry, confessed the faith in Christ, and was baptized. She was duly groomed for her appearance in England, becoming very formal and civil after the English manner and speaking her husband's language acceptably. When the party on its arrival at Plymouth June 12, 1616, especially Lady Rebecca and her child, made a considerable stir, Captain John Smith hastened to link his name with the celebrity and bask in the warmth of reflected glory. In his *Generall Historie* he claims that he wrote and sent to the queen a little book in order to acquaint her majesty with the qualities of his protégée. In the "abstract" of the pamphlet inserted in the history he speaks of "Pocahontas, the Kings most deare and wel-beloved daughter, being but a childe of twelve or thirteene yeeres of age, whose compassionate pitiful heart, of my desperate estate, gave me much cause to respect her." He tells how "after some six weeks fatting amongst those Salvage Courtiers, at the minute of my execution, she hazarded the beating out of her owne braines to save mine, and not onely that, but so prevailed with her father, that I was safely conducted to James towne, where I found about eight and thirtie miserable poore and sick creatures, to keepe possession of all those large territories of Virginia, such was the weaknesse of this poor Commonwealth, as had the Salvages not fed us, we directly had starved." He recites other instances of her services and is fulsome in his praise of her as the instrument that preserved the colony from death, famine, and utter confusion. After Lady Rebecca had been fêted and presented at court, she embarked for the return voyage to Virginia, but, in the words of Smith, "it hath pleased God at Gravesend to take this young Lady to his mercie, where shee made not more sorrow for her unexpected death, than joy to the beholders, to heare and to see her to make so religious and godly an end."

For more than two hundred years Captain Smith's story of his dramatic rescue by the chief's daughter remained unchallenged. When, however, in 1860 Charles Deane edited a newly discovered manuscript entitled "A Discourse of Virginia" written by Edward M. Wingfield, the first President of the Virginia Colony, he noted the fact that no mention is made of the famous incident, which is likewise omitted from *A True Relation* of 1608 and in the narrative of his companions appearing in the Appendix of *A Map of Virginia* of 1612, although in neither "is any attempt made to conceal his valient exploits and hair-breadth escapes." In view of these facts he drew the conclusion: "No one can doubt that the earlier narrative contains the truer statement, and that the passage last cited is one of the few or many embellishments with which Smith with his strong love of the marvellous, was disposed to garnish the stories of his early adventures, and with which he or his editors were tempted to adorn particularly his later works." The silence of Ralph Hamor, who as secretary of the colony came to Virginia in 1610 and whose history of 1615 is largely devoted to Pocahontas, was to Mr. Deane equally significant. When in 1866 he edited Smith's *A True Relation of Virginia,* he repeated and re-enforced his former charge. He pointed out that the account of the capture and release of Smith had been written by him on the spot, and that no story inconsistent with this had been told on his return to Jamestown might be inferred from Wingfield, who in his version says nothing of Pocahontas. And the only other contemporary account of Smith's capture, written by his companions and published in 1612 in the Appendix of *A Map of Virginia,* naturally repeats what the captain had told on his return; but though it is a continued eulogy of Smith, the reader will not find the least indication on which to found the romantic story.

Other historians and writers were quick to accept the opinion of Deane brushing aside Smith's claim as a mere fabrication, and for a long time it became the fashion to speak of the " Pocahontas Legend." However, not a few, and among them some of the best historians, have risen in defense of Smith. True, at first blush the doughty captain's case looks bad; but not as bad as some would have us believe. The absence of any references in Smith's first book proves nothing, for the settlers were expressly enjoined from " writing any letters of anything that may discourage others." Even if Smith had mentioned Powhatan's hostility and Pocahontas' help, that information was not to be brought to the attention of the public. As a matter of fact, Smith's long letter was published without his knowledge or permission. The editor J. H. remarks in his preface: " Happening upon this relation by chance, as I take it, at second or third hand, I thought good to publish it." He expressly indicates omissions by the further statement: " Somewhat more was by him the author written, which being as

I thought fit to be private, I would not adventure to make public." Some have even thought that Smith did not at first tell his companions about the adventure, as the probability of a woman's favor was apt to cause desertions to the Indians, and he himself might be accused of forming an alliance with the natives, a charge not to be lightly taken in view of the fierce quarrels among the leaders.

Even if Wingfield knew of the happening, his silence as a bitter enemy of Smith is to be expected. Having been fined £200 for slander in bringing the charge of mutiny against the strongheaded captain, he almost certainly would omit reciting an occurrence reflecting credit upon one he bitterly hated. The injunction against unfavorable reports may have remained in force a number of years, and Hamor's work does not go into the details of Smith's stay in Virginia, but covers mainly the period subsequent to 1610. It is true that Smith's supposed letter or booklet to the queen in 1616 rests entirely upon the authority of his *Generall Historie,* but nevertheless it is somewhat extraordinary that Purchas and others who were in a position to know the facts should not have challenged his statements if he had deliberately uttered falsehoods. No attempts were evidently made to discredit Smith's narrative. As John Fiske has pointed out, within a year of the publication of the history, George Percy, one of the original company in Jamestown, wrote a pamphlet for the express purpose of picking Smith's work to pieces and discrediting it in the eyes of the public. " If Smith had not told his comrades of the Pocahontas incident as soon as he had escaped from the Powhatan's clutches, if he had kept silent on the subject for years, Percy could not have failed to know the fact and would certainly have used it as a weapon."

There is of course no question that Smith as a lady's man saw a fine opportunity to link his name with a famous member of the fair sex, which according to his statements in numerous instances had come to his rescue. Thus in the dedication of the *Generall Historie* where he asks " so piercing and so glorious an Eye, as your Grace, to view these poore, ragged lines," he directs attention to the fact that heretofore honorable and virtuous ladies have offered him rescue and protection in his greatest dangers. When he was a slave to the Turks, the beauteous Lady Tragabigzanda did all she could to secure him; when he overcame the Bashaw of Nalbrits in Tartaria, the charitable Lady Callamata supplied his necessities; when he escaped the cruelty of pirates and most furious storms, a long time alone in a small boat at sea, and driven ashore in France, the good Lady Madam Chanoyes beautifully assisted him. No wonder that he also mentions that the "blessed Pokahontas" oft saved his life, giving later in the work itself the details of the one much fought over rescue.

Whatever may be adduced in favor of Smith's veracity in general and in regard to the Pocahontas incident in particular, falls still short of being entirely convincing, for a number of troublesome points remain unexplained and inexplicable. But to brand the captain's statements falsehoods and to call him a liar leads to difficulties which the unprejudiced investigator in all fairness and justice must avoid. The truth will probably never be known, and as the pros and cons carry about equal weight, judgment may well be suspended. As far as Smith's experience itself is concerned, there is nothing inherently improbable in it; on the contrary, as Fiske remarks, it is precisely in accord with Indian usage. A case rather similar to that of John Smith and Pocahontas occurred in 1528, when John Ortiz, one of the soldiers of Narvaez captured by the natives of Florida, was rescued from a fiery death by the daughter of the chief. Smith's rescue by Pocahontas also would in part explain the close relationship that later existed between the two.

The romantic story of Smith and Pocahontas, true to Indian character and so appealing to human nature, has had a remarkable influence in American literature as the favorite and recurring theme of writers dealing with the Indian. Toward the end of the 18th century the figure of the chief's daughter began to appear in dramas, and during the early part of the following century she became the center of a large number of plays with the rescue of the captain generally forming the climax. The fact that this rescue comes at the beginning, with her later life forming an anti-climax, inconvenienced the playwrights not a little, a difficulty they sought to overcome by various means. Poems and novels also featured the Nonpareil of Virginia who had caught the imagination not only of Smith, but of countless others. If none can be classed as really first rate literature, the large number attest to the widespread interest. With the passing of the Indian drama about 1850, Pocahontas also practically passes as a literary figure. However, as of old, her story perennially fascinates the youthful mind, and of late her romantic person has again been put before the eyes of the public, proof sufficient of the vitality of the intriguing material.

CHAPTER II

PURITAN WRATH AND INDIAN CAPTIVITIES

The bleak shores of New England were less hospitable to the idealization of the Indian than the sunny clime of Virginia. From the very beginning the stern character of the Puritan probably precluded a sympathetic relationship to the race soon to become his opponent and bitter enemy. In his struggle for his very existence the Calvinist who had looked upon the native as a being to be redeemed from the power of Satan soon became satisfied that the enemy of God was to be exterminated at any cost, and that the only good Indian was a dead Indian. In his peculiar religious intolerance and fanaticism he reputedly fell first upon his knees and then upon the aborigines, prompted to do the first in the hope that the second might be more successful.

The altruistic motive as the moving cause of New England colonization has often been unduly emphasized. When we read in the Charter of the Colony of Massachusetts Bay: " To win and to invite the natives of this country to the knowledge and obedience of the only true God and Saviour of mankind and the Christian faith, in our royal intention, and the adventurer's free profession is the principal end of this Plantation," we wonder whether these pious sentiments had not for the time being obscured the economic mainspring prompting nearly all actions. Whatever the royal or other intentions may have been, so much is certain: missionary endeavors on the part of the Puritans are conspicuous mainly by their absence. The noble John Eliot and Roger Williams in no way fairly represent the New England attitude toward the aborigines, who were regarded as fit objects of exploitation and forced to serve as slaves for lack of other help. Soon they became enemies in the eyes of the Pilgrim fathers, who believed that the New World was the promised land which was theirs to possess

PURITAN WRATH AND INDIAN CAPTIVITIES 11

even if every one of the Canaanites perished at the point of the sword.

No outstanding work either of a romantic or realistic nature dealing with the relationship between the settlers and the natives of New England was produced in this period. The stark reality of the earlier chroniclers is hardly ever lit up by a bright spot, except by a grim humor that makes us nowadays shudder. For those early historians told with a frankness bordering on brutality of the slaughter of the natives. The depredations of the newcomers from the first foreshadowed tragic results, though it is likely that sooner or later the struggle for the possession of the country would have begun even without any overt act. But just such an act had occurred shortly before the settlement in 1620, for in 1614 Thomas Hunt, whom Captain Smith had left in charge, had taken away twenty-seven inoffensive Indians. In spite of such highhanded behavior no serious clash threatened at first, since the Pilgrims settled in a region from which the Indians had been swept by the terrible plague of 1616–17, an occurrence which to the English seemed providential. To put it into the words of Johnson: " God cast out the heathen to make room for his people."

However, as soon as the increasing number of the whites made migration to the fertile Connecticut Valley desirable, a conflict known as the Pequot War was precipitated. The high spirited and warlike Pequots naturally resented the intrusion of the whites into their hunting-grounds. Although there may be a difference of opinion as to the rightful ownership of the soil, any fairminded person will accord the natives the right to oppose the further expansion of undesired newcomers. The new England conscience was not troubled by any scruples, for public opinion was practically unanimous in favor of *Christian* rights. Events moved with lightning-like rapidity for those early days, and though the wily chief Sassacus was able to avert personal disaster for some time, the year 1637 marked the extermination of the main Pequot strength at Fort Mystic and the passing of the danger to the settlements.

Among the narratives of the memorable war, those written by

Mason and Underhill are most interesting and illuminating, Mason's account being especially vivid. According to his *Brief History of the Pequot War,* Major John Mason was " a principal Actor therein, as then Chief Captain and Commander of Connecticut Forces." His observations had been penned with no idea of publication, for in his address " To the Judicious Reader " he remarks: " I never had thought that this should have come to the Press, until of late: If I had, I should have endeavored to have put a little more Varnish upon it." So much the better for the reader who is more interested in unvarnished facts than in efforts to embellish or to distort the real happenings.

By the year 1637 about two hundred and fifty English families had settled in the Connecticut Valley. The murder of about thirty persons by the Pequots, though not wholly unprovoked, and their intimidation of other Indians made inevitable the grim determination of the Puritan to root out Sassacus and his band, for otherwise destruction stared the English settlers in the face. When on May 1, 1637, the General Court of Connecticut convened at Hartford, it declared an offensive war against the Indians, levied and provisioned a force of ninety men, and placed the whole under the command of John Mason. The other settlements were quick to come to the rescue of the sister colony: already on April 18 Massachusetts Bay had ordered a levy of one hundred and sixty men, while on June 7 the Plymouth Company also took warlike measures.

Acting with his characteristic vigor and disobeying definite instructions, Mason struck almost at once. The Pequots were gathered in two principal places. As the wily Sassacus held a stronghold farther away and more dangerous to approach, Mason in the hope of easier success singled out the fort at Mystic for his first attack. In all, he was able to marshal seventy-seven white soldiers, only twenty men from Massachusetts Bay having arrived for the expedition. Fortunately, he had succeeded in enlisting sixty Mohegans with their chief Uncas and two hundred Narragansetts, the whole number of supporting Indians later reaching five hundred. The help of these Indians, however, was at first more than doubtful, since at the approach of danger many of the frightened

Narragansetts either fell to the rear or openly deserted. Chief Uncas, whose unfaltering courage Mason highly commends, proved to be of real assistance. To bolster up the flagging spirit of the others, the indomitable white leader admonished the allied natives " that they should by no means fly, and stand at what distance they pleased, and see whether English men would fight or not."

All night long the assembled allies, unsuspected by their enemies, had listened to the merrymaking of the Pequots in their fort. Led by friendly Indians, they approached the stronghold before dawn. After commending themselves to God, the Puritans divided their forces: Captain Mason was to rush the north-east entrance, while Underhill endeavored to make his way from the south. Mason in his narrative gives a graphic description of the attack. According to the original plan the Indians were to be destroyed by the sword, and the plunder was to be saved. And when the surprise attack of the whites threw their enemies into indescribable confusion, an easy victory seemed assured. But as the immense advantage gained by firing the flimsy structures of the Indians flashed upon his mind, Mason accordingly gave that command, thereby abandoning whatever booty might otherwise have been his. The object was accomplished, for he exultingly exclaims: " And indeed such a dreadful Terror let the Almighty fall upon their Spirits, that they would fly from us and run into the very Flames, where many of them perished." When the fort had been thoroughly fired, the soldiers fell back, " while God . . . laughed his Enemies and the Enemies of his People to Scorn, making them as a fiery Oven." Underhill graphically describes the result: " Many were burnt in the fort, both men, women, and children. Others forced out, and came in troops to the Indians, twenty and thirty at a time, which our soldiers received and entertained with the point of the sword. Down fell men, women, and children; those that scaped us, fell into the hands of the Indians that were in the rear of us." Between six and seven hundred Indians perished, while the English loss was confined to two killed and twenty wounded.

In his narrative published the year following the slaughter,

Underhill meets the criticism of unnecessary fury on the part of the English by referring to the wars of David. ' When a people is grown to such a height of blood, and sin against God and man, and all confederates in the action, there he hath no respect to persons, but harrows them and saws them, and puts them to the sword, and the most terriblest death that may be. Sometimes the Scripture declareth women and children must perish with their parents. Sometimes the case alters; but we will not dispute it now. We had sufficient light from the word of God for our proceedings." And Mason rejoices that God had crushed those who were once a terror to their neighbors and who had resolved to destroy " all the English and to Root their very Name out of this Country," a God who had visited their iniquity upon their own heads, " burning them up in the fire of his Wrath, and Dunging the Ground with their Flesh: It was the Lord's Doings, and it is marvellous in our Eyes It is He that hath made his work wonderful, and therefore ought to be remembered."

The blow dealt the Pequots at Fort Mystic involved them in irreparable disaster. They were scattered and became a prey to all their enemies. Hardly a day passed without a head being brought to Windsor or Hartford in return for the reward offered. Their chief Sassacus was drawn into the ruin. He had to flee the ancient hunting-grounds and fell in the same year under the tomahawks of the Mohawks, who were probably eager to take possession of the large quantity of wampum he had carried along in his flight. With his death ended all hope of resistance for the unfortunate Pequots. And as a fitting climax to his book, Mason can break out in this pæan: " Thus we may see, How the Face of God is set against them that do Evil, to cut off the remembrance of them from the Earth. Our Tongue shall talk of thy Righteousness all the Day long; for they are confounded, they are brought to Shame that sought our Hurt! Blessed be the Lord God of Israel, who only doth wondrous Things; and blessed be his holy Name forever: Let the whole Earth be filled with his Glory! Thus the Lord was pleased to smite our Enemies in the hinder Parts, and to give us their Land for an Inheritance: Who remembered us in our low Estate, and redeemed us out of our Enemies Hands:

PURITAN WRATH AND INDIAN CAPTIVITIES 15

Let us therefore praise the Lord for his Goodness and his wonderful Works to the Children of Men!"

By his daring success in the conduct of the expedition, which easily might have turned out differently, Mason became the hero of the war and was enrolled among New England's great men. As a fitting reward of his prowess he was made the Major General of all the forces of Connecticut, a position which he held till his death. According to Thomas Prince, who a century later wrote the introduction to a new edition of Mason's history, " The Rev. Mr. Hooker of Hartford, being desired by the Government in their Name to deliver the Staff into his Hand; We may imagin he did it with all that superior Piety, Spirit, and Majesty, which were peculiar to him: Like an ancient Prophet addressing himself to the Military Officer, delivering to him the Principal Ensign of Martial Power, to Lead the Armies and Fight the battles of the Lord and of his People."

The tide that had threatened to overwhelm the young colony had been turned, and a peace was established that remained unbroken for nearly forty years, or until King Philip made his desperate attempt to overthrow white supremacy. Yes, peace reigned, but it was the peace of the graveyard!

Had the Puritans been confronted by a real confederacy of tribes pledged to the destruction of the whites, they probably could not have survived. A combination of circumstances, however, worked in their favor during the initial and crucial period of the settlement. Benefiting in the beginning from the effects of the terrible plague of 1617, they also gained the friendship and alliance of important tribes. The adhesion to their cause by Uncas, chief of the Mohegans, and the favor of the Narragansetts have already been mentioned. The friendship of Massasoit, the Wampanoag chief, proved to be especially valuable. In spite of occasional ill treatment at the hands of the English, he remained steadfast in his devotion to the time of his death, which occurred in 1662.

That date marks the waning of the friendship of the Wampanoags. After the death of Massasoit's eldest son, the chieftainship devolved upon Metacom, better known as Philip of Pokanoket or King Philip. Without question he must be regarded the most remarkable of all the Indians of New England. He not only clearly foresaw that the encroachment of the whites would inevitably lead to the downfall of the Indians, but he also matured a plan to prevent such a disaster. For nine years he devoted all his energies to the preparation for the mighty conflict, and furthered his designs with remarkable patience and insight. Since his own tribe numbered only about five hundred warriors, it was necessary that he find allies, and he actually succeeded in winning over the principal tribes from the Merrimac River to the Thames. The white population in the united colonies was between thirty and forty thousand, of whom about seven thousand were able to bear arms. The Indians were about equal in numbers, but were not as closely united as Philip ardently desired, and treachery on the part of some of the natives probably prevented that measure of success which otherwise might have been expected. Finally in 1675 the war broke out in all its fury, and for two years the carnage went on. Of the ninety towns fifty were attacked, and twelve completely destroyed. Though the bravery of the Indians was remarkable, it proved to be no match for the better armed colonists, once they had been sufficiently warned.

After the first furious assault, of which the whites were happily forewarned, the final result was never in doubt, though the war dragged on through many months. At last, beaten and harassed, Philip was overtaken by disaster in his swamp fortress in Rhode Island during the night of August 12, 1676. With the Indians practically surrounded, confusion and consternation reigned in his camp, each man seeking safety in flight. To quote from the history of Church: " They were soon in the swamp, and Philip the foremost, who starting at the first gun, threw his petunk and powder-horn over his head, catch'd up his gun, and ran as fast as he could scamper, without any more clothes than his small breeches and stockings, and ran directly on two of Capt. Church's ambush . . . ," an Englishman and an Indian. When the Englishman's gun failed at the critical moment, the Pocasset Indian, named *Alderman* by the English, shot the dreaded Philip and thus sent down to defeat and ruin a man who had succeeded in killing

PURITAN WRATH AND INDIAN CAPTIVITIES 17

from six to eight hundred white settlers. No wonder that the grim Puritan was unwilling to accord this hated man decent treatment even in death. In his *History of King Philip's War,* Increase Mather thus gloats over the decisive event: " And in that very place where he first contrived and began his mischief, he was taken and destroyed, and there was he (like as Agog was hewed in pieces before the Lord) cut into four quarters, and is now hanged up as a monument of revenging justice, his head being cut off and carried away to *Plymouth,* his hands were brought to *Boston. So let thine Enemies perish, O Lord!* "

King Philip's War was the most disastrous experienced by the hostile Indians. All the leading chiefs were killed, and the Wampanoags and Narragansetts practically exterminated. Some of the survivors fled to the interior tribes; those that surrendered were either sold into slavery, among them Philip's wife and little son, or allowed to join the various Praying Villages in southern Massachusetts. Philip's name remained for many years on the lips of those who had been participants in the stirring events. Later he became the subject of numerous stories, poems, and dramas, some of which, as the poem *Yamoyden* and the play *Metamora* attained wide popularity. In Cooper's *Wept of the Wish-ton-Wish* he appears as one of the three chief persons of the novel. His character has been variously estimated by different historians. The Puritans naturally looked upon him as the incarnation of the devil, but it cannot be denied that he was a man of remarkable abilities, who had the welfare of his race at heart, and who, but for the treachery of his own people, probably would have swept the colonists from the New World.

However, long before the character of Philip and his heroic struggle had become the subject of sentimental poetry and song in the 19th century, realistic descriptions of the stirring events began to appear. Already in 1682 there was printed *The Narrative of the Captivity and Restauration of Mrs. Mary Rowlandson,* written by the wife of the minister of the church at Lancaster, Massachusetts, which gives a first hand account of her experiences following her capture in February 1676. The editors of the facsimile reproduction of the 1682 edition, published in 1903 at

Lancaster, not ineptly call it " an authentic and graphic contemporary delineation of the manners and customs of the primitive children of the soil, from whom our ancestors relentlessly wrested their beautiful and beloved heritage, in order to enrich us and our posterity; it is an eloquently pathetic record of grave perils bravely encountered, and terrible sufferings patiently borne with unswerving faith in the wisdom and mercy of an overruling providence." As the first and probably the best of the many so-called Indian captivities, it became immensely popular, at least thirty reprints being known to have appeared. The opening sentences of this remarkably graphic account have often been quoted: " On the 10th of February, 1675, came the Indians with great numbers upon Lancaster: their first coming was about sunrising; hearing the noise of some guns, we looked out; several houses were burning, and the smoke ascending to heaven. There were five persons taken in one house, the father and mother, and a sucking child they knocked on the head, the other two they took and carried away alive. There were two others, who being out of their garrison upon occasion, were set upon; one was knocked on the head, the other escaped: Another there was who running along was shot and wounded, and fell down; he begged of them his life, promising them money (as they told me) but they would not hearken to him, but knocked him on the head, stript him naked, and split open his bowels."

Then follow the various " removes " or changes in camping sites, twenty in all, the happenings connected with each being given in considerable detail. For instance, under the first remove Mrs. Rowlandson reports: " This was the dolefulest night that ever my eyes saw. Oh the roaring, and singing, and dancing, and yelling of those black creatures in the night, which made the place a lively resemblance of hell: And miserable was the waste that was there made, of horses, cattle, sheep, swine, calves, lambs, roasting pigs and fowls (which they had plundered in the town) some roasting, some lying and burning, and some boiling, to feed our merciless enemies: who were joyful enough, though we were disconsolate."

We see later the resolute woman with her wound growing stiff, and her sick and wounded child dying a lingering death in her arms. During the seven weeks and five days of her captivity until her ransom there are intense suffering from trips, rain, snow, and cold, difficulty in procuring food, clothing and shelter, coupled with the mental anguish about the fate of relatives and friends, and the constant expectation that her Bible as the source of strength might be snatched away. And yet, in spite of privations and dangers, life is made more endurable by her personal honor remaining inviolate, as she is happy to report: " I have been in the midst of those roaring lions, and savage bears, that feared neither God, nor man, nor the devil, by night and day, alone and in company; sleeping all sorts together, and yet not one of them ever offered the least abuse of chastity to me, in word or action."

If we make allowance for Mrs. Rowlandson's peculiar brand of religion, which permits her to exhaust the vocabulary in vituperation of the cruel and pagan enemies, the narrative throughout breathes a deep piety and reliance upon God, an expression of the true Puritan spirit which with the graphic and realistic delineation of an eye witness makes the booklet an exceedingly valuable historical and literary production.

Among the " captivities " that began to follow the first in never-ending succession for the next hundred and fifty years, only two comparable in intrinsic value and literary importance need be mentioned here: Jonathan Dickinson's *Narrative of a Shipwreck in the Gulph of Florida*, 1699, and *The Narrative of the Captivity and Adventures of John Tanner*, 1830, which latter served Longfellow as a veritable mine in writing his *Song of Hiawatha*. Dickinson's account of the shipwreck and enforced stay among the hostile Indians until he and his party reached hospitable Carolina and proceeded to Pennsylvania gives a vivid picture of the dangers and hardships encountered as well as of the wretched state of the natives of Florida. Though some of the experiences were undoubtedly distressing in the extreme, they appear from the distance in a humorous light. " We all sat expecting death, and that in a most barbarous manner . . . ; they rushed violently on us, rending and tearing those few clothes we had; they that had breeches had so many about them that they hardly touched the ground till they were shaken out of them; they tore all from my wife, and espying her hair lace some were going to cut the hair away to get it, but like greedy dogs, another snatched and tore it off. As for our poor young child, they snatched from it what little it had, as though they would have shaken and torn it limb from limb." Cold, hunger, and thirst add their terrors to the often imminent danger of a violent death. As a vivid and interesting first hand account of actual experiences, Dickinson's work ranks only second to Mrs. Rowlandson's narrative, and, like it, is pervaded by the same religious atmosphere and trust in God's protecting providence, which proved to be the surest help and defense in times of greatest difficulty.

CHAPTER III

THE INDIAN COMES INTO HIS OWN

"The Father of American Poetry," Philip Freneau (1752-1832), fittingly is also the pioneer figure in the use of Indian material for poetical purposes. Though he may have realized only dimly the value of this material, the poems dealing with the natives are unquestionably among his finest and best. His interest in the aborigines developed early, for he had published already before the age of twenty a work of about four hundred and fifty lines entitled *The American Village,* in which the Indian is given a prominent place. The character of the native appears in a rather favorable light:

>Nor think this mighty land of old contained
>The plundering wretch, or man of bloody mind:
>Renowned SACHEMS once their empires rais'd
>On wholesome laws; and sacrifices blaz'd.
>The gen'rous soul inspir'd the honest breast,
>And to be free, was doubly to be blest.

Conditions changed when the invaders came,

>And rav'nous nations with industrious toil,
>Conspir'd to rob them of their native soil:
>Then bloody wars, and death and rage arose,
>And ev'ry tribe resolved to be our foes.

The breast of the simple native was filled with a high and noble resolve, for

>Full many a feat of them I could rehearse,
>And actions worthy of immortal verse:
>Deeds ever glorious to the INDIAN name,
>And fit to rival GREEK or ROMAN fame.

One story only, representative and heroic though sad, he tells of the possible many. The Indian hunters in the Hudson Bay region bring their beaver pelts to Port Nelson in their boats. In sight of the shore the bark of Caffraro, who is accompanied by his consort Colma and their little son, springs a leak, and the three stoically await death. His brother pushes off from shore in a small boat, but it can save only two. Heroically and unselfishly the wife and mother implores her husband to save the little son. She prevents her own rescue at the expense of others by leaping into the water, and raising her head from the flushed wave, addresses her life companion at great length on the life to come and other subjects, and then at last

> . . . downward in the hoary deep
> Plung'd her fair form to everlasting sleep;
> Her parting soul its latest struggle gave,
> And her last breath came bubbling thro' the wave.

Like Rousseau and other writers of the 18th century, Freneau was fascinated by the thought of innocence and bliss of man's natural state. In glowing terms the discoverer of America speaks in *The Pictures of Columbus* of the native's paradise before the arrival of the whites:

> Sweet sylvan scenes of innocence and ease,
> How calm and joyous pass the seasons here!
> No splendid towns or spiry turrets rise,
> No lordly palaces — no tyrant kings
> Enact hard laws to crush fair freedom here;
> No gloomy jails to shut up wretched men;
> All, all are free! — here God and nature reign;
> Their works unsullied by the hands of men. —

In the melancholy mood of the *Caribbeana* Freneau mentions the fair West India islands, their once happy inhabitants now crushed under the Spanish tyrant's heel, and "the harmless Indian race torn by his dogs in every chace." Similarly in *Sketches of American History,* after alluding to the Indian's happy existence in a rural domain, he gives scant credit to benevolent intentions of explorers and settlers, who by their actions convinced the native that he had better rid himself of such dangerous neighbors. The Pilgrims with their peculiar notions of righteousness boded no good for the dissenting savage, for

THE INDIAN COMES INTO HIS OWN   23

> Some, came on the Indians to shed a new light,
> Convinced long before that their own must be right,
> And that all who had died in the centuries past
> On the devil's lee shore were eternally cast.

Even under the most favorable conditions of white domination, nature alone remained as the native's peculiar realm, and this he preferred to the learning and civilization of the newcomer. That fact is poignantly and concretely expressed in *The Indian Student, or Force of Nature*. Shalum, a "copper-coloured boy" from among the savage tribes of the Susquehanna, is persuaded by a wandering priest to leave "Satan's waste" and at Harvard College acquire learning. For a while he submits to the boredom of classical studies, engaging as a relaxation in his favorite hunting:

> No mystic wonders fired his mind:
> He sought to gain no learned degree,
> But only sense enough to find
> The squirrel in the hollow tree.
>
> The shady bank, the purling stream,
> The woody wild his heart possessed,
> In dewy lawn, his morning dream
> In fancy's gayest colours dressed.

Overcome at last by regret of having sought civilization, he determines to return to the old charms:

> "And why (he cried) did I forsake
> My native wood for gloomy walls;
> The silver stream, the limpid lake
> For musty books and college halls.
>
> A little could my wants supply —
> Can wealth and honour give me more;
> Or, will the sylvan god deny
> The humble treat he gave before?
>
> Let seraphs gain the bright abode,
> And heaven's sublimest mansions see —
> I only bow to Nature's God —
> The land of shades will do for me.

>These dreadful secrets of the sky
>Alarm my soul with chilling fear —
>Do planets in their orbits fly,
>And is the earth, indeed, a sphere?
>
>Let planets still their course pursue,
>And comets to the centre run —
>In Him my faithful friend I view,
>The image of my God — the Sun.
>
>Where Nature's ancient forests grow,
>And mingled laurel never fades,
>My heart is fixed; — and I must go
>To die among my native shades."

A grosser materialism is exhibited in a later poem entitled *The Indian Convert,* which portrays the native in an unfavorable light. By persuasion and constant harassing the parson has at last induced an Indian to be *good,* although he had long esteemed the preaching and singing as less attractive than his fishing and fowling. One day the quasi convert, seeking something substantial, interrupts the parson's discourse on the beautiful things of heaven, and the ensuing dialogue inevitably leads to the termination of a relationship entered into under false conceptions as to the rewards available.

>Said he, Master *Minister,* this place that you talk of,
>Of things for the stomach, pray what has it got;
>Has it liquors in plenty? — If so I'll soon walk off
>And put myself down in the heavenly spot.
>
>You fool (said the preacher) no liquors are there!
>The place I'm describing is most like our meeting,
>Good people, all singing, with preaching and prayer;
>They live upon these without eating or drinking.
>
>But the doors are all locked against folks that are wicked;
>And you, I am fearful, will never get there: —
>A life of REPENTANCE must purchase the ticket,
>And few of you, Indians, can buy it, I fear.
>
>Farewell (said the Indian) I'm none of your mess;
>On victuals, so airy, I faintish should feel,
>I cannot consent to be lodged in a place
>*Where's there's nothing to eat and but little to steal.*

THE INDIAN COMES INTO HIS OWN 25

No wonder that the materialistic native with his scorn of the white man's gifts became enamoured of his present existence, and that in spite of the occasional stress which savage life entailed he tenaciously clung to this earth. *The Dying Indian: Tomo-Chequi* voices the lament of the aged chief who is reluctant to leave the Huron shore, the charming solitudes of the tall ascending woods, the glassy lakes and prattling streams, and the mountain's lofty swell, to be exchanged for a shadow land with its uncertain activities, since no ghost has returned to confirm the fine tales about the world beyond. It is indeed a dreary prospect that faces the old man, with vigor, youth, and active days a thing of the past.

> To what strange lands must Chequi take his way!
> Groves of the dead departed mortals trace:
> No deer along those gloomy forests stray,
> No huntsmen there take pleasure in the chace,
> But all are empty unsubstantial shades,
> That ramble through those visionary glades;
> No spongy fruits from verdant trees depend,
>   But sickly orchards there
>   Do fruits as sickly bear,
> And apples a consumptive visage shew,
> And withered hangs the hurtle-berry blue.

The once dauntless warrior chief shrinks before the unknown dangers that are likely to confront the departed. But as he gives directions for the preparation of his hollow tomb, to be provided with the trusty bow and arrow, the cheerful bottle and venison for the long, lonesome journey, a single ray of light pierces the gloom, the hope that nature may at last repair the ruins, and that a real world and a newborn mansion may somehow once more be assigned to the immortal mind.

The parting moments of another leader are recounted in *The Prophecy of King Tammany*, a Delaware chieftain who is said to have been the first Indian to welcome William Penn to America, and who appears as the aged arbitrator Tamenund in Cooper's *The Last of the Mohicans*. In uncontrolled rage the still vigorous warrior laments the irresistible onward march of the white invader and the native's helplessness in the face of superior numbers and weapons. As a way out of the intolerable situation he decides to join as an unexpected guest the far-famed sachems in the gardens of the west, despite the dark horrors of the path. But before he goes, he denounces the Christians and prophesies that also their civilization will be devastated and drowned in blood with many led captive, and that at last a sordid race will succeed to slight the virtues of a firmer generation. Then he calmly raises the funeral pyre and as the crackling flames ascend, smiles in anticipation of the end,

> 'Till the freed soul, her debt to nature paid,
> Rose from the ashes that her prison made,
> And sought the world unknown, and dark oblivion's shade.

The last poems may fittingly be counted as belonging to the so-called Indian deathsongs, a type once popular both in England and America. Of these numerous deathsongs, so well discussed by Professor Farley in his article entitled *The Dying Indian*, few possess literary merit. Probably one of the best occurs in Mrs. Morton's long tale of four cantos named *Quâbi or the Virtues of Nature*, 1790, in which we are told that fierce sachems

> Midst the flames their fearless songs begin —
> Pain has no terrors to the truly brave.

The noble and generous Illinois chieftain Quâbi has a worthy mate in Azakia, who is not only noted for her beauty, as

> Her limbs were straighter than the mountain pine,
> Her hair far blacker than the raven's wing;
> Beauty had lent her form *the waving line*,
> Her breath gave fragrance to the balmy spring,

but also willing and anxious to join her supposedly dead husband by committing suicide. Quâbi himself exhibits all the grandeur and manly defiance expected of a warrior in the deathsong before the Huron enemies, his bosom scorning the throbs of pain:

> No griefs this warrior-soul can bow,
> No pangs contract this even brow;
> Not all your threats excite a fear,
> Not all your force can start a tear.

THE INDIAN COMES INTO HIS OWN

>Think not with me my tribe decays,
>More glorious chiefs the hatchet raise;
>Not unreveng'd their sachem dies,
>Not unattended greets the skies.

Unquestionably the most popular and famous poem belonging to this type, in which the victim derides his enemies and spurs them on to greater efforts, is *The Deathsong of a Cherokee Indian*, here given in the form ascribed to Freneau:

>The sun sets in night, and the stars shun the day,
>But glory remains when their lights fade away.
>Begin, ye tormentors: your threats are in vain
>For the son of Alknomock can never complain.
>
>Remember the woods, where in ambush he lay,
>And the scalps which he bore from your nation away!
>Why do ye delay? — 'till I shrink from my pain?
>Know the son of Alknomock can never complain.
>
>Remember the arrows he shot from his bow,
>Remember your chiefs by his hatchet laid low,
>The flame rises high, you exult in my pain?
>Know the son of Alknomock will never complain.
>
>I go to the land where my father is gone:
>His ghost shall rejoice in the fame of his son.
>Death comes like a friend, he relieves me from pain
>And thy son, O Alknomock, has scorned to complain.

The authorship of this spirited poem, with differences in refrain, stanza arrangement, and word order in the various versions, is still in doubt. It has been attributed not only to Freneau and Mrs. Hunter, but also to Royall Tyler. The claims of the latter, however, have very little weight. The poem appears, it is true, as a song in his prose play *The Contrast,* which was first published in 1790, but there is no reason to believe that it was his own; it likewise was sung in the same year in an English opera entitled *New Spain; or, Love in Mexico.*

The English origin of the song is less doubtful, although by no means certain. One version of the poem is found as early as 1783 in Joseph Ritson's " Historical Essay on the Origin and Progress of Natural Song" published in *A Select Collection of English Songs with their Original Airs,* but with no indication of authorship. In 1802 it appeared in a volume of poems by Mrs. John Hunter, with the following note: " The idea of this ballad was suggested several years ago by hearing a gentleman, who had resided several years in America amongst the tribe or nation called the Cherokees, sing a wild air, which he assured me it was customary for those people to chaunt with a barbarous jargon, implying contempt to their enemies in the moments of torture and death. I have endeavoured to give something of the characteristic spirit and sentiment of those brave savages. We look upon the fierce and stubborn courage of the dying Indian with a mixture of respect, pity, and horror; and it is to those sensations excited in the mind of the reader, that the Death Song must owe its effect. It has already been published with notes to which it was adapted." The gentleman from whom the information might have been secured was William Augustus Bowles, who styled himself " Ambassador from the United Nations of Creeks and Cherokees to the Court of London." Some find it hard to believe that such a respectable lady as Mrs. Hunter should have been mistaken as to the origin of the poem even nineteen years after its first publication, or that she should deliberately have claimed what was not her own. Her statement that the ballad was suggested " several years " ago when in fact it had been published nineteen years ago, is loose and inexact, to say the least.

Not a few authorities assert that Freneau is the author of the poem. In America it is found in the initial number of Matthew Carey's *American Museum,* January 1, 1787, and there assigned to P. Freneau. Professor Pattee includes it in his edition of Freneau's poems, but with this qualifying statement: " The testimony of Carey's as to its genuineness carries with it considerable weight. . . . The poem, however, is not included in any of the poet's collections and I can find no earlier newspaper appearance, although my search has not been exhaustive. The authenticity of a poem suspected to be Freneau's may always be gravely doubted if it is not found to be included in his collected works, for he hoarded his poetic product, especially in his earlier period, with miserly care."

This statement as to the non-inclusion in a collection carries less weight if we remember, for instance, that, according to Pattee himself, *The American Village,* " Freneau's first distinct poetical publication, was for many years known only from his description of it in a letter to Madison. It was supposed to have been lost, until a copy was discovered in a volume of miscellaneous pamphlets which had been purchased by the Library of Congress in November, 1902." If he did not trouble himself further about this early poem of about four hundred and fifty lines, he might certainly have overlooked a deathsong with its paltry sixteen. Some infer that Carey erroneously assigned the poem in question to Freneau, probably confusing it with one of his two deathsongs, *The Dying Indian,* or *The Prophecy of King Tammany.* In the absence of conclusive evidence as to whom the song belongs, the question of authorship must remain unanswered.

There is no question, however, that Freneau wrote *The Indian Burying Ground,* probably his finest short poem, which for delicacy of touch, sympathetic portrayal, and pious sentiment has seldom been equalled. The aptness of the line " The hunter and the deer, a shade! " appealed so much to Thomas Campbell that he concluded the fourth stanza of his *O'Connor's Child* with that verse.

> In spite of all the learned have said,
>   I still my old opinion keep;
> The posture, that we give the dead,
>   Points out the soul's eternal sleep.
>
> Not so the ancients of these lands —
>   The Indian, when from life released,
> Again is seated with his friends,
>   And shares again the joyous feast.[1]
>
> His imaged birds, and painted bowl,
>   And venison, for a journey dressed,
> Bespeak the nature of the soul,
>   Activity, that knows no rest.

---

[1] " The North American Indians bury their dead in a sitting posture; decorating the corpse with wampum, images of birds, quadrupeds, &c: And (if that of a warrior) with bows, arrows, tomhawks, and other military weapons."

His bow, for action ready bent,
    And arrows, with a head of stone,
Can only mean that life is spent,
    And not the old ideas gone.

Thou, stranger, that shalt come this way,
    No fraud upon the dead commit —
Observe the swelling turf, and say
    They do not lie, but here they sit.

Here still a lofty rock remains,
    On which the curious eye may trace
(Now wasted, half, by wearing rains)
    The fancies of a ruder race.

Here still an aged elm aspires,
    Beneath whose far-projecting shade
(And which the shepherd still admired)
    The children of the forest played!

There oft a restless Indian queen
    (Pale Shebah, with her braided hair)
And many a barbarous form is seen
    To chide the man that lingers there.

By midnight moons, o'er moistening dews;
    In habit for the chase arrayed,
The hunter still the deer pursues,
    The hunter and the deer, a shade!

And long shall timorous fancy see
    The painted chief, and pointed spear,
And Reason's self shall bow the knee
    To shadows and delusions here.

    The student of Freneau's Indian poems is struck by the fact that the attitude of the poet is both romantic and realistic. He looks upon the native as predominantly nature's nobleman, exhibiting all the qualities with which travellers and romancers were wont to invest the lord of the forest. His delicate fancy surrounds him even in death with a sentiment at once tender and pious. This attitude had its roots in the naturalism of the period and a poetic imagination truly romantic. When in the Indian death-songs Freneau expresses the " savage notions and romantic heroism " so " horrible to the imagination," the transition to realism had been made. One could of course hardly blame the child of nature if he shrank from the rude touch of the white intruder of the Ohio valley, and thus

> From these fair plains, these rural seats,
> So long concealed, so lately known,
> The unsocial Indian far retreats,
> To make some other clime his own.

But by no means did he always thus easily relinquish his hunting-grounds to the grasping newcomer, for the author records how " the murderous Indian " struck down the twin brothers Sevier as they were assisting a new settler with a numerous family to cross the Cumberland River in North Carolina. In view of the bitter satires directed by the outspoken patriot against the cruel white enemy, his restraint in the face of savage atrocities is truly remarkable. Only incidentally does he mention " the indian, to the english true," in the army of Burgoyne, while the reference to Indian butcheries in *America Independent* involves both sides, and in its specific application loyalists and not patriots are the victims:

> Full many a corpse lies mouldering on the plain
> That ne'er shall see its little brood again:
> See, yonder lies, all breathless, cold and pale,
> Drenched in her gore, Lavinia of the vale;
> The cruel Indian seized her life away,
> As the next morn began her bridal day! —

The Lavinia of the vale is one Jenny M'Rea, affianced to a loyalist officer, who with her whole family was brutally murdered, scalped, and mangled in a most horrible manner near Fort Edward, an incident exploited by several writers. Thus delicate fancy and stern reality alike find expression in the lines of Freneau, just as blatant war songs and the productions of a poetic imagination had appeared side by side.

The pioneer in the poetic delineation of the native is less successful when he chooses prose as his medium. On May 23, 1795, Freneau began to publish as a covenient filler in the *Jersey Chronicle* a series of sketches under the caption *Tomo-Cheeki, the Creek Indian in Philadelphia.* The letter writer is identical with the famus chief Tomo Chachi who under the direction of General Oglethorpe had visited England in 1734. Although he is said not to have criticized the ways of civilization on that memorable visit, in Freneau's letters the " manners and absurdities of the Americans are described from the standpoint of the observant savage."

However, these letters or prose sketches form only an insignificant part of Freneau's portrayal of the red man. It is in verse that his delicate fancy and wistful sentiment brood over the passing of a race once the proud possessor of a marvellous heritage. Only now and then does the savage in hopeless despair strike back at the despoiler; more often, he stoically resigns himself to what seems an inexorable fate. Over both, Freneau weaves the delicate and glamorous threads of his poetic imagination.

CHAPTER IV

FICTION DISCOVERS THE NATIVE

It was only natural that the red man, who had played such a conspicuous part in the wars of the last half of the 18th century, should have attracted the attention of the reading public turning to fiction after those stirring events. Accordingly we find that his exploits, his customs and manners form the subject of numerous anecdotes and short stories in the magazines of that day. Occasionally he was also introduced in attempted historical novels dealing with the period, as for instance in the *Female Review*, a tale published in 1793. During the same year he actually appeared as the central figure in a curious tale by Mrs. Ann Eliza Bleeker, entitled the *History of Maria Kittle,* written in the manner of the Indian captivities. Evidently based upon the experiences of the author's husband during an Indian raid, it graphically describes what would arouse and satisfy the curiosity of the reader. In keeping with the practice of the times, the period selected is that of the French and Indian War. The bloodthirsty savages mercilessly butcher all but one of a family they had previously befriended. Only Mrs. Kittle is saved by an old Indian who had promised her protection before the raid, and who cares for her as she is carried off to Canada. Though not lacking in some vivid passages, this ambitious tale like so many other attempts has little literary significance.

The distinction of having first successfully utilized the Indian as fiction material really belongs to Charles Brockden Brown (1771–1810), even if others before him had sensed his literary possibilities. Like a miner who discovers precious ore, Brown, the first professional man of letters in America, deliberately introduced and exploited native material, chief among which was the red man. In his preface to *Edgar Huntley, or Memoirs of a Sleep-Walker,* 1799, he tells the public that he wants to profit by some of the numerous and inexhaustible sources of amusement to the fancy and instruction to the heart peculiar to America, and to exhibit a series of adventures growing out of the conditions of the new country. The writer claims at least one merit, " that of calling forth the passions and engaging the sympathy of the reader by means hitherto unemployed by preceding authors. Puerile superstitions and exploded manners, Gothic castles and chimeras, are the materials usually employed for this end. The incidents of Indian hostility, and the perils of the western wilderness, are far more suitable; and for a native of America to overlook these would admit of no apology. These, therefore, are, in part, the ingredients of this tale, and these he has been ambitious of depicting in vivid and faithful colors."

The candid critic will readily admit that Brown, a lover of nature and acquainted with his section of the country, did not fail. It is true, the Clithero story introduces European material, and sleepwalking is made the source of chief interest, but the scene of the tale is distinctively American, laid in or near the primeval forests of Pennsylvania. With considerable skill Brown describes the wild country west of Norwalk, the wilderness of early times. As a fitting background of Indian depredations, there are the almost impenetrable fastnesses, the valleys and hills in their original state as they came from the hand of the creator, the solitudes with their panthers, their crevices and subterranean channels: these are typically American and far removed from the conventional characteristics of the Old World.

The claim sometimes made and thoughtlessly repeated that the author of *Edgar Huntley* began the idealization of the Indian rests upon the most insubstantial basis. Old Deb, the hag who has instigated the Indian depredations, Huntley in a whimsical mood designates by a fanciful name: " The wildness of her aspect and garb, her shrivelled and diminutive form, a constitution that seemed to defy the ravages of time and the influence of the element; her age which some did not scruple to affirm exceeded an hundred years, her romantic solitude and mountainous haunts suggested to my fancy the appellation of *Queen Mab*." But the progress of the story with Old Deb's supposed end makes it clear that she is viewed in anything but a romantic light.

The whole situation is rather one of grim reality and reflects the implacable hatred of a race driven from its hunting-grounds by the steady march of the white man. All the districts mentioned in *Edgar Huntley* comprised at one time the domains of the Delaware Indians to which Old Deb belonged. When the encroachments of the English colonists brought about a crisis, Old Deb stoutly opposed the decision to abandon their ancient seats and to retire to the banks of the Wabash and the Muskingum. Though her birth, talent, and age gave her great influence and authority among her people, all her zeal and eloquence failed to persuade them to abandon their scheme.

Old Deb tenaciously maintained her view and her position. She burnt the empty wigwams of her departing kinsfolk and claimed possession of overlordship of the country. Issuing from her hut in the fastnesses of Norwalk and guarded by three wolf-like dogs, she demanded from the neighboring inhabitants the necessities of life as her just due. She claimed that by remaining behind her countrymen she had succeeded to the possession of the region and that the government had devolved upon her. The English colonists she regarded as intruders, who were suffered to remain temporarily only on condition of supplying her wants as a sovereign. Later she had occupied the lonely hut of a luckless Scotchman whose life she probably had taken and whose homestead she had appropriated in the course of what she considered legitimate confiscation.

The outbreak of Indian atrocities seems to have been the direct result of the refusal on the part of the people of Chetasco to honor the regal claims of Old Deb, accentuated of course by the many injuries and encroachments that had exasperated the tribes. Brooding over her contemptuous or neglectful treatment, Old Deb had conceived schemes of revenge. When her kinsfolk visited her, she so inflamed the mind of one that he murdered Huntley's friend Waldegrave. Nevertheless, the sagacity of the ruffian was such that he refrained from tearing away the usual trophy from the dead in order not to arouse the suspicions of the whites. Later the whole band returned and opened hostilities.

Nothing could be clearer than the definiteness of the views Huntley entertains regarding the Indians, opinions which probably should be identified with those of Brown. He had been a grievous sufferer of their frequent and destructive inroads into the heart of the English settlement during the late war. Only by the intervention of a kind Providence he and his two sisters had been saved when his father's house on the verge of the wilderness was assailed by eight assassins during the dead of night, his parents and an infant child murdered in their beds, the house pillaged and burnt to the ground. Since then, even the image of a savage made him shudder. No wonder that Edgar applies to the Indians such terms as " inexorable enemies," " miscreants," savages who pursue a sanguinary trade, to drink the blood, and exult in the lament of their unhappy foes and of his own brethren, merciless enemies who would tear away the skin from his brows.

Edgar Huntley's acquaintance with the natives is not confined to reports and casual meetings, but deepened by personal and bloody encounters. At the end of one of his sleepwalking rambles, he suddenly finds himself confronted by " four brawny and terrific figures," who block his exit from the cave. Like one fascinated by strange wild beasts, he views their profound if light slumber and calculates his chances to escape without being detected. He is impressed by the gigantic form and fantastic ornament of the savage who awakens and upon leaving the cavern for a moment neglects to take his gun and hatchet along. As Edgar meets him outside a little later, the only means of escaping undetected is to bury his hatchet in the breast of the potential enemy, who expires without a groan. The party, whose fair captive our hero succeeds in rescuing, was returning from a murderous raid of the white settlements.

In their precipitous flight the two reach safely the cottage of Old Deb, but when Edgar contemplates that his uncle and sisters may have shared the fate of other settlers, he regrets having spared the three Indians and even considers returning to the cave for bloody revenge. However, they soon favor him with their presence, and are dispatched in a thrilling encounter. Edgar is visibly impressed by the physique and mentality of his enemies: he speaks of the "tawny and terrific visage," and the "three beings, full of energy and heroism, endowed with minds strenuous and lofty," "their huge limbs inured to combat and *war-worn*." Later upon leaving the neighborhood of the hut he met another bloodthirsty foe who moved on all fours. "His disfigured limbs, pendants from his ears and nose, and his shorn locks, were indubitable indications of a savage. Occasionally he reared himself above the bushes and scanned, with suspicious vigilance, the cottage and the space surrounding it. Then he stooped, and crept along as before." Him he bayonets, not, however, without paying a tribute to the Indians as "distinguished by prowess and skill, equally armed against surprize and force." Afterwards he comments upon their marvelously accurate sense of sight. It should be noted, however, that we look in vain for detailed descriptions of the native, so much in vogue at a later period.

But the tributes to enemies proficient in their nefarious trade never blunt a settler's sense of justice to be visited upon the heads of a murderous crew. Gruesome evidences of the Indian's ruthlessness are found at Selbys in the mangled form and gory head of the scalped victim and the frustrated attempt of the wily savage to obliterate all traces of his pillage and murder by means of fire. The report of his uncle's death and the supposed capture of his sister tend only to heighten the unspeakable horror of one who knows only too well the fate of such unfortunate captives, "to gratify the innate and insatiable cruelty of savages by suffering all the torments their invention can suggest or to linger out years of weary bondage and unintermitted hardship in the bosom of the wilderness."

Charles Brockden Brown has the colonist's conception of the Indian as a murderous savage, whose every action if not closely circumscribed leads to tragedy. Edgar's nearest relatives and dearest friends fall under the red man's tomahawks, and only resolute action and a kind Providence save him from a similar fate. Though the treacherous native inspires him with amazement and wonder, and Indian warfare is not without its romantic aspects, the sense of terror predominates, and of idealization in the strict sense of the term there is little or nothing.

CHAPTER V

FATE FROWNS UPON MISCEGENATION

In 1820 *Yamoyden, A Tale of the Wars of King Philip,* in six cantos, attracted the attention of the reading public, and for some time maintained its position as America's most popular literary production. This long poem was the work of two friends, both under twenty years of age. While pursuing his studies for the ministry at Bristol, Rhode Island, James W. Eastburn (1797–1819) was impressed by the story of King Philip, whose chief stronghold had been in the neighborhood. He conceived the plan of the poem and communicated it to Robert C. Sands (1799–1832). The two divided the material and interchanged and read the parts as they were finished. During the revision Eastburn, who in the meantime had taken orders in the Protestant Episcopal Church, died at sea on a voyage to Santa Cruz undertaken for the benefit of his health.

Yamoyden is based upon a hasty reading of Hubbard's *Narrative of the Indian Wars* and other works, many of which are cited. Under these circumstances it was perhaps only natural that not a few errors should have crept in, which are frankly attributed by Sands to the authors' ignorance of the subject. Various inconsistencies also occur in the tale covering only a period of forty-eight hours, and in addition there is at least one long passage of irrelevant matter which the pious hand of Sands felt not called upon to remove. Aside from these and other shortcomings which mar the story, it appears as a remarkable piece of work of the two young friends whose enthusiasm for the nobility of the Indian and indignation at his shameful treatment knew no bounds.

As indicated by the title, King Philip is not the main character, though he plays a very prominent part. Curiously enough, he plots to rob the Nipnet or Nipmuc chief Yamoyden of his white

FATE FROWNS UPON MISCEGENATION 39

wife and child, so that by sharing the common bond of grief the exasperated husband and father will join in the campaign of vengeance and liberty. This from the outset puts the plot under a severe strain, for otherwise Philip appears as a hero, wise, bold, and true, who

> ... fought, because he would not yield
> His birthright, and his father's field;
> Would vindicate the deep disgrace,
> The wrongs, the ruin of his race; —
> He slew, that well avenged in death,
> His kindred spirits pleased might be; —
> Died, for his people and his faith,
> His sceptre and his liberty!

Yamoyden, King Philip, and other persons are the characters in the tragic drama of a people sent down to destruction by the greed and cruelty of the white man. As the authors so well express it,

> 'Tis the death wail of a departed race, —
> Long vanished hence, unhonored in their grave;
> Their story lost to memory, like the trace
> That to the greensward erst their sandals gave;
> — Wail for the feather-cinctured warriors brave,
> Who, battling for their father's empire well,
> Perished, when valor could no longer save
> From soulless bigotry, and avarice fell,
> That tracked them to the death, with mad, infuriate yell.

Throughout the poem, the Puritan settlers are represented as entirely in the wrong, and the Indians as wholly in the right. The stern father of the heroine Nora believes that under the guise of friendship for the white man's race and an expressed desire to learn Christian usages, the tawny chief Yamoyden by fiendish craft has won his daughter's heart and left him lonely in his grief. Even when at the end his son-in-law has rescued him from the murderous ax that instead descends into the Indian's breast, Fitzgerald knows nothing more charitable than to call his rescuer a misguided man, along whose path dim light was shed, and who possibly may receive mercy in the world to come.

Certainly in this world the Puritan offered none. Before the fight with the natives the embattled host sings a war hymn and seeks the blessing of God upon its bloody work:

> No throb was there of pity's mood,
> For native of the solitude;
> Doomed to the carnage of the sword
> They deemed the country and its lord;
> And bigot zeal, to bosoms brave,
> The callous thirst of slaughter gave.

The plot of the poem is not particularly impressive. The imaginary hero, bearing the fictitious name of Yamoyden, has placed his wife and child in an island grove near Mt. Hope, the stronghold of King Philip. Even before the kidnapping of his child he remains obdurate to his wife's plea not to stain his Christian hands with Christian blood; essentially noble, he once more wants to speed his brethren's flight and then far from the sounds of war enjoy home life.

A softer and more lyric strain blends with the harsh notes when the mother in putting her child to sleep sings the song based upon a passage found in Bartram's *Travels,* a poem that glorifies the Creeks' most blissful spot on earth:

> They say that afar in the land of the west,
> Where the bright golden sun sinks in glory to rest,
> Mid fens where the hunter ne'er ventured to tread,
> A fair lake unruffled and sparkling is spread;
> Where, lost in his course, the rapt Indian discovers,
> In distance seen dimly, the green isle of lovers.
>
> There verdure fades never; immortal in bloom,
> Soft waves the magnolia its groves of perfume;
> And low bends the branch with rich fruitage deprest,
> All glowing like gems in the crowns of the east;
> There the bright eye of Nature, in mild glory hovers:
> 'Tis the land of the sunbeam, — the green isle of lovers!
>
> Sweet strains wildly float on the breezes that kiss
> The calm-flowing lake round that region of bliss;
> Where, wreathing their garlands of amaranth, fair choirs

Glad measures still weave to the sound that inspires
The dance and the revel, mid forests that cover
On high with their shade the green isle of the lover.

But fierce as the snake with his eyeballs of fire,
When his scales are all brilliant and glowing with ire,
Are the warriors to all, save the maids of their isle,
Whose law is their will, and whose life is their smile;
From beauty there valor and strength are not rovers,
And peace reigns supreme in the green isle of lovers.

And he who has sought to set foot on its shore,
In mazes perplext, has beheld it no more;
It fleets on the vision, deluding the view,
Its banks still retire as the hunters pursue;
O! who in this vain world of wo shall discover,
The home undisturbed, the green isle of the lover!

Later the child is robbed in order that it may be offered as a sacrifice to the evil spirit in return for success in battle. Possibly as a consequence of religious interests on the part of the authors, the supernatural and especially the dæmonical element bulks larger than in most works dealing with the aborigines.

According to Dr. Palfrey's historic review of the poem published in the April 1821 number of the *North American Review*, its strength lies in the fourth canto, in which use is made with great felicity of the customs, rites, and superstitions of the Indians. The rites he finds described with a prodigious aptness for the terrible. "We do not remember anything finer of the semi-infernal sort, except Shakespeare's witches. We are at a loss to praise this part of the poem sufficiently to satisfy ourselves, without seeming extravagant." The Song of the Pow-wahs, with incantations based upon passages from Charlevoix, is especially impressive:

> " Beyond the hills the spirit sleeps,
> His watch the Power of evil keeps;
> The spirit of fire has sought his bed,
> The Sun, the hateful Sun, is dead.
> Profound and clear is the sounding wave,
> In the chambers of the Wakon-cave;
> Darkness its ancient portal keeps;
> And there the Spirit sleeps — he sleeps.

The Pow-wahs are summoned:

> Come ye hither, who o'er the thatch
> Of the coward murderer hold your watch;
> Moping and chattering round who fly
> Where the putrid members reeking lie,
> Piece-meal dropping, as they decay,
> O'er the shuddering recreant day by day.
>
> . . . .
>
> Come ye who give power
> To the curse that is said,
> And a charm that shall wither
> To the drops that are shed,
> On the cheek of the maiden
> Who never shall hear
> The kind name of Mother
> Saluting her ear;
> But sad as the turtle
> On the bare branch reclining,
> She shall sit in the desert,
> Consuming and pining;
> With a grief that is silent,
> Her beauty shall fade,
> Like a flower nipt untimely,
> On its stem that is dead.

After the baby has been lulled to sleep, there follows the dedication song of the priestess before the sacrifice; but before the latter can take place, a storm suddenly breaks, during which the child is rescued by a stranger.

In the next two cantos the story hastens to a dramatic close, as Yamoyden, believing his wife and children stolen, longs to fight, and Philip in a doleful deathsong prepares for the end. Nora witnesses how her people surround the unfortunate Indians and how a native wounds Philip, until

> . . . in the moor's dank, miry bed,
> Deep fell the indignant chieftain, dead.

She sees her father rescued by her beloved Yamoyden, who instead receives the deadly stroke. The re-united lovers die, but the child is safe.

Historically *Yamoyden* proved to be of the greatest importance, since its popularity augured well for those desirous of utilizing material from what seemed to be a rich mine. In his famous article in the *North American Review* Dr. Palfrey praised the choice of the subject in unmeasured terms. " We are glad that somebody has at last found out the unequalled fitness of our early history for the purposes of a work of fiction. For ourselves, we know not the country or age which has such capacities in this view as N. England in its early day; nor do we suppose it easy to imagine any element of the sublime, the wonderful, the picturesque and the pathetic, which is not to be found here by him who shall hold the witch-hazel wand that can trace it."

He regarded the Puritan characters fit and interesting subjects for delineation, and then " there are the Indians, a separate and strongly marked race of men, — with all the bold rough lines of nature yet uneffaced upon them, — phlegmatic but fierce, inconstant though unimpassioned, hard to incite and impossible to soothe, cold in friendship and insatiable in revenge, yet, though manifesting little sensibility to the wonders of art, alive to the impressions of natural grandeur and beauty, and speaking even in their common affairs the rich language of a sententious poetry. . . . He who shall give them their just place in poetry, will differ from any delineator of artificial manners almost as much as a landscape of Salvator Rosa differs from an artist's draught of a modern house. Their superstitions furnish abundant food to an imagination enclined to the sombre and terrible, their primitive habits admit of pathos in the introduction of incidents of private life, and in public there occurred events enough to find place for the imposing qualities of heroism. The attitude of the Indian tribes for nearly a century after the landing at Plymouth, was one of high practical interest. The prince saw his followers half alienated, the priest his faith supplanted, the patriot his race declining towards political annihilation; and innumerable must have been the designs of valor, endlessly discordant the counsels of interest, deep the forebodings of despair, bitter the menaces of vengeance, sharp the contests of discordant policy throughout that anxious period."

The reviewer concludes his discussion with this significant prophecy: " Whoever in this country first attains the rank of a first rate writer of fiction, we venture to predict will lay his scene here. The wide field is ripe for the harvest, and scarce a sickle has yet touched it."

Spurred on by the success of *Yamoyden* and the invitation of such a distinguished reviewer, not a few eagerly set to work in order to take advantage of the discovery. Among them was Lydia Maria Francis (Child), at that time a young woman of twenty-two. One Sunday noon in 1824 she came across Palfrey's article in her brother's study, who served the First Parish in Watertown, read it, and before the afternoon service wrote the first chapter of a two hundred page novel entitled *Hobomok, a Tale of Early Times,* which was published in the same year.

The scene of the story, ostensibly based upon an old Puritan manuscript and covering several years after 1629, is mainly laid at Salem and Plymouth. Delicate Mary Conant, overwhelmed by the report of the loss at sea of her betrothed Charles Brown, hastily accepts as husband the sympathetic chief Hobomok, who is described as cast in nature's noblest mold. " He was one of the finest specimens of elastic, vigorous elegance of proportion, to be found among his tribe. His long residence with the white inhabitants of Plymouth had changed his natural fierceness of manner into haughty, dignified reserve; and even that seemed softened as his dark expressive eye rested on Conant's daughter." Early she had begun to prefer to those around her the Indian, " whose language was brief, figurative, and prophetic, and whose nature was unwarped by the artifices of civilized life." And as a wife she learns to love better every day the kind, noble-hearted creature, who becomes the father of her hopeful son.

But soon complications arise. Hobomok on a brief hunt in very un-Indian like fashion " pursuing his way through the woods, whistling and singing as he went, in the joyfulness of his heart " comes across Charles Brown, who after escaping shipwreck with his life had been held for three years as prisoner in Africa. Both men are willing to give up the lady, but finally the generous chief commends his son to the rival's care and suggests that the handsome English bird sing the marriage song in the wigwam of the Englishman. Divorcing his wife after the manner of the Indians, and catching one last glimpse of Mary and his boy, he leaves never to return. The two lovers are speedily re-united; little Hobomok later becomes a distinguished graduate at Cambridge, and finishes his education in England.

That a young girl of twenty-two, wholly unacquainted with the Indians and with boyish love in her head, should have produced a masterpiece, was more than could be expected under the circumstances. Though not without some stylistic merit, *Hobomok* is hastily written, entirely improbable in plot, and peopled with Indians that never existed. But as one of the first fictitious productions with its scene laid in Puritan days and marking the " very dawn of American imaginative literature," which launched Mrs. Lydia Francis Child on her literary career, it is of considerable historical interest and importance.

CHAPTER VI

IN PAULDING'S HUMOROUS VEIN

About a century ago, James Kirke Paulding (1779–1860) was a prominent figure in American letters as well as in politics. His original satirical humor manifested itself early in collaboration with Washington Irving, whose brother William had married James' sister. In spite of various public offices such as that of secretary to the board of navy commissioners, navy agent at the port of New York, and Secretary of the Navy under Van Buren, he found time for literary matters, shifting the details of his political offices to subordinates. Among his numerous writings, once popular but in most cases long since overtaken by complete neglect, is *Koningsmarke, The Long Finne,* 1823, one of the finest composed in his lighter vein. Written in imitation of Fielding's *Tom Jones,* which he considered one of the most consummate works of fiction ever produced, the story deals mainly with life among the Swedish settlers of Delaware and the Indians of central Pennsylvania about 1660. The fortunes of Christina, Governor Peter Piper's comely daughter, are linked with those of the Long Finne, who in spite of various vicissitudes among the Swedes, the Indians, and later in New York, finally succeeds in claiming his bride.

As might be expected in a work pervaded by satiric humor, the passages dealing with the natives are not without laugh-provoking elements, even though the warriors are grim fighters and savages with revengeful spirits. When well treated, as by the Big Hats or Quakers, they are kind, liberal, and hospitable to strangers, ever mindful of benefits received; but on the other hand, they are reserved and fiercely resentful of wrongs suffered, breathing an undying vengeance especially against the whites who plowed up the ground where the bones of their fathers had been deposited. The people of the town of Elsingburg on the

Delaware, Governor Piper's capital, lived in peace with the neighboring redskins except when the latter occasionally took little miffs, and committed depredations on the cattle and fields. According to Paulding, before the contact with the whites the Indians had few vices, the state of their society furnishing them few temptations; and even these were counterbalanced by many good and great qualities. But the universal curse of their race, spirituous liquors, gradually debased the minds and degraded to a miserable remnant of degenerate beings the tall and stately monarchs of the forests.

For the purpose of settling various religious and economic matters, the colonists arranged a conference with their Indian neighbors, whose gravity of deportment and expression of habitual melancholy represented a fitting counterpart to the stolid Swedes. The council was not without its humorous aspects, when there appeared among others " ten or a dozen of the monarchs of the new world, whose names and titles, translated into English, equal those of the most lofty and legitimate kings of the east . . . the Big Buffalo, the Little Duck Legs, the Sharp Faced Bear, the Walking Shadow, the Rolling Thunder, the Iron Cloud, the Jumping Sturgeon, the Belly Ache, and the Doctor, all legitimate sovereigns, with copper rings in their noses, blanket robes of state, and painted faces." The speeches and discussions gradually become more serious and even threatening as the natives complain that they are deprived of their fish by a dam, and the Dominie denies their right to a country they neither plow nor fence so that they grow neither rich nor are happy as the people of Europe. To this the exasperated natives reply that if the settlers were so happy at home, there is no reason why they should have come over. The Indians finally demand that they be left in undisturbed possession of their woods, their waters, their ancient customs and gods, whereupon they withdraw with warwhoops and the chanting of bloody songs.

As a natural consequence of such feelings, the attack on Elsingburg quickly follows, and the explosion of the powder magazine makes Piper's retreat to the boats necessary. However, not all are as fortunate as Lob Dotterel on a former occasion, who, his queue having been seized by a savage, left only his wig in the hands of the astonished warrior as a trophy. With grim humor Koningsmarke begins to cut off both hands and the head of a savage who tried to seize his boat, but he and Christina are made prisoners when Indian reenforcements arrive. He is immediately claimed as a slave by the widow whom he had bereft of a provider.

The redskins are now in an ugly mood. They fire the town and tomahawk women and children. The fate of Claas Tomeson and Councilor Varlett indicates the extremes to which the savages would go when aroused. Claas had successfully run the gauntlet of his tormentors and gained temporary refuge in the council house when the doctor or conjurer claimed all his effects for services rendered, and having carefully gathered together the various items of the fee, marched with astonishing dignity and gravity out of the wigwam. Next Paulding inserts a scene of horror, " which has been often witnessed by the dauntless spirits who marched in the van, to the exploring and settling of this new world, and which may perhaps, in some measure, serve to excuse their harshness to that unhappy race, by whom their friends and brothers had so often suffered." Tomeson had been stripped, painted black, and beaten with sticks by the women and boys. His hands were tied behind his back with a rope, the other end of which was fastened to a stake about fifteen feet high. As he went around the stake, the men fired powder into his naked skin and thrust burning brands into his body, while the squaws were busy throwing hot ashes and burning coals upon his bare head. When almost senseless from the suffering he lay down upon the hot ground, an old hag placed " burning coals on a piece of bark, threw them upon his back, which was now excoriated from head to foot." Since he is no longer susceptible to pain, a chief kills him with a tomahawk.

Such tortures Councilor Varlett avoids by pretending that rifle balls cannot hurt him. When their bullets kill him, the Indians comprehend, but too late, that a victim has escaped them. Mad with rage and disappointment, they tear his body to pieces, scoop up his blood with their hands, and drink it smoking hot, finally tossing his limbs into the flames. Then follows a night scene baffling all description, brought on by strong drink, and the morning finds the wretched bacchanals dejected, worn out, and melancholy in the extreme; some are wounded, others crippled, or dead.

The scene just described marks the extreme of horror. Paulding pens other passages of a bloody nature that would warm the heart of every red-blooded warrior. After his initiation into the Muskrat tribe, Lob Dotterel fights under the name of Jumping Sturgeon against enemies on the banks of the Ohio, and the description of his successful encounter with a tall Indian is especially spirited and interesting. Likewise Koningsmarke's combat with a chief and his supporting boy hardly ever has been excelled in the description of battle scenes anywhere.

But this is only one side of Indian life depicted by Paulding; another is that of affectionate tenderness. He tells us that the " Indian women are as remarkable for the tenderness and warmth of their affection, as the Indian men are for their coldness and indifference. They become suddenly and strongly attached, especially to white men, and being entirely governed by the feelings of nature, do not hesitate to take upon themselves those advances, which, among civilized people, are the province of men alone." Once having secured their prize, they are all gentle and tender simplicity. The afore-mentioned widow had cast her eyes upon Koningsmarke as a suitable substitute for her former spouse, whose place he is assigned in consideration of the fact that he is responsible for her lonely condition. But he not unnaturally demurs and during a drunken debauch escapes with another white man and with Christina, who had been lodged conveniently nearby with a widow. Unfortunately they chance to kill the brother of Aonetti or Deer Eyes who had befriended the lovers, and are recaptured. Christina is rescued by Deer Eyes, but the two men are to undergo torture and death at the stake. The pleas of Deer Eyes are in vain, and all is in readiness when the loud and sharp crash of thunder halts the gruesome ceremony. The Indian maiden skilfully interprets the thunderclap as a manifestation of the divine will: " Hark! The Great Spirit bears testimony against this deed. You heard his voice in the air. It came not from a cloud in the skies. It is the great Master of Life, that cries out from above against his people that have offended him. In his name I command you to stop — in his name I command you to spare these white men." Terror-struck, the chiefs decide to learn more fully the will of the Great Spirit before they proceed with the ceremony. When next day the frantic priest turns against the prisoners, they seem lost, but at the opportune moment a party of Big Hats sent by William Penn arrives. With gifts of coats, glass beads, and tobaccos — the kegs of whiskey are conspicuously lacking — they succeed in placating the Indians who allow their captives to return to Delaware.

Only once more the natives appear in the story. When Governor Lovelace of New York threatens Governor Piper, that worthy warrior despatches the Long Finne and a party with presents to the neighboring savages, asking them to take up arms in his behalf. This the wily redskins decline to do, with the secret wish, however, that the two belligerents would mutually exterminate each other.

Paulding has given us a rather comprehensive picture of the natives. On the one hand, they are not saints by any means, for at times their cruelty knows no bounds. Their grimmer moods are portrayed with considerable skill: the burning at the stake, if horrible, is yet unforgettable; the personal encounters are described in a way that compels joyous attention; the thunder scene is especially fine in the skilful blending and counteraction of the chief primary emotions. The natives partake somewhat of the Dutch character with their awkwardness and mental dullness. On the other hand, they are not simply bloodthirsty savages, but are open to persuasion and reasonableness. They exhibit even a few of those characteristics that make life more endurable or joyous. The aggression of the whites the author by no means condones. He believes that the policy of William Penn can never be sufficiently praised or admired. The latter's acquisition and retention of the confidence and good-will of the Indians was almost unexampled, for none " without resorting to the agency of superstition or fear ever attained so great an influence over the violent capricious and intractable tempers of the savages of North

America." Strangely enough, Paulding closes with the melancholy reflection that the natives are "a singular race, with whom all attempts at civilization only seem to destroy their good qualities, and convert them from barbarians into beasts," certainly a pessimistic statement denying the very foundation of progress under the tutelage of the more advanced white settler.

CHAPTER VII

THE NATIVES THROUGH THE EYES OF AN OPTIMIST

Even though he did not utilize them as material for fiction, the natives of America repeatedly attracted the attention of the kind and genial nature of Washington Irving (1783-1859). And no wonder, for his brother William was an Indian trader, and from his close friend Henry Brevoort, engaged with John Jacob Astor in the fur trade, he received long letters dealing with the natives. Irving's early interest found expression in the two papers " Indian Traits " and " Philip of Pokanoket," which he later incorporated in the *Sketch Book*. The few occasional and humorous references to the original owners of Manhattan Island in *Knickerbocker's History of New York* betray a natural, if faint, acknowledgment of the disregarded rights of the aborigines. In his *Life of Washington* the Indians are frequently mentioned. And in three works the Indian plays a major part, namely in *A Tour of the Prairies*, 1835, *Astoria*, 1836, and *The Adventures of Captain Bonneville*, 1837. The first is based upon his own experiences in the Far West, while the other two are the reshaping of diaries and reports of travellers, hunters, and trappers.

The two essays entitled " Traits of Indian Character " and " Philip of Pokanoket " were inspired by a romantic enthusiasm for primitive tribes, which was prevalent in those days. In the former Irving speaks of the traits then generally attributed to the Indian, as for instance his " proud stoicism and habitual taciturnity," an opinion which closer contact hardly upheld. The author also glorifies his proud independence, his reverence, and his lofty contempt of death. While thus at practically every turn he defends the native, he magnifies the wrongdoings of the newcomer, who is said to have hunted the aborigines like wild beasts.

In the paper entitled " Philip of Pokanoket," which as one of his juvenile efforts appeared as early as 1814, Irving incidentally glorifies on the basis of slight reading Conanchet, the Narragansett chief. Whatever admirable qualities this Indian brave may have possessed, he hardly fits into the heroic picture when slipping on a stone and wetting his gun he was so unnerved as to become " like a rotten stick, void of strength," a fatal weakness in the hour of peril. The figure of King Philip appears as one of grand and heroic proportions. He is characterized as " a true born prince, gallantly fighting at the head of his subjects to avenge the wrongs of his family; to retrieve the tottering power of his line; and to deliver his native land from the oppression of usurping strangers." Irving admires his traces of amiable and lofty character, the feelings of connubial love and paternal tenderness, and the generous sentiments of friendship, his proudness of heart and untamable love of natural liberty — along with the qualities of the warrior and statesman. The Puritan writers he makes out as grossly unfair, for to him Philip is a patriot, a true prince, and a great soldier, embodying a lofty spirit and an ambitious temper. Irving considered the Indians " worthy of an age of poetry, and fit subjects for local story and romantic fiction," though he himself strangely enough never worked this supposedly rich mine of native material.

In the introduction to *A Tour of the Prairies* Irving tells us that the book was written in response to public expectations aroused by an extensive journey he made to the West in 1832. Without much enthusiasm he turned to his memoranda covering a month's " foray into the Pawnee Hunting Grounds," watered by the Arkansas, the Grand Canadian, and the Red River. As would seem natural, the record of this four weeks' expedition, led by a Government Commissioner and protected by army rangers, does not at all compare in interest and importance with the material available for the two other more ambitious works.

Since the untamed Pawnees, the terror of the border, were not even sighted, the one alarm of their approach proving to be a false one, they play a rather inconspicuous part. The references to them are largely confined to a recital of their prowess and skill by a half-breed guide, who regales the inexperienced rangers with tales of their exploits. The gaily bedecked Creeks and the more austere Osages, border tribes which had come under the direct influence of the whites, figure much more in the work, especially in the beginning. Irving speaks enthusiastically of the Osages as the finest looking Indians he had ever seen in the West, admiring especially " the finely shaped heads and busts of these savages, and their graceful attitudes and expressive gestures." He praises the glorious independence of man in his savage state, who in the absence of the enslaving artificial wants of society possesses the great secret of personal freedom.

Irving evidently believed in the innate goodness of many of the natives, and he condemned strongly the border propensity of charging everything to the Indians. His utterance was occasioned by the threat of a squatter to give a sound lashing to a young Osage whom he suspected of having lured away his horse in order to reap a substantial reward for its return. " Such, however, is often the administration of law on the frontier, ' Lynch's Law,' as it is technically termed, in which the plaintiff is apt to be witness, jury, judge, and executioner, and the defendant to be convicted and punished on mere presumption; and in this way, I am convinced, are occasioned many of those heart-burnings and resentments among the Indians, which lead to retaliation, and end in Indian wars."

Throughout the work, the author gives his observations and interpretation of native traits, which are not always those found in fiction. For instance, the Indians are by no means " the stoics they are represented, taciturn, unbending, without a tear or a smile." They may be taciturn and grave among strangers, but gay and even garrulous when with acquaintances. At times there is humor and laughter; and then again tears flow in abundance at the death of a relative or friend. " As far as I can judge, the Indian of poetical fiction is like the shepherd of pastoral romance, a mere personification of mere attributes."

The romantic and striking in Indian character Irving left largely unelaborated. He noted, however, the " superstitious propensity, common to the solitary and savage rovers of the wilderness, that gives such powerful influence to the prophet and dreamer." To illustrate their superstitions, he adds a little story current among the Osages, who tell how the Flower of the Prairies, a beautiful girl affianced to the bravest and most graceful hunter of the tribe, seemingly meets her intended on his return from St. Louis; but when later he wants to lead her to the camp, her spirit from the shadow world has vanished, and as the fatal truth dawns upon him, he joins her in death. From the anecdotes of the intrepid Delawares he mentions how the guardian spirit in the form of a great eagle is supposed to lend protection to those in danger. In such a perilous hour the chief warrior of a band surrounded by foes sacrificed his horse to the tutelar spirit, who took up the gift and shed the magic feathers that enabled the whole party to escape unharmed from the deadly ring of the Pawnees. Surely, material in abundance there was for a creative work, had the author chosen to use it; but evidently such a possibility either did not occur to him or lacked sufficient appeal.

Astoria is an exceedingly readable account of the establishment and fortunes of the fur-trading station at the mouth of the Columbia River named after its promoter John Jacob Astor. Not only does it deal with the voyage of the " Tonquin " from the Atlantic to the Pacific and its fate, but it also describes the overland journey of one of the partners, Mr. Hunt, the return trip of Mr. Stuart, and the capture of the trading post during the war of 1812 by the Hudson Bay Co., the powerful rival of the American association. The work is based mainly upon material put at Irving's disposal by Mr. Astor, who was anxious that the services he incidentally had rendered his country be immortalized. Irving himself, assisted by a nephew, sufficiently worked over the material so as to give a literary flavor to the narratives of traders, hunters, and trappers. Still, the whole is invested with that peculiar interest ordinarily inherent in first hand accounts of hardy pioneers.

It is but natural that the Indians should appear on many pages of this history of the early fur industry in the American Northwest. Since the work occupies the border line between history and literature, we may appropriately confine ourselves to the discussion of the more important aspects of the natives, who are described in great detail. As in *A Tour of the Prairies,* the aborigines appear generally in a rather favorable light, and the ensuing difficulties and conflicts are laid more often at the door of the whites than of the red men.

Take for instance the fate of the good ship Tonquin, whose crew was massacred by the enraged natives and later blown up by its wounded clerk with terrible consequences to the new possessors. Setting out from Astoria, it had anchored at Vancouver's Island in the face of the warnings of the Indian interpreter; its captain Thorn, deficient in patience and pliancy and also in the chicanery of traffic, had lost his temper, snatched the proffered otter skins from the hands of an insolently bargaining chief, " rubbed it into his face, and dismissed him over the side of the ship with no very complimentary application to accelerate his exit. He then kicked the peltries to the right and left about the deck, and broke up the market in the most ignominious manner." The furious Indians returned next day under the pretext of trade, were admitted, and when through barter they had secured weapons, slaughtered the crew with the exception of five members who succeeded in barricading themselves in the captain's cabin and who cleared the deck with firearms. During the night the four sailors slipped away in the ship's boat, and in the morning the disabled clerk lured the savages on board and then took terrible vengeance by setting fire to the powder magazine, the explosion of which resulted in the death of more than one hundred savages. The natives on their part exacted a ghastly toll when in the morning they captured the four sailors, prevented by a stiff wind from getting out of the bay, and sacrificed them to the manes of their kindred with all the lingering tortures of savage cruelty. According to Irving, the melancholy story of the Tonquin, more thrilling than the adventures of a dime novel, need never have been told but for its headstrong and tactless commander, who had offered a direct insult so wounding to savage pride.

Of absorbing interest are also the experiences of Mr. Hunt's party which proceeded overland from St. Louis in 1810. The antics of the half-breed interpreter Dorian and his intractable Sioux squaw cast a lurid light upon the life and morals of the mongrel

NATIVES THROUGH THE EYES OF AN OPTIMIST

offspring. The story of one of the trappers, retold by Irving from Bradbury's *Travels in America,* deserves to be given verbatim as one of the most stirring episodes enacted among the proud and vindictive Blackfeet, who had suffered the loss of a warrior while attempting to steal horses from Captain Lewis.

" Colter, with the hardihood of a regular trapper, had cast himself loose from the party of Lewis and Clark in the very heart of the wilderness, and had remained to trap beaver alone on the head-waters of the Missouri. Here he fell in with another lonely trapper, like himself, named Potts, and they agreed to keep together. They were in the very region of the terrible Blackfeet, at that time thirsting to revenge the death of their companion, and knew that they had to expect no mercy at their hands. They were obliged to keep concealed all day in the woody margins of the rivers, setting their traps after nightfall, and taking them up before daybreak. It was running a fearful risk for the sake of a few beaver skins; but such is the life of the trapper.

They were on a branch of the Missouri called Jefferson's Fork, and had set their traps at night, about six miles up a small river that emptied into the fork. Early in the morning they ascended the river in a canoe, to examine the traps. The banks on each side were high and perpendicular, and cast a shade over the stream. As they were softly paddling along, they heard the trampling of many feet upon the banks. Colter immediately gave the alarm of ' Indians! ' and was for instant retreat. Potts scoffed at him for being frightened by the trampling of a herd of buffaloes. Colter checked his uneasiness, and paddled forward. They had not gone much further when frightful whoops and yells burst forth from each side of the river, and several hundred Indians appeared on either bank. Signs were made to the unfortunate trappers to come on shore. They were obliged to comply. Before they could get out of their canoes, a savage seized the rifle belonging to Potts. Colter sprang on shore, wrested the weapon from the hands of the Indian, and restored it to his companion, who was still in the canoe, and immediately pushed into the stream. There was the sharp twang of a bow, and Potts cried out that he was wounded. Colter urged him to come on shore and submit, as his only chance for life; but the other knew there was no prospect of mercy, and determined to die game. Levelling his rifle, he shot one of the savages dead on the spot. The next moment he fell himself, pierced with innumerable arrows. The vengeance of the savages now turned upon Colter. He was stripped naked, and, having some knowledge of the Blackfoot language, overheard a consultation as to the mode of dispatching him, so as to derive the greatest amusement from his death. Some were for setting him up as a mark, and having a trial of skill at his expense. The chief, however, was for nobler sport. He seized Colter by the shoulder, and demanded if he could run fast. The unfortunate trapper was too well acquainted with Indian customs not to comprehend the drift of the question. He knew he was to run for his life, to furnish a kind of human hunt to his persecutors. Though in reality he was noted among his brother hunters for swiftness of foot, he assured the chief that he was a very bad runner. His stratagem gained him some vantage ground. He was led by the chief into the prairie, about four hundred yards from the main body of savages, and then turned loose to save himself if he could. A tremendous yell let him know that the whole pack of bloodhounds were off in full cry. Colter flew, rather than ran; he was astonished at his own speed; but he had six miles of prairie to traverse before he should reach the Jefferson Fork of the Missouri; how could he hope to hold out such a distance with the fearful odds of several hundred to one against him! The plain, too, abounded with the prickly pear, which wounded his naked feet. Still he fled on, dreading each moment to hear the twang of a bow, and to feel an arrow quivering at his heart. He did not even dare to look round, lest he should lose an inch of that distance on which his life depended. He had run nearly half way across the plain when the sound of pursuit grew somewhat fainter, and he ventured to turn his head. The main body of his pursuers were a considerable distance behind; several of the fastest runners were scattered in the advance; while a swift-footed warrior, armed with a spear, was not more than a hundred yards behind him.

Inspired with new hope, Colter redoubled his exertions, but strained himself to such a degree that the blood gushed from his mouth and nostrils and streamed down his breast. He arrived

NATIVES THROUGH THE EYES OF AN OPTIMIST 59

within a mile of the river. The sound of footsteps gathered upon him. A glance behind showed his pursuer within twenty yards, and preparing to launch his spear. Stopping short, he turned round and spread out his arms. The savage, confounded by this sudden action, attempted to stop and hurl his spear, but fell in the very act. His spear stuck in the ground, and the shaft broke in his hand. Colter plucked up the pointed part, pinned the savage to the earth, and continued his flight. The Indians, as they arrived at their slaughtered companion, stopped to howl over him. Colter made the most of this precious delay, gained the skirt of cotton-wood bordering the river, dashed through it, and plunged into the stream. He swam to a neighboring island, against the upper end of which the driftwood had lodged in such quantities as to form a natural raft; under this he dived, and swam below water until he succeeded in getting a breathing place between the floating trunks of trees, whose branches and bushes formed a covert several feet above the level of the water. He had scarcely drawn breath after all his toils, when he heard his pursuers on the river bank, whooping and yelling like so many fiends. They plunged in the river, and swam to the raft. The heart of Colter almost died within him as he saw them, through the chinks of his concealment, passing and repassing, and seeking for him in all directions. They at length gave up the search, and he began to rejoice in his escape, when the idea presented itself that they might set the raft on fire. Here was a new source of horrible apprehension, in which he remained until nightfall. Fortunately, the idea did not suggest itself to the Indians. As soon as it was dark, finding by the silence around that his pursuers had departed, Colter dived again and came up beyond the raft. He then swam silently down the river for a considerable distance, when he landed, and kept on all night, to get as far as possible from this dangerous neighborhood.

By daybreak he had gained sufficient distance to relieve him from the terrors of his savage foes; but now new sources of inquietude presented themselves. He was naked and alone, in the midst of an unbounded wilderness; his only chance was to reach a trading post of the Missouri Company, situated on a branch of the Yellowstone River. Even should he elude his pursuers, days must elapse before he could reach this post, during which he must traverse immense prairies destitute of shade, his naked body exposed to the burning heat of the sun by day, and the dews and chills of the night season; and his feet lacerated by the thorns of the prickly pear. Though he might see game in abundance around him, he had no means of killing any for his sustenance, and must depend for food upon the roots of the earth. In defiance of these difficulties he pushed resolutely forward, guiding himself in his trackless course by those signs and indications known only to Indians and backwoodsmen; and after braving dangers and hardships enough to break down any spirit but that of a western pioneer, arrived safe at the solitary post in question."

The experiences of the party making its way to the Pacific Coast contradicted the descriptions of the idyllic life sometimes attributed to the natives in their primitive state. For every Indian tribe seemed to show implacable hostility to some rival tribe, a situation which tended to the extinction of the native even before the advent of the white man. Mr. Hunt gives a sad account of the Indian tribes bordering on the Missouri River. " They are in continual war with each other, and their wars were of the most harassing kind; consisting not merely of main conflicts and expeditions of moment, involving the sackings, burnings, and massacres of towns and villages, but of individual acts of treachery, murder, and cold-blooded cruelty; or of vaunting and foolhardy exploits of single warriors, either to avenge some personal wrong, or gain the vainglorious trophy of a scalp. The lonely hunter, the wandering wayfarer, the poor squaw gathering wood or cutting corn, was liable to be surprised and slaughtered. In this way tribes were either swept away at once, or gradually thinned out, and savage life was surrounded with constant horrors and alarms. . . . It is rather a matter of surprise that so many should survive . . . for the existence of a savage in these parts seems little better than a prolonged and all-besetting death. It is, in fact, a caricature of the boasted romance of feudal times, chivalry in its native and uncultured state, and knight-errantry run wild."

Even within the tribes themselves despotic chiefs would assume the power of life and death. The Omahas, for instance, had been under the sway of the famous Blackbird, about whom savage and romantic stories were told. When his people began to show signs of discontent over his highhanded way of enriching himself and the white traders at the expense of his subjects, he had by means of arsenic obtained undisputed control over the ignorant and superstitious. In the eyes of his people he seemed to be endowed with supernatural powers and with the gifts of a prophet. Whoever questioned his authority, was certain to be smitten by a strange and sudden disease in accordance with the prophecy of the great chief, and perish from the face of the earth. No wonder that all dreaded such supernatural power and were unwilling to incur the displeasure of so mighty a being.

The surrounding tribes, such as the Pawnees and Poncas, had felt the heavy hand of this wily and warlike chief. With all his savage and terrifying qualities, however, he was not insensible of the power of female beauty and love. A Ponca chief, for instance, had purchased immunity only by the gift of his beautiful daughter arrayed in her finest ornaments. But even she, his favorite wife, fell a victim to a fit of insane rage. The great chief, however, was helpless in the face of the dreaded small-pox, which swept him and two thirds of his people away. His burial mound on the banks of the Missouri, towering four hundred feet above the waters, at that time still remained as a memorial of the grim chieftain.

As an instance of white man's wanton attacks upon the native, an episode involving a Mr. Carson and the Sioux is cited as illuminating. When Mr. Hunt reproached them for having killed three white men the previous summer, the chief explained that the three were slain to avenge the death of one of the brethren at the hands of one of Mr. Hunt's companions, who being with a party of Arickaras had fired a random shot at the Sioux across the Missouri, without much expectation of effect at such a distance. But it had brought down a Sioux warrior, for whose wanton destruction threefold vengeance had to be taken. Irving concludes: " In this way outrages are frequently committed on the natives by thoughtless or mischievous white men; the Indians retaliate according to a law of their code, which requires blood for blood; their act, of what with them is pious vengeance, resounds throughout the land, and is represented as wanton and unprovoked; the neighborhood is roused to arms; a war ensues, which ends in the destruction of half the tribe, the ruin of the rest, and their expulsion from their hereditary homes. Such is too often the real history of Indian warfare, which in general is traced up only to some vindictive act of a savage; while the outrage of the scoundrel white man that provoked it is sunk in silence."

The filth of the Indian village, as well as his innate hospitality before he has mingled to any considerable extent with the white man, is duly noted. The emotional nature of the Indian is exhibited in the description of the successful return of a Arickara war-party which proved the fallacy of the old fable of Indian apathy and stoicism. The most rapturous expressions of joy as well as doleful wailings and lamentations greeted the victors and the dead. The perfidy and thievery of the Crows and other tribes impressed themselves forcibly upon the party, as also the mischief occasioned by half-breeds and white ruffians, outcasts of civilization, and heartless desperadoes who sow the seeds of enmity and bitterness among the unfortunate tribes.

No doubt the natives of the Northwest had often evil and malicious intentions, though at times they were more the gay and mischievous ruffians than bloodthirsty savages. They were quick to avenge an insult and injury which are often at the bottom of what may seem unprovoked and wanton cruelty. For instance, Mr. Clarke as a firm believer in the doctrine of intimidation, and holding the life of a savage extremely cheap, had executed a thief of the Pierced-Nose tribe. Later a number of companions were killed on the Snake River in what seemed an act of butchery, but which the Astorians ascribed as a measure on the part of the offended tribe in revenge for the death of their comrade. Irving draws this conclusion: " If so, it shows that these sudden and apparently wanton outbreakings of sanguinary violence on the part of the savages, have often some previous, though perhaps remote, provocation."

The Adventures of Captain Bonneville is in many respects an echo of the experiences of Astor's men, since the area traversed between May 1832 and August 1835 covered approximately the hunting-grounds of the same Northwest tribes. As far as the natives are concerned, the exploration two decades later often repeats the sentiments of the men connected with the earlier venture. For instance, the Crows and Blackfeet still appear as horse-thieves, rogues, and ruffians of the first order, from whose predatory habits the trappers especially suffer. Sometimes they seem to be in a jocose rather than sanguinary mood, as when in the Wind River Valley they stripped an unfortunate trapper of absolutely everything till he appeared stark naked, and then dismissed him among universal laughter with a buffalo robe. Others again, as the Pends Oreilles, are said to abstain from all aggressive action displeasing to the Great Spirit. At times, Bonneville's opinion is more favorable than that of the earlier pioneers, though in the case of the Nez Percéds he seems to have been over-enthusiastic. While Astor's men had found them extremely difficult to handle, Bonneville, who resided for some time among them and had repeated opportunities to ascertain their real character, " invariably speaks of them as kind and hospitable, scrupulously honest, and remarkable, above all other Indians that he had met with, for a strong feeling of religion. In fact, so enthusiastic is he in their praise, that he pronounces them, all ignorant and barbarous as they are by their condition, one of the purest-hearted people on the face of the earth." But unfortunately for his judgment, one of them steals a rare skin from one of the captain's men, for which the soldier-diplomat executes a poor innocent dog. Truly, tact never scored a greater triumph.

This does not mean that the worthy captain was ignorant of the treacherous nature or underestimated the fighting qualities of potential enemies. As a matter of fact, he respected the Indian as a vigilant and crafty foe who was by no means given to hair-brained assaults and who seldom attacked when he found his foe well prepared and on the alert. But in dealing with him he considered diplomacy and caution at least as efficacious a protection as courage.

As in *Astoria*, Irving condemns the perfidy and cruelty of white men, which often led to bloody reprisals. The encounter involving a Blackfeet chief as also the Battle at Pierre's Hole was the fault of the whites, who at the moment of friendly overtures began hostilities. He indignantly arraigns the firm and resolute trappers who refused to free two Arickara spies except on condition that all and not merely some of their stolen horses be returned by the party. In order to impress the savage mind properly, they dragged the two prisoners to the blazing pyre, and burned them to death in sight of their retreating comrades. " Such are the savage cruelties that white men learn to practice, who mingle in savage life; and such are the arts that lead to terrible recrimination on the part of the Indians. Should we hear of any atrocities committed by the Arickaras upon captive white men, let this signal and recent provocation be borne in mind. Individual cases of the kind dwell in the recollections of whole tribes; and it is a point of honor and conscience to revenge them."

Though Washington Irving had only a vicarious acquaintance with the natives of America, his delineations on account of that very fact surpass in faithfulness the writings of many who could boast of a wider personal experience, but which on the other hand constituted the limits of their knowledge. The sentimentalism of the first decades of the 19th century had early exacted from him its tribute in the form of praise for the New England Indians defending their soil against the invader. But interest in European subjects soon crowded out what he himself had declared to be fit subjects for romantic fiction. When finally he fixed his gaze again upon America, the literary possibilities of the picturesque native somehow failed to fascinate the cultured cosmopolitan, eliciting only perfunctory expressions of a benevolent attitude.

CHAPTER VIII

THE INDIAN DRAMA

While as early as 1766 the American Indian furnished the material for a native play, it was not till the 19th century that the dramatic value of the picturesque red man was fully realized. During the first three decades the Indian drama began to gain a hearing, and about 1830, especially through the masterful acting of one of America's great tragedians, it became immensely popular and for a dozen years retained its hold upon the theatergoers. Gradually the obvious defects of the stage Indian, notably a sentimental idealization and his strained and bombastic speech, furnished clever burlesque the means to drive him from the stage. As one of the outstanding figures of America's early native drama, the stage Indian is of more than passing interest to the student of literature.

Nearly three score of plays dealing primarily with the native seem to have been written or produced, but of them fewer than twenty have survived. Among those either imperfectly recorded or entirely vanished, a bewildering array of titles greets our eyes: *The Manhattoes; Narramattah; The Maid of Wyoming; The Wigwam; The Indian Wife; The Last of the Mohicans; Miantanimoh; The Liberty Tree; Lamorah; Wacousta; The Pioneers; Oronaska or the Chief of the Mohawks; Kairrissah; Outallissi; The Yemassee; Sassacus; Tippecanoe; Sharratah; Osceola; Telula, or the Star of Hope; Onoleetah; The Eagle Eye; OuaCousta, or the Lion of the Forest; The Star of the West; The Silver Knife, or the Hunters of the Rocky Mountains; Onylda, or the Pequot Maid; Oroonoka; Tuscatomba; Tutoona; Wissahickon; Mioutoumah.* Even if these have left hardly a trace behind, there is little reason to believe that their passing represents any considerable literary loss, as the extant plays may be counted among the best and most representative.

The first American drama dealing primarily with the Indians is *Ponteach, or the Savages of America,* 1766, by Major Robert Rogers. Born in New Hampshire in 1727, already as a boy Rogers had fought against the savage warriors, and later as commander of " Rogers' Rangers " he played a conspicuous part during the siege of Detroit by the great Ottowa chief Pontiac and his allies. Soon afterwards he conceived the great Indian as the hero of a play he published in London, which, however, does not seem to have been produced.

Ponteach, written in the traditional blank verse, is a drama of no great literary value, and the early reviews were anything but favorable. *The Monthly Review* called it " one of the most absurd productions we have ever seen," and " even the *Critical Review,* which had suggested the topic . . . pronounced the drama unreservedly insipid and flat," a statement rather too severe. Though *Ponteach* ranks higher than most Indian plays, fine passages are comparatively rare, and the temptation to quote is not strong. On the other hand, the play shows real insight into native character, and the portrayal with its aim to " give a just idea of the genius and ideas of the Indians " is on the whole true to life.

The first two acts with their wealth of material and fidelity to truth effectively lay bare the causes of Ponteach's warlike attitude. The frontier characters appear in the worst possible light. The traders' fundamental maxim is shown to be

> That it's no Crime to cheat and gull an Indian.

They sell adulterated rum at exorbitant prices, and the scales of McDole are so contrived

> That one small Slip will turn Three Pounds to One.

The English hunters look upon the savages, who have killed some of their near relatives, as revengeful, cruel, and faithless devils. Without provocation they shoot down what they term " a Brace of Noble Bucks," rob them of their valuable fur packs, and conceal the " tawny Dogs " after they have taken their scalps, which they intend to sell for at least two hundred crowns during the next war. Honeyman, the chief offender, scoffs at the English law pro-

THE INDIAN DRAMA 67

tecting the persons of the Indians, and regards their wanton slaying as no more murder than the cracking of a louse. Equally callous are Colonel Cockum and Captain Frisk, the latter wishing that

> God send the Day that puts them all to Sleep.

The appropriately named Governors Sharp, Gripe, and Catchum, sent by the King to distribute presents, appropriate two thirds for themselves and give away only the things that won't do to sell. The accusations and entreaties of the Indians, who are by no means as naïve as often represented, go for nought. Throughout, the contrast between the liberal treatment of the French and the miserly and haughty conduct of the English is painfully evident, and the whole is shot through and enlivened with a grim humor.

A large part of the drama deals with the attempt of Chekitan, one of Ponteach's sons, to win as his bride the comely Monelia, loyal daughter of the English loving Mohawk chief Hendrik. The great Ottowa chief invites and welcomes the help of the Mohawks, but his boundless ambition will brook no rival once the Indian power has become supreme. Another son, Philip, sets out both to win Hendrik and to destroy Monelia and her brother, in order that the enraged Chekitan may expose himself to mortal danger, and he himself become the sole heir. The proud Ponteach, who occasionally vents his wrath in long bombastic speeches, is greatly troubled by a peculiar dream of an immense elk, the meaning of which both the native conjurer and the French priest in vain try to reveal, although they diplomatically predict success in the impending war against the English.

Events begin to move fast when the murdered Indian hunters are found. Although the much travelled King Astinaco counsels to punish only the guilty, his humane desire does not prevail, especially as several chiefs in long speeches contrast their former happiness under the French with the present sadly changed conditions. In a very effective address the unscrupulous French priest, who claims that " he that shall kill a Briton, merits Heaven," succeeds in arousing the Indians to the frenzy of war. Colonel Cockum and Captain Frisk as well as the deceitful traders are scalped, and their brains and blood fed to the dogs. Honeyman's repentance in the face of death, after a vigorous denunciation of his cruelty by his wife has brought him to his senses, avails him nothing. Ponteach releases her, but the trader expiates his crime through a death by torture. Through the treachery of Philip tragic disaster overtakes not only Chekitan and Monelia, but also the traitor himself.

Weighed down by private sorrows and public calamities, the afflicted monarch gives unrestrained expression to his grief. With his sons dead and the chiefs in revolt, his cause is lost. Though forced to withdraw before the victorious English, the still defiant chief gives vent to his emotions in the rhetoric of the closing speech of the drama:

> I will not fear — but must obey my Stars:
> Ye fertile Fields and glad'ning Streams, adieu;
> Ye Fountains that have quench'd my scorching Thirst,
> Ye Shades that hid the Sun-beams from my Head,
> Ye Groves and Hills that yielded me the Chace,
> Ye flow'ry Meads, and Banks, and bending Trees,
> And thou proud Earth, made drunk with Royal Blood,
> I am no more your Owner and your King.
> But witness for me to your new base Lords;
> That my unconquer'd Mind defies them still;
> And though I fly, 'tis on the Wings of Hope.
> Yes, I will hence where there's no British Foe,
> And wait a Respite from this Storm of Woe;
> Beget more Sons, fresh Troops collect and arm,
> And other Schemes of future Greatness form;
> Britons may boast, the Gods may have their Will,
> Ponteach I am, and shall be Ponteach still.

The hero of the play exhibits all the qualities history has ascribed to the great Algonquin leader, whose remarkable gifts and personality marshalled the numerous and diverse tribes for the one supreme purpose of destroying the English, after the French-Indian War had deprived the native of his indulgent Gallic brothers. Lofty pride and unbounded ambition, implacable hatred and a cruelty seldom tempered with mercy, genuine patriotism and far-sighted statesmanship, all appear in the excessively long speeches, which at times degenerate into empty rhetoric and meaningless bombast, longwinded utterances characteristic of both warriors and women alike.

The play breathes the stern reality of conflict and strife, as the white invaders and their unhappy enemies repay each other in kind. The former appear decidedly more blameworthy than the cruel and treacherous natives. Under guise of love a " Christian " captain tried to stain Monelia's honor, while the equally corrupt French priest attempted to ravish the pure maiden, who is thus led to believe that every Christian is a foe to virtue. No wonder that under such conditions conciliation became utterly impossible, and that force and bloodshed had to decide the issue.

The same subject was treated by General Alexander Macomb sixty years later in his *Pontiac, or the Siege of Detroit,* a prose drama in three acts, which did not appear in print till 1835. In striking contrast to Rogers' production, all the material is historical with the exception of Pontiac's capture on board the Gladwin and the manner of his death, changes which were made for the sake of dramatic effectiveness. The Prologue is written in a vein sympathetic to the native, who may be now

> Revengeful, cruel, — not by nature so,
> But 'tis because depressed by us so low.
> When first we saw him in his pristine state,
> The native knew not what it was to hate.

The author gives high praise to savage virtues and hospitality, which were sorely tried by the newcomers, especially the English, who unlike the French did not join the native in his savage law. Soon the possessor of the soil felt himself compelled to fight against the invader, and the brave chief skilled in warlike enterprise defied each foe:

> He stakes his life his country to defend,
> And in that noble duty finds his end.

The experienced Major Rogers, author of the first Pontiac play, is one of the principal characters and by his shrewd advice and resolute action saves the English from disaster. The American author-general characterizes the British officers as haughty and inefficient, totally lacking in an understanding of the savages, who in turn despise the redcoats. The wily Indian leader exhibits the traits history and tradition have attributed to him, but for all his cunning the English under the direction of Rogers entrap him on board the Gladwin, and but for Rogers' intervention he would have received short shrift. The major's plan to keep him as a hostage in order to guarantee the fulfillment of treaty stipulations is repugnant to the officers who regard the tawny rascals as serpents lurking in the grass and bushes. The problem is quickly solved by Augushway, who as a sacrifice to his country's peace kills his friend, whose warlike ambitions knew no bounds and who never would have extended his hand to an invader except to strike deep the tomahawk or the knife.

General Macomb's *Pontiac* falls considerably below its more distinguished predecessor in diction as well as in dramatic effectiveness. Nevertheless, it was acted with great success at the National Theater in Washington in 1838, which was probably due chiefly to the participation of the United States Marine corps in the play.

The second extant Indian play, but the first actually performed and also the first dealing with the important Pocahontas material, is *The Indian Princess; or La Belle Sauvage,* written by J. N. Barker, who under President Van Buren became the first Comptroller of the Treasury at Washington. Barker, who is the author of several plays, at first had intended to make of *The Indian Princess* a regular drama, but at the request of the composer Bray he worked it up into an opera, called on the title page of the printed play " An Operatic Melo-Drame." It was first performed April 6, 1808, at the Chestnut Street Theater, Philadelphia, to a crowded house; but the opposition to Webster, the singer, caused such a tumult that the author directed the curtain to be dropped. Since that time, Barker tells us, it was frequently acted in all the theaters of the United States. It also seems to have been given, though in a much changed form, at Drury Lane, London, on December 15, 1820, which according to Professor Quinn would appear to be the first well authenticated instance of an original American play being produced in London after an initial performance in America.

In the words of the author, " the principal materials that form this dramatic trifle are extracted from the General History of Virginia, written by Captain Smith, and printed London, folio, 1624; and as close an adherence to historical truth has been preserved as dramatic rules would allow of." This is borne out by the drama, which skilfully combines the most picturesque details, only slightly altered, into an effective play. The love element dominates throughout; not only are there five pairs of lovers, but incidents such as Smith's dramatic rescue by Pocahontas are sufficiently toned down so as not to obscure the main interest. The romance of Rolfe and the princess reaches its dramatic climax at Powhatan's banquet, when, after the intervention of Pocahontas has saved the Europeans, and the rival suitor has obligingly removed himself by suicide, the happy pair is united. The humorous elements, mainly contributed by the English settlers, and the dramatically and psychologically effective passages with the romantic setting would doubtless even now please the general run of play-goers.

Captain John Smith, somewhat theatrical and bombastic in his speech and characterized as

a man of might
In Venus' soft wars or in Mars' bloody fight,

is shown here only in the latter rôle, since Pocahontas looks upon him as a brother rather than as a lover. His stoic indifference to pain and torture is at least equal to that of his savage enemies. Lieutenant Rolfe rather early reveals the bent of his mind by his conduct, especially evident in his disdainful attitude toward European dames with their whimsies and caprice, their variance and wildness, and his preference for the squaws of the woods.

Throughout the play Pocahontas is shown to be of a kind and merciful disposition, so un-Indian like that in the beginning she grieves over the flamingo she has shot to death, and intends henceforth to lay aside bow and arrow. It is this creature of gentleness, sweet simplicity, and angel softness that saves Smith from savage tomahawks. Soon she discovers the first advances of love in a heart of perfect simplicity which shrank before the advances of the fierce Miami, his boasts as a mighty hunter and invincible warrior all to no avail. With the naïveness of a child she responds to the ardent wooing of a gentleman, while the rejected chief in a jealous rage sends the red hatchet as a sign of war. Powhatan, her indulgent father, readily accepts the challenge, whereupon his superstitious priest Grimesco puts the warriors into a frenzy.

Meanwhile in a scene of glamorous poetry lover and lass breathe their tenderest sentiments into each other's ear, Pocahontas in particular being profuse in her expression:

> Thou art my life!
> I lived not till I saw thee, love; and now
> I live not in thine absence. Long, Oh! long
> I was the savage child of savage Nature,

viewing the changing brow of her wild mother with neither love nor dread until she met him whose presence transformed for her the very earth:

> O! 'tis from thee I draw my being:
> Thou'st ta'en me from the path of savage error,
> Blood-stained and rude, where rove my countrymen,
> And taught me heavenly truths, and fill'd my heart
> With sentiments sublime, and sweet, and social.
> . . . .
> Guided by thee, has not my daring soul,
> O'ertopt the far-off mountain of the east,
> Where, as our fathers fable, shad'wy hunters
> Pursue the deer, or clasp the melting maid
> 'Mid everblooming spring?

Such Old World love making stands in sharp contrast to the efforts of the treacherous forest-priest to inflame the mind of Powhatan against the newcomers, in which the eloquent savage so well succeeds that the selfish chief is unwilling to sacrifice the happy hunting-grounds in the life beyond for the friendship of the palefaces. However, an aboriginal sense of justice in the person of the princess prevents the contemplated massacre of the unsuspecting Englishmen at the banquet tendered them by Pocahontas' friendly brother Nantaquas. Unwilling that his torture shall feast the eyes of his foes and upholding the best traditions of his nation, the

Susquehannock chief Miami stabs himself, and thereby obligingly clears the ground for the embrace of Rolfe and Pocahontas, quickly followed by that of Robin and Nima, attendant of the forest princess.

Pocahontas but little resembles the Indian maid — she is too civilized, too sentimental, and too favorably disposed to European men and ways, however much her sentiments may please the romantically inclined. Her brother Nantaquas exudes some of the same un-savage spirit. More typical and realistic is the tribal chief Powhatan, the fierce and energetic suitor Miami, and last but not least the calculating and treacherous priest Grimesco. But the romantic heroine rather than the stern savage warrior gently sways a play that in song, in prose, and in blank verse of considerable merit irresistibly moves toward its pleasing dénouement.

The dramatist who made the Indian play really fashionable, which was soon to receive an even more powerful impetus through Forrest's masterful acting of *Metamora*, was George Washington Parke Custis, son of John Park Custis, the stepson of Washington. His first play, *The Indian Prophecy*, was produced at the Chestnut Street Theater, Philadelphia, July 4, 1827, and published the following year. It is based upon an incident related to Custis by Dr. James Craik, an intimate friend of Custis' famous stepfather. In 1770 an Indian chief is said to have informed Washington how at Braddock's defeat he and his braves had vainly tried to kill the young officer, but baffled at his miraculous escape they finally had given up, believing him immune through divine intervention. The chief prophesied that Washington was destined to survive all battles and become the head of a mighty state. This prophecy forms the climax of a play that consists almost wholly of conversations and is of such a character that a detailed discussion may be dispensed with.

Little is known about *The Pawnee Chief*, which is also ascribed to Custis. More important and influential was his *Pocahontas, or the Settlers of Virginia*, which beginning with January 16, 1830, had an unusually long run of twelve nights at the Walnut Street Theater in Philadelphia and was also produced elsewhere. It is entirely written in prose, with excessively long speeches especially on the part of the main characters. Aside from the absence of blank verse, it differs chiefly from other Pocahontas plays in that Smith's rescue by the Indian maiden does not occur until the last and final act. Though this device violates the chronology of Smith's *General History*, it gives to the drama a unity and climactic force commonly lacking in the other plays dealing with the same material. The love story of Rolfe and Pocahontas, foreshadowed almost from the first, finds in the pledge of Powhatan's friendship immediately following Smith's rescue, and in the union of the two as the binding tie between native and Englishman its fitting climax.

Pocahontas with her form and feature, her gentleness, grace, and courtesy early attracts the attention of Smith. With her companion Omaya, an imaginative and fiery-loving girl, she seems rather sophisticated and civilized, having imbibed from a survivor of a former settlement Christian doctrines and friendship for the English. Totally lacking in savage traits, she refuses even to consider becoming the wife of the fierce chief Metacoran, who, though renowned in war and wise in council, " lacks the best attribute of courage — mercy." However, the young Namautac in his wide travels has lost none of his love of forest life in preference to civilized ways. Powhatan, peaceloving but suspicious, treacherous and cruel when occasion affords, shares with the other Indians a natural desire to rid the country of the troublesome whites possessing the dreaded fire arms. He is overshadowed by his chief counselor Metacoran, a fierce warrior and crafty diplomat alike, who finds it inexplicable that Englishmen professedly loving their country so much should want to cross the wide sea to deprive the poor Indian of his rude and savage forests. Anxious to win Pocahontas' favor and even magnanimous to a brave and fearless foe, " eternal enmity to the invader, and devoted fidelity to his king and country " ever remain his guiding star. When offered in the general reconciliation at the end freedom and honors, he remains obdurate, and his " brave, wild, and unconquerable spirit " drives him to seek unmolested liberty in the west.

On the whole, Custis has rather skilfully utilized the historic material and in his Indian portrayals puts only a fair strain upon

THE INDIAN DRAMA

credulity except that in some instances the native ideas are too much colored by white civilization.

The play that gave the Indian drama its greatest impetus and prolonged its popularity for two decades, was *Metamora, or the Last of the Wampanoags,* by John Augustus Stone. In the November 22, 1828, issue of the *Critic* the famous actor Edwin Forrest had offered five hundred dollars and half the proceeds of the third night for the " best tragedy, in five acts, of which the hero, or principal character, shall be an original of this country." The committee of award, with Bryant as chairman and Halleck a member, chose Stone's *Metamora* from among the fourteen submitted. At its first production December 15, 1829, in the Park Theater in New York, it was vigorously applauded, and the actor scored an even greater triumph when he staged it on January 23, 1830, at the Arch Street Theater in his native city of Philadelphia. For hundreds of nights Forrest played the title rôle in all parts of the United States and reaped wealth and fame from this stage sensation. The author of the drama, however, benefited little from its success. Despairing of recognition and mentally deranged, he drowned himself on May 29, 1834, when barely thirty years old, in the Schuykill River at Philadelphia. Under a handsome monument " Erected to the memory of the Author of *Metamora* by his friend, Edwin Forrest," the unhappy man found an appropriate resting place.

It is not unlikely that Custis' *The Indian Prophecy* and the reading of Bird's unpublished *Sagamore* induced Stone to produce his famous prize play. The name Metamora is patterned after Metacomet, son of the great sachem Massasoit, and by the English generally called King Philip. The play was never published, and only the part of the hero has been preserved in manuscript form. However, from descriptions of William Alger, Forrest's biographer, and others we can largely reconstruct the play at least in outline and recover not a few of the speeches. It is generally agreed that the play itself had little literary value, and that it owed its fame entirely to Forrest's masterful acting of the part of Metamora, which, beautifully conceived and written to order, fitted the personality of the great tragedian to perfection. While Professor Quinn claims that Metamora is a type, not a real Indian, with every admirable characteristic intensified, Forrest's contemporary and biographer Alger asserts that " it was the genuine Indian who was brought upon the stage, merely idealized a little in some of his moral features," and that " with the single and very proper exception of this partially heightened moral refinement, the counterfeit was so cunningly copied that it might have deceived nature itself." However, its alleged idealization and the somewhat bombastic speeches did not detract from its popularity even among Indians, for delegations from various tribes were much impressed, and their pleasure and approval unqualified. While *Metamora* was one of Forrest's greatest drawing cards throughout his career, it died with him for the reason that no other actor was able to make the title rôle a success.

Since *Metamora* is of such historic importance, it is worthwhile to follow its action, speeches, and characterizations mainly under the guidance of William Alger, whose knowledge of the play and its production was complete. It will convey to us some of the effect that was responsible for the numerous Indian plays in which other actors sought similar profit and fame.

The opening scene of *Metamora* was a glen, with ledges of trees, stones, bushes, running vines and flowers, the leading character seen, in his picturesque, aboriginal costume, standing on the highest rock in an attitude that charmed the eye. Leaning forward on his firmly-planted right foot, the left thrown easily back on its tip, he had a bow in his hand, with its arrow sprung to its tip. As the arrow sprang from the twanging string, he raised his eyes with an eager gaze after it, gave a deep interjection, " Hah! " bounded upon a rock below, and vanished. In a few moments he re-entered, with his left arm bleeding, as if it had been bitten in a struggle with a wild beast. Oceana, a white maiden, passing, sees his wound and offers him her scarf to bind it up. The mother of Oceana had once befriended Massasoit when he was sick. Metamora, in his gratitude, had visited her grave with offerings for the dead, and, on such an occasion, had rescued Oceana from a panther. He hesitates before accepting, and fills the delay with a by-play of pantomime so true to Indian nature, so new and strange to the spectators, that it was invested with an absorbing interest. At length he says: "Metamora will take the white maiden's gift." He then gives her an eagle's feather, bids her wear it in her hair, and if she is ever in danger he will fly to her rescue at the sight of this pledge of his friendship.

As the play moves on, the audience are gradually borne back to the early days of their fathers, and their dread struggle to establish themselves on these Western shores. We see the thin and thriving settlements constantly augmented with reenforcements, pushing the natives before them. We are taken within the homes of the Indians, shown their better qualities, their hopeless efforts, their mixed resolution and misgiving before their coming fate. Our sympathies are enlisted, before we know it, with the defeated party against ourselves; and thus the author and actor won their just victory. For the English are made to represent power and fraud, the Indians truth and patriotism, and when their fugitive king pauses on a lofty cliff in the light of the setting sun, gazes mournfully on the lost hunting-grounds and desecrated graves of his forefathers, and launches his curse on their destroyers, every heart beats with sorrow for him.

The speeches in which the instinctive love of nature that unconsciously saturated the Indian soul is expressed, and in which the closeness of their daily life to the elements of the landscape and the phenomena of the seasons is revealed, were delivered with matchless effect. Metamora, poised like the bronze statue of some god of the antique, says, "I have been upon the high mountain-top when the gray mists were beneath my feet, and the Great Spirit passed by me in wrath. He spoke in anger, and the rocks crumbled beneath the flash of his spear. Then I felt proud and smiled. The white man trembles, but Metamora is not afraid." And again: "The war and the chase are the red man's brother and sister. The storm-cloud in its fury frights him not; and when the stream is wild and broken, his canoe is like a feather that cannot drown."

Another class of speeches, equally unique in character, and breathing with compressed passion, were those in which the relative positions of the intruding race and the native lords of the soil were described. The style with which these were pronounced made the form of the actor seem a new tenement in which the departed Sachem of the Pequots lived and spoke again. " Your lands? " he exclaims, with sarcastic disdain. " They are mine. Climb upon the rock and look to the sunrise and to the sunset, — all that you see is the land of the Wampanoags, the land of Metamora. I am the white man's friend; but when my friendship is over I will not ask the white man if I have the right to be his foe. Metamora will love and hate, smoke the pipe of peace or draw the hatchet of battle, as seems good to him. He will not wrong his white brother, but he owns no master save Manito, Master of Heaven." Another time he delivers himself of this rhetoric utterance: " The pale-faces are around me thicker than the leaves of summer. I chase the hart in the hunting grounds; he leads me to the white man's village. I drive my canoe into the rivers; they are full of the white man's ships. I visit the graves of my fathers: they are lost in the white man's cornfields. They come like the waves of the ocean forever rolling upon the shores. Surge after surge, they dash upon the beach, and every foam-drop is a white man. They swarm over the lands like the doves in winter, and the red men are dropping like withered leaves."

To these may be added a passage quoted by Quinn in which Metamora points out the kind reception his people had given the Europeans: " Then would you pay back that which fifty snows ago you received from the hands of my father Massasoit. You had been tossed like small things on the face of great waters and there was no Earth for your feet to rest on. Your backs were turned on the land of your fathers and the son of the forest took ye as a little child and opened the door of his wigwam. The keen blast of the north howled in the leafless woods, but the Indian covered you with his broad right hand and put it back." As an example of the rhythmic antithesis with which the author endowed the Indian and which is at times effective, Professor Quinn cites from a speech of Metamora: " Your great Book, you say, tells you to give good gifts to the stranger and deal kindly with him whose heart is sad. The Wampanoag needs no such counsellor, for the Great Spirit has with his own finger written it on his heart."

A wonderful interest, too, was concentrated in the personal traits of Metamora himself as an individual; so true to his word, so faithful to his friend, so devoted to his wife and child, so proud of his land and his fathers, so fearless of his foe, so reverential before his God. " To his friend Metamora is like a willow, — he bends ever at the breath of those that love him. To others he is an oak. Until with your single arm you can rive the strongest tree of the forest from its earth, think not to stir Metamora when his heart says No."

In scenes with his wife Nahmeokee and his child he showed conjugal affection and parental tenderness. The expression of human love was so simple and complete, and so exquisitely set in the wild seclusion of nature, suggestive of the self-sufficingness of this little nest of affection embosomed in the wood and forgetful of all else in the world, that it made many a soft heart beat fast with an aching wish that stayed long after the scene was gone. But sterner moods also grip him, as when in a vision he sees the white man's scalp in his hand, and in a bitter rejoinder to his wife about the enemy's spirit of mercy exclaims: " Yes, when our fires are no longer red in the high places of our fathers, — when the bones of our kindred make fruitful the fields the stranger has planted amid the ashes of our wigwams, — when we are hunted back like the wounded elk far towards the going down of the sun — our hatchets broken, our bows unstrung, and our war-whoops hushed, — then will the stranger spare; for we shall be too small for his eye to see! "

Defiantly he meets the English settlers in council and strikes the traitor Aganemo dead before the astonished eyes of the whites. When Fitz Arnold orders his men to seize the high-handed executioner of their witness, Metamora, towering alone in solitary and solid grandeur, with accents and gestures whose impassioned sincerity painted every thought as a visible reality and made the excited audience lean out of their seats, hurls back his electric defiance: " Come! my knife has drunk the blood of the traitor, but it is not satisfied. Men of the pale race, beware! The mighty spirits of the Wampanoags are hovering over your heads. They stretch their shadowy arms and call for vengeance. They shall have it. Tremble! From East to West, from the South to the

North, the tribes have roused from their slumbers. They grasp the hatchet. The palefaces shall wither under their power. White men, Metamora is your foe." Suddenly seizing a white man and putting him as a living shield before himself to receive the bullets, he darted away, leaving the enemies dumb with astonishment.

When later a peace-runner brings Metamora the news that Nahmeokee is a captive in the power of his enemies, he leaves fifty white men bound as hostages to secure his own safety, and starts alone to deliver her. As he approaches the English camp, he hears Nahmeokee shriek. Bursting in upon them, he awes his enemies and rescues her. But at the wigwam his wife informs him that his son has been killed by the whites a few hours before. There follows a pathetic scene, and his manner now changes. Some great resolution seems to have arisen in him. His words have a tender yet ominous meaning in their inflection as he asks Nahmeokee: " Do you not fear the power of the white man? He might seize thee and bear thee off to his far country, bind those arms that have so often clasped me, and make thee his slave. We cannot fly; our foes are all about us. We cannot fight, for this [drawing his long knife] is the only weapon I have saved unbroken from the strife. It has tasted the white man's blood and reached the cold heart of the traitor. It has been our best friend, and it is now our only treasure." Here he drew her still closer, and placed her head on his bosom, and with the long knife in his hand, pointed upwards, and with an alluring, indescribably sweet and aerial falsetto tone, painted a picture that seemed to take form and color in the very atmosphere: " I look through the long path in the thin air, and think I see our little one borne to the land of the happy, where the fair hunting grounds never know snows or storms, and where the immortal braves feast under the eyes of the Giver of Good. Look upward, Nahmeokee! See, thy child looks back to thee, and beckons thee to follow." Drawing her closer to his left arm, and lowering his right, he whispers, " Hark! In the distant wood I faintly hear the tread of the white men. They are upon us! The home of the happy is made ready for thee! " While this picture of fear and hope is vivid before her mind, he strikes the blow, and in an instant she is dead in his arms. He clasps her to his breast, presses his lips on her fore-

THE INDIAN DRAMA

head, and gently places her beside the dead child. He then shudders and draws forth the knife sheathed in her side, and kisses its blade in a sudden transport, exclaiming, " She knew no bondage to the white men. Pure as the snow she lived, free as the air she died! "

At this moment the hills are covered with the white men, pointing their muskets at his heart. He proudly denies that he is their prisoner and haughtily defies them: " I live, the last of my race, live to defy you still, though numbers and treachery overpower me. Come to me, come singly, come all, and this knife, which has drunk the foul blood of your nation, and is now red with the purest of mine, will feel a grasp as strong as when it flashed in the glare of your burning dwellings or was lifted terribly over the fallen in battle." When the order is given to fire upon him, he replies: " Do so. I am weary of the world; for ye are dwellers in it. I would not turn on my heel to save my life." They shoot, and he staggers, but in his dying agonies launches on them his awful malediction: " My curses on ye, white men! May the Great Spirit curse ye when he speaks in his war-voice from the clouds! May his words be like the forked lightnings, to blast and desolate! May the loud winds and the fierce red flames be loosed in vengeance upon ye, tigers! May the angry Spirit of the Waters in his wrath sweep over your dwellings! May your graves and the graves of your children be in the path where the red man shall tread, and may the wolf and the panther howl over your fleshless bones! I go. My fathers beckon from the green lakes and the broad hills. The Great Spirit calls me. I go, — but the curses of Metamora stay with the white men! "

He crawls painfully to the bodies of his wife and child, and, in a vain effort to kiss them, expires, with his last gasp mixing the words, " I die — my wife, my queen — my Nahmeokee! "

It may readily be seen how effective a play *Metamora* must have been under the masterly acting of the great Forrest. But, on the other hand, the inherent difficulties of the principal rôle were such that no other actor proved equal to the demand. And thus, after the matchless popularity of two score years, the creation of one personality was destined to die with its dissolution.

One of the best plays dealing with the native was produced

by Robert Dale Owen, born in England but later a member of Congress, who in 1837 published his *Pocahontas: A Historical Drama* in five acts and with an introductory essay and notes. According to the author, the play was the result of a winter's leisure spent in a careful study of the historic material. He believed that the public would derive from the perusal of the play a benefit similar to the one he had experienced from his preparatory work. The subject itself seemed appealing, for it deals with the well known story of the heroine so intimately connected with the very first effort to colonize North America, and the " fates of a noble race, which is fast fading away from the earth; and that, through our agency: a race, the savage magnificence of whose character appears to me indifferently well adapted to dramatic effect." Of *Pocahontas'* success as an acted drama he was not sanguine, since it appeared to be lacking in two elements, important from a technical point of view. Its scenes embodied little deep tragedy, and less broad humor. He also felt it to be deficient in that bold, startling style of finish, which shows so much better than it reads. For even moderate success on the stage he considered it essential that the play be curtailed and be partially recast, on account of its length if for no other reason. The author's remarks, sensible and modest as they are, put the reader into a sympathetic mood to approach the one hundred and eighty page drama of alternating prose and blank verse.

The quarrels and discussions of the colonists, often long drawn out and too prominent, concern us only as they shed light upon the aborigines. The conspirators plot to leave the country with its rude, stern, and free inhabitants, both of which are defended by Smith who says of the native that

> His sense of courtesy is strong;
> Stronger, perchance, if in less courtly garb,
> Than under damasks, taffeties, and tissues,

to which Archer replies that

> These savages are worse than Turks to deal with;
> Their scalping knives are sharp.

Appealing from the first is the figure of Matokes or Pocahontas with her sister shooting at a mark and in true modesty declining

THE INDIAN DRAMA

to accept as a prize the pair of moccasins. Her attitude toward the newcomers is truly benevolent. Though not unfriendly toward the whites, Powhatan, spurred on by his hostile counsel or Utta Maccomac, becomes incensed over their increasingly defiant attitude. And when Smith is brought in, he is ready to have him clubbed to death, from which fate the gentle and just Pocahontas saves him.

The groundwork of Rolfe's love for the Indian princess the author lays in determined, though perhaps too obvious a fashion. For when Smith asks the newly arrived gentleman whether he will stay, Captain Newport significantly remarks:

> Show him some dark-haired, bright-eyed Indian girl —
> Some graceful mermaid of these ocean-forests —
> And ask him then, whether he sails with me,
> Or anchor here among you.

In telling of his escape, the doughty explorer describes Pocahontas in glowing terms, mentioning in particular her dark flashing eyes, her slender form, her raven tresses, her wonderful brow, her clear, dusk cheek, her graceful limbs, and her musical voice. No wonder that Rolfe is impressed and immediately upon her appearance sighs:

> Th' embodied spirit of her forest race!

On her part, she is pleased with the Yengeese face and eagerly accepts his offer to be her brother, upon which the more experienced Smith breathes the pious prayer:

> Sweet wild flower!
> May the cold touch of icy-hearted doubt
> Ne'er reach thy pure, warm spirit!

In a discussion of love and kindred subjects the aspiring Pocahontas expresses the wish to cross the Great Salt Lake, and when her sister Nomony in answer to the question

> Thinkest thou
> Woman was made to be the friend of man,
> To share man's confidence — win his respect —
> To be — to be — his equal?

indicates that she herself is satisfied with the position of squaw, the future wife of the white man feels that

> I am born
> To aid, but not to slave.

After various vicissitudes the two lovers are united, and the match is approved by Indians and Smith alike, who in pointing to the ardently embracing pair draws this moral:

> Look on that Yengeese chief;
> His heart and Pocahontas' heart are one.
> They have joined hands and hearts. So let it be
> With Red Men and Yengeese. Let them sit down
> Within the lodge of peace, and let their hearts
> Henceforth be one.

The material of the play, which disregards the time order of Smith's history, is skilfully arranged. Though the interest is somewhat divided between Smith and Rolfe, the love of Pocahontas, triumphing over all obstacles, serves as the connecting link. The Indian characters are well drawn, from the guileless, humane chief Paspaho and the artless Pocahontas, " reflecting the beauty, simplicity, and purity of her natural environment," with her gentleness, faith, justice, and fidelity, to the crafty and revengeful Powhatan and the still more hostile, suspicious, and custom bound priest and counselor Powah.

Probably influenced by Custis' *Pocahontas,* in which her mother had played the title rôle, Charlotte M. S. Barnes (Conner) produced *The Forest Princess, or Two Centuries Ago,* 1848, a historical play of alternating prose and blank verse in three parts. The author characterizes her work as an " ephemeral production," a judgment with which the average reader will heartily agree, for the play has little literary or other value. Its unconquerable defect, rhetorically speaking, she considered the division of interest between Smith's adventures and the love interest centering in Pocahontas. In distinction from practically all other plays on the same theme, the last act is laid in England. There Rolfe, who plays a rather prominent part, even saving Pocahontas from a panther, espouses Raleigh's cause and is accused of treason, but soon freed.

The manifest weaknesses of Stone's *Metamora* as well as the absurdities of other Indian plays were certain to bring down upon them the ridicule of the seriously minded dramatist and the comedian. In 1846 the playwright James Rees wrote that in his opinion the Indian drama " had of late become a perfect nuisance," and soon after John Brougham began to belabor it in his two act burlesque *Metamora; or The Last of the Pollywoags*, according to a statement in the printed copy originally produced in Boston in 1847 and since performed throughout the Union by various companies. The play contains a great deal of rime, and the bombastic Metamora or King Philip speaks as a rule in couplets. Indignantly he demands to know the source of gin among his people:

> Who was it changed the Indian's native hue,
> With such vile stuff, making the red man blue?
> The mountain rivulet is made impure
> By the foul steam that rises from your door.

The French speaking Fitzfaddle, who does not seem to have injured the squalling squaw of the king, before being stabbed by the monarch is frightened by the fearful threat:

> One tear from Tapiokee, and, by thunder,
> The axe shall hew your quivering limbs asunder.
> One hair from Tapiokee's head, you'll find
> The ashes of your bones upon the wind!

Both Metamora and his wife fall, the latter through the knife of her husband, only to rise again before the play ends in a Comic Dance and Tableau, but not until the author has seen fit to fling a gratuitous insult at the whites in the closing lines:

> The red man's fading out, and in his place
> There comes a bigger, not a better race.
> Just as you've seen the squirming Pollywog
> In course of time become a bloated frog.

The plot is exceedingly thin, and the play does not bear comparison with the author's production soon to make stage history.

For in 1855 Brougham returned to the attack with one of the greatest burlesques ever produced in this country, a curious concoction entitled "An Original Aboriginal Erratic Operatic Semi-Civilized and Demi-Savage Extravaganza, being a Per-Version of Ye Trewe and Wonderfulle Hystorie of a Rennowned Princesse *Pocahontas: or The Gentle Savage,*" a title that admirably characterizes the contents. Aside from the novel and startling plot, surprising at every turn, the effect is mainly produced by the scintillating wit generally taking the form of puns. Thus, for instance, O-po-dil-doo asks,

> Are *not* soaps made from *lyes?*

to which Col-o-gog replies,

> May I ask in the word *lie,*
> What vowel do you use, sir, *i* or *y?*

to be answered in turn by the former,

> *Y* sir, or *i* sir, search the Vowels through,
> And find the one most *consonant to you.*

The popularity of the piece was immense, and it may be said to have given the deathblow to the more serious Indian drama of which the theater-goers by this time had begun to get tired.

The characters are undeniably interesting with their lively humor and the brilliant wit that flashes throughout the play. Captain John Smith appears as "The Undoubted Original, vocal and instrumental, in the settlement of Virginia, in love with Pocahontas, according to *this* story, though somewhat at variance with *his* story." His contact with Pow-Ha-Tan I — King of the Tuscaroras — a crotchety Monarch, in fact, a Semi-Brave," played by Mr. Brougham himself, assumes a serio-comic aspect. Their first meeting the ambitious captain describes as follows:

> I visited his majesty's abode,
> A portly savage, plump, and pigeon-toed,
> Like *Metamora* both in *feet* and *feature,*
> I never *met — a — more — a-musing* creature.

The latter appears as a seemingly genial, tobacco smoking monarch, loud in his praise of the Nicotine weed:

THE INDIAN DRAMA

> While other joys one sense alone can measure,
> This to all senses gives extatic pleasure.
> You *feel* the radiance of the glowing bowl,
> *Hear* the soft murmurs of the kindling coal,
> *Smell* the sweet fragrance of the honey-dew,
> *Taste* its strong pungency the palate through,
> *See* the blue cloudlets circling to the dome,
> Imprisoned skies up-floating to their home —
> I like a dhudeen myself!

His dialogue with Smith later under a humorous form has more serious implications:

> King. What *iron* fortune led you to our shores?
> Smith. *Ironic* Monarch, 'twas a pair of *oars*.
>   Between ourselves, though, if the truth be told,
>   Our *goal* we'll reach when we have reached your *gold*.

Upon being questioned further, Smith admits:

> The seas we *clove* in hopes to live in *clover*.
> Befriend us, and we'll try and be of use,
> Even to cooking of your royal goose.
> King. Don't put yourself into a stew, my friend,
>   My *Kitchen Cabinet* to that attend.

The adventurer offers to marry any red queen that might fall in his way, accepting her scepter, crown, and all, but is warned to go slowly, for

> If any jokers dare to run their rigs
> Near our *wigwams*, we're sure to *warm their wigs!*

When all the natives demand that he be hanged, he calls a halt, and asked by the king the reason for his faltering, rejoins:

> I fain would *halt* before I reach the *halter*.
> That *cord* is not my *line* in any sense,
> I'd rather *not* be kept in such suspense.

The " vociferous irruption of Juvenile Squaw-lers," as the emancipated maidens are designated, soon brings Pocahontas into the foreground. Powhatan evidently does not favor the bold captain as a suitor, though he mockingly bids his favorite to prepare for the ceremony:

> Now, daughter dear, prepare,
> With orange-wreaths *array* your *raven* hair;
> To *prove* I love *you,* Smith, before you wed,
> We'll take a *proof* impression of your head,
> In our approved new lithographic style.

With singing and joking the action proceeds, Rolfe, though not favored by the maiden, gradually gaining the ascendency, while the fettered Smith seems to be at the end of his resources, but still begs

> A few last words, I trust, you'll let me say?
>
> King. We're *tied* to *time,* and *time* and *tide* wont wait,
> You must *die early* so you can't dilate!
> Our *Indian* laws are *some,* there's no receding!
>
> Smith. Why what a *Indian summary* proceeding.

However, Pocahontas and the clamoring and threatening maidens demand the right to choose their own husbands, and as a concession Smith's fate is to be decided through a pack of cards. He wins, and in his closing speech remarks in subdued triumph:

> I have *won fairly,* I appeal to you (To King).
> And *fair one,* I have *fairly won you, too,*
> So let us *two* make one.

Thus by gentle ridicule, wit and humor, offending and shocking no one with his puns, anachronisms, and allusions, Brougham in a single night's entertainment laughed the serious and dignified Indian off the stage.

However, that the Pocahontas material did not entirely lose its attraction even during the second part of the 19th century is shown by the fact that as late as 1875 S. H. M. Byers published *Pocahontas, A Melo-Drama* in a stage edition of five acts, which curiously enough never seems to have been acted. The character of the work, with the monotony of blank verse and prose frequently broken by songs, is appropriately indicated by its subtitle. At the Governor's feast the natives are mostly represented by " tramps and vagabonds tricked out with fancy ribbons, bells, and paint. Yet there was one, a girl, with form as light as some young antelope, with glowing eyes, and hair as black as night. The men are wild in love with her, and follow round as if she were the lode star of the North." As a fortune teller the young maiden early informs Rolfe that the favor of the fates shall be his and that even now his love is near him, whereupon the smitten lover promptly puts a ring upon her finger. But before the lovers can unite, many trials intervene on account of the hostility of the savages, who believe that the gods frown upon the presence of the white invaders.

Captain Smith's capture presents a serious problem dramatically and otherwise until the versatile and impulsive maiden rescues him by the novel device of threatening suicide. Thereupon the captain recedes into the background, only to make way for Argall, a troublesome suitor promptly dispatched by Rolfe, who, ravished by the maiden's beauty, also expresses his sentiments in song. The play ends with a tableau of the marriage of Rolfe and Pocahontas; Powhatan and Smith, Harkluyt and Helen also forming part of the group.

The interest of the drama is too much divided. The intrigues of the colonists and the efforts of various suitors for the hand of Helen, Governor Wingfield's ward, fill many pages, in which Helen and her favorite lover Harkluyt at times rise to poetic heights. Captain Smith likewise occupies the stage too much especially in the first part, while Pocahontas and her lover do not achieve that prominence which they rightfuly deserve.

Another melodrama, but published fifty-four years earlier, is *Oolaita, or the Indian Heroine,* in which Lewis Deffebach takes his readers to the West. The scene of the play, mostly written in blank verse, is laid among the Sioux on or near Lake Pepin, where curiously enough there is a palmetto's shade. The heroine, daughter of the Sioux king, with a soul as pure and spotless as the snow, would willingly die for unthinking Christians, but her father characterizes them as vile reptiles, spies, marauders, thieves, and plunderers of honest toil and labor's fruit, who on their part return the compliment by speaking of the merciless fangs of mud-colored rascals.

As so often in works dealing with the emotional life of the Indian, melancholy love forms the theme of the play. The suit of the renowned but aged, crafty and treacherous Monona is repugnant to the gentle maiden in love with the young and merciful chief Tullula, and she would rather die than marry a withered limb, and embrace deformity, declining years, and second childhood. Even though the murderous plot of the old chief against his young rival is only partly successful, the unhappy girl when faced by the forced marriage throws herself into Lake Pepin, and the wounded and disappointed Tullula stabs himself during the universal lament.

Not less unsatisfactory than this ending, with the intrigues of the chief strangely remaining unpunished, are most parts of the play. The plot is rather improbable, and the Indians are too much like white men.

Noteworthy as showing the influence of Christianity upon the Indians is *Carabasset,* 1830, a tragedy in five acts, which deals with the destruction of the chief village of the Norridgewoks in Maine by the English in 1724. Although the author, N. Deering, adheres in the main to historical facts, he introduces the villain Ravillac as the instigator of the tragedy. In the preface he asserts that, if the language of his Indians is less figurative than that usually ascribed to them, figurative language is not the language of passion; and if his Indians bear but little resemblance to the sons of the forest, the asperities of the Norridgewoks were at least softened, if not removed, by the influence of the French priests.

However, the Jesuit Rallé well knows the fierce, uncontrolled passions of the uncivilized natives, and he opposes their use in war after the English fashion. For they are

>   A wild, revengeful race, to fire at night
>   The widow's humble cot, and steep their hands
>   In the life-blood of helpless innocence.

Among those partly civilized by the self-sacrificing priest is Carabasset, the best and bravest of them all. But here as so often elsewhere, degenerate white men destroy the fruit of missionary endeavors. In this case it is Ravillac, who by raping and killing the convert Rena, the kind and virtuous wife of the chief, incites the infuriated Indians to wholesale revenge in spite of the priest's warning that such measures are dangerous as well as unjust. Despairingly the good man is forced to cry out:

> Who can control the savage in his fury!
> Then he is like the tiger who had drank
> Of human blood — nought else can satisfy.

The author incidentally pays a well deserved tribute to the Jesuits when he has Rallé steadfastly refuse to desert his charges at the approach of the white troops under Ravillac. He falls a victim to this his erstwhile protégé, an ingrate to the man who had saved his life.

Carabasset witnesses the to him incomprehensible slaughter and outrages committed by Christian whites, until at last in his mad desire to kill a member of that hated race he succeeds in stabbing the traitor, who escapes the well deserved torture only through the nearness of the English troops. The proud chieftain repudiates the doctrine of weak submission to vile cords, as he, the last of all the Norridgewoks, leaps from a cliff to his death, after hurling this defiance:

> Tell them he scorn'd to be the sport of slaves;
> Of those whom he had trampled on — of those,
> Whom he had dragg'd as captives — ay, of those,
> Whose lips do quiver when they mention him.
> Go, tell them this.
> Tell them that thus a Norridgewok hath liv'd,
> And thus — can die.

The play *Carabasset* is interesting for the fact that it shows an Indian convert who, brooding over the mistreatment and duplicity of the whites, finds it hard to comprehend the Christian doctrine of returning good for evil. The native instincts of the heart, which are only subdued, but by no means rooted out, powerfully re-assert themselves under the stress of circumstances.

Likewise a tragedy, but with a *mise-en-scène* in the extreme South, is the unpublished five-act play *De Soto,* written by George H. Miles for James E. Murdoch, who staged it in the Chestnut Street Theater, Philadelphia, on April 19, 1852. Above the average in literary value and attractive as a play, it found applause also in New York and New Orleans, the subject matter and atmosphere naturally appealing to Southern audiences.

The action as well as the delineation of character impresses the reader. A center of interest and especially appealing is Ulah, supposedly a daughter of chief Tuscaluza, but in reality the child of a murdered survivor of the expedition of Narvaez. Listen to the enthusiastic praise of her charms as uttered by the chief of the Floridas:

> I looked upon her —
> She moved among my daughters like the moon
> Amid the stars — her eyes were dark and moist
> As night: on her white cheeks red roses lay,
> Her breath was perfume, and her laughter music.

No wonder that when the warriors had demanded that the stake blaze for the paleface, he had acknowledged her as his queen and daughter and claimed the beautiful flower as his own. When the maiden later suspects her origin and anxiously inquires whether her mother lives, in four brief sentences the author superbly lays bare the tragedy enacted many years before:

> Tuscaluza. Beneath yond tree I met her. Ask these leaves
> How fared the Spanish woman on that night.
> Ulah. You slew her?
> Tuscaluza. She is sleeping at thy feet.

Her impulsive and revengeful Spanish nature finds due expression in her rejection of all the advances of a murderer — even more, biding her time, she reveals Tuscaluza's plot, saves the Spanish army, and betrays the hiding place of the Indian band. But for her the Florida chief would have been a victor monarch, at his belt De Soto's scalp.

Tragic and melodramatic elements galore crowd the last part, as upon Ulah's invitation the great chief kills her, and he himself in turn is dragged by De Soto to the grave of his victim and cut down. The last speech of the famed chieftain pleading with the Great Spirit to take him to the happy hunting-ground of his fathers contains a note of mingled reproach and regret when he mournfully observes:

> Was there no room
> Beyond the wave — no other Ulah there,
> That he must come for mine? Alas, she's dead!

THE INDIAN DRAMA 93

Another glamorous touch the author adds in the passing of De Soto himself, who at midnight, the scene lit up by the moon and the flares of his companions, is buried in the Mississippi, and thus with a dirge and a volley of muskets Miles brings to a fitting close the prose-verse tragedy built around the great adventurer into Indian haunts.

From a survey of the Indian plays it is evident that favored dramatic material and characters were largely historical, however much some playwrights might deviate in details from the sober facts of history. Others believed that a strict adherence to events was essential, sometimes to their own discomfiture. A play with all historical allusions claimed to be accurate is *Logan, The Last of the Race of Shikellemus, Chief of the Cayuga Nation*, 1821, by Dr. Joseph Doddridge, who thought that the bravery, talents, and misfortunes of the chief were worthy of commemoration.

Interest in the native centers largely in Logan, the unprovoked slaughter of whose family in April 1774 near Wheeling, W. Va., determined him upon bloody revenge, and during that summer more than thirty whites are said to have fallen by his hand. In long, pathetic speeches he voices his undying hostility to the white man, whose friend he had once been called, but who had bereft him of all his kindred so that as the last of the long race of chiefs renowned in peace and war he will leave like the shooting star no track behind. After the defeat of the Indians and toward the close of the play the author lets Logan read from a belt of white wampum his well known and extravagantly praised speech beginning: "I appeal to any white man to say, if ever he entered Logan's cabin hungry, and he gave him not meat; if ever he came cold and naked, and he clothed him not." Another main character is Shahillas, chief of the Ottoways, a more restrained and calculating savage, but unafraid and anxious to reap full advantage of circumstances once hostilities become inevitable.

Dr. Doddridge trusts that he has done justice to the customs and the phraseology of the native sons of the forest, which is apparent in the correct coloring of the Indian dialogue as shown by such phrases as "Long-knives" for Englishmen and "for ten snows and ten ears of corn." In regard to the backwoodsmen he felt himself on safer ground, for he insists that his delineation cannot be wrong, as he was brought up among them.

The feelings of these ruthless characters are shared by the military who regard the Indian's claim to the country as feeble as that of the buffalo which has marked the earth with his feet, eaten the weeds, brushed the bushes with his tail, and made paths to the salt licks. A captain appropriately called Furioso objects even to this comparison, for in his eyes the native is a beast of prey like the wolf and bear that live upon the destruction of life. The objection of Captain Pacifimus that the slaughter of women and children would be inhuman, he callously brushes aside with his remark: " I would kill all, nits will be lice." With sentiments such as these prevalent among the borderers and troops the conflict was bound to result in a fight to the finish.

It may readily be admitted that Dr. Doddridge has gathered together a respectable body of basic material on a subject possessing dramatic possibilities, but he did not fashion it into a work of art. The main objection to the production as a play lies in its almost total lack of action and its colorless pedestrian prose.

In 1836 Dr. William Emmons published " a national drama " in five acts called *Tecumseh: or the Battle of the Thames,* on a subject he had dealt with in a pamphlet issued in 1822, and which in 1827 appeared as the seventeenth canto of his long poem *The Fredoniad: or, Independence Preserved. An Epic Poem of the Late War of 1812.* The author's excursion into the field of drama, with a plot both lurid and improbable and teeming with red and white characters, exhibits the worst features of chauvinism and is unblushing in its exaltation of Kentucky. The broken and choppy bombastic prose is heavily freighted with peculiar fanciful figures of speech on the part of native and invader alike.

The former need not fear comparison in the exhibition of cruelty and ruthlessness, in which both parties, including the scalp-buying English, indulge. If anything, the Indians are more considerate. Of interest are especially Maypock, an impulsive and cold-blooded warrior, the great chief himself, and his brother the Prophet. The latter is rather superstitious and cruel, sacrifices playing an important part in his religion. Tecumseh appears as high-tempered, brave, and fearless in the face of superior numbers. Deeply revering the beliefs of his ancestors and determined to make good his stand against the encroaching whites, he is yet not without humane qualities. Brought down in an interchange of shots by the American commander Colonel Johnson, his embittered soul takes flight with this curse upon the enemy: " May the hawk flap his wing over his steaming carcass! The wolf lap up his — his — blood! " Over him Edward, whom the fallen leader had rescued from a painful sacrifice, pronounces the verdict: " The mighty man Tecumseh! rude, yet great — most towering chief that ever hatchet raised against the white man."

It was but natural that such literary successes as *Nick of the Woods* and *Hiawatha* and books of outstanding writers generally should have been exploited by the shrewd and vainglorious dramatist. But the three extant imitations, while for a time popular to a greater or lesser degree, fall measurably below the qualities of the novels and the poem they sought to embody.

For a score of years Louisa H. Medina's *Nick of the Woods,* 1838, maintained its place as one of America's most popular melodramas. It is comparatively short, and its prose is enlivened with considerable music. The more colorful elements like the exploits of " Salt River Roarer " Ralph Stackpole, Nathan's terrible revenge, and the village of Wenonga, the " black Vulture of the Shawnees," are skilfully played up. The main action of the famous story is fairly closely followed, and a surprisingly large number of highly interesting incidents are embodied in the play. No wonder that such a drama held the boards for a long time. However, the ending is needlessly abrupt, and the suspense of the novel has been sacrificed by the early identification of Nathan with the Jibbenainosay or the Nick of the Woods. While an effective play, Medina's melodrama for these reasons if for no other is less satisfying than Bird's moving and powerful novel.

The short, two-act prose play *The Wept of Wish-ton-Wish,* 1851, based upon Cooper's novel of the same name, is claimed to have been performed in all the principal theaters in the United States. Though in the main it follows the action of the novel, there are not a few changes. The regicide Gough is less obscure and more prominent, and the first attack on Wish-ton-Wish is merely related in a report. Some of the persons assume a different rôle from that played in the novel. Narramattah, the Wept of Wishton-Wish, becomes a daughter of Gough, and her sister Faith the wife of Captain Content Heathcote. A humorous element is introduced in the person of Skunk, who as selectman had appropriated the community treasury of New London, turned Indian, and become prime minister of the Mudturtles. His wife Abundance pays tribute to her name by bearing fifteen children, twelve of them to Skunk. Music plays a not inconsiderable part in the drama, and there is plenty of action, though at times somewhat complicated. But on the whole, this short play is only a faint echo of an improbable and mediocre story.

Interesting as an exploitation of Longfellow's famous poem is the Musical Extravaganza *Hiawatha; or Ardent Spirits and Laughing Water,* 1856, by Charles M. Walcot. The author frankly and humorously acknowledges his dependence upon the song of the professor, but justifies his rape on account of the scarcity and dearth of striking subjects, the knowledge of its value, and its value for its title.

The playlet incidentally features modern conditions and tends toward the glorification of the American Union, which Walcot thought endangered by treasonable conduct. However, the humorous mood prevails almost throughout. For example, Minnehaha is distinctly husband-minded and boldly facilitates Hiawatha's proposal through the unmistakable implication of her speech:

> Why, I'm sixteen, and that's no laughing matter.
> Then father's such a grumphy slow old poke,
> Living with him, I tell you, now's no joke.
> There's never any fun in our house —
> I really sometimes wish I were a mouse,
> That other little mice might come and play with me,
> Or else some great big pussey run away with me,

to which the wooer instantly replies,

> My darling, look at me! Behold your cat!

The arrowmaker Dammidortur, who opposes the match, is speedily overruled, and the action hurries to the end with none of the tragic complications of Longfellow's epic.

Walcot himself correctly characterized his production as " necessarily but a poor offering," written " in thirty-four hours, during eight days of almost constant suffering from rheumatism." One can only hope that the composition gave him at least some measure of mental relief.

The popularity of the stage Indian was strictly limited to the first half of the 19th century, for after 1850 he appears only at rare intervals. During more recent years aboriginal material has been utilized comparatively seldom in plays, and we may appropriately confine our discussion to the two most successful of these attempts, each dealing effectively with a certain phase of Indian life and activity. They are William C. De Mille's *Strongheart* and *The Arrowmaker* by Mary Austin, the latter probably being the best Indian drama produced during the last eighty years.

The Arrowmaker, 1911, deals with " aboriginal life in the Southwest, anywhere between the Klamath River and the Painted Desert," prior to the white occupation of California. Its many characters Mary Austin has portrayed with a fidelity to truth characteristic of the scientific investigator and delineator she has shown herself to be in painting the Mohave Desert Indian. Chief among them are Simwa, the Arrowmaker, and Chisera, young medicine woman, personifying aboriginal ambition and love. Though her duties as " Friend of the Soul of Man " are manifold and keep her fully occupied, Chisera resents that her mind on that account should remain far away from love. " If I have walked in the midnight and heard what the great ones have said, is that any reason I should not know what a man says to a maid in the dusk? " In her womanly desire to occupy his wickiup as wife, she has used her medicine to draw to herself the young man who is anxious to be chosen leader in the impending war against an enemy tribe. However, the calculating brave, sacrificing on his part all to ambition, is less sanguine to enter such a permanent alliance, which according to him has serious drawbacks. " But what service could you do me when you had lost the respect of the tribesmen? You know the tribal custom. It is not for the Friend of the Gods to dig roots and to dress venison." In spite of this, the medicine woman does not lose hope, and a rival candidate fails to bribe her with two doeskins, tanned white and fine, a blanket of the Navajos, four strings of shells, and a cake of mesquite meal. So the honor of leadership goes to Simwa, who almost immediately strives to entrench himself still more by marrying the chief's daughter. But during the wedding, at which the determined Chisera appears uninvited, rather embarrassing scenes occur when the former lover repudiates her and vehemently denies the charge that he owes everything to the medicine woman. The woman scorned now vows that she will make no more medicine for the Arrowmaker, who is admonished to look well to himself.

The refusal of the Friend of the Gods to make medicine is followed by evil days and defeat, whereupon the old chief presents to her the alternatives, either death or good medicine. Womanlike her emotions give way, and she asks in an injured tone: " Are my breasts less fair that there should never be milk in them? " Like others she desires " love, and sorrow and housekeeping, a husband to give me children, even though he beat me." Of this the tribe deprived her, and she resentfully exclaims: " Did ever woman serve them [the gods] the less because she had dwelt with a man? Nay, all the power of woman comes from loving and being loved, and now the bitterest of all my loss is to know that I never had it." Evidences, however, multiply that the Arrowmaker has only married the chief's daughter for political purposes, and when Chisera by dancing tries to regain her power, he shoots at her the " magic arrow against my evil hour " which unwisely she had entrusted to him. Aboriginal jealousy in his former rival promptly removes him who is declared a traitor dishonest even in his unbelief. The woman thwarted in her love life recovers her power of leadership and with the assurance of victory leads her people against the foe.

The Arrowmaker, wrought with colorful details true to aboriginal life, richly deserves the praises showered upon it. In view of the fact that it deals probably more with woman's thwarted desire for a love life than with ambition, this might properly have found expression in the title. In regard to the two greatest themes of modern drama, love and ambition, the author recognizes the fact that the latter is modified by the " more or less communal nature of tribal labour," and the former by " the plain fact that in the simple, open air life of the Indian the physical stress of sex is actually much less than in conditions called civilized." Among Indian plays *The Arrowmaker* is almost unique in that woman unblushingly demands as her right marital life and the bearing of children, experiences of which the savage probably deprived very few.

" The Law of the Races " which frowns upon miscegenation forms the theme of William C. De Mille's *Strongheart,* 1905, which places the Indian in the very current of modern university life. Soangataha, sent east by his people to be educated as a wise chief, finds himself the mainstay of Columbia's football team and the cynosure of feminine eyes. Like an athlete he readily responds by falling in love with Dorothy Nelson, whose brother Frank he had saved in the West. The Indian now has every reason to believe that his desire to form an intimate connection with the white race will not be rejected, for his beloved assures him that the advantages of civilization enjoyed by the aborigines will cause her people to call his brothers, and furthermore, her brother Frank and her admirer Dick Livingston have become his fast friends as a result of their having faced common dangers in the West. This supposition is strengthened by his noble conduct when the falling of the football signals into the hands of the opposing team had thrown a dark shadow upon his character. Even Dorothy's chum advises her not to let the difference of race stand in the way of love, but to accept the proposal of the Indian, who has a great purpose and absolute truth in his eyes.

In a setting appealing to an Indian and romantic alike, De Mille allows the football star to put the crucial question. The white girl is tired of the noise and the rush of the city and her thoughts go out to " those great, silent mountains, smiling up at the sun, or showing to the dark, gray clouds a face as stern and grim as their own, but always peaceful." Exactly such a girl, rising above the effete East, the native wants as a companion, loving her with a love as great as his mountains and as pure as the air about them.

Racial prejudice lying dormant in the white man immediately

rouses itself, for brother Frank and suitor Dick forbid him to make love to a white woman. But he as *the* American boldly claims it as his right, he who has now the same education, the same customs, and the same feelings as the white man. The latter has been false to his race, robbed him of everything, and now, even though the red man lives by the laws of the palefaces, they refuse to look upon him as a brother and deny him the right to love. After having called him from the mountains and showed him what modern life is like, they now try to keep him back — an injustice the red man keenly feels and indignantly resents. Thus does the play denounce the racial prejudice of the white man that lurks in the most of us. Still, it is overcome as the love of the white girl hurdles the barriers of race, for she is willing to share Strongheart's life among his people.

A more formidable barrier to amalgamation the red man himself erects. The messenger Black Eagle, notifying the Indian of his own elevation to the chieftainship after the death of his father, maintains that his people will not receive the white woman, and their claim is the stronger, since they have paid for his wisdom. Aboriginal prejudice at last prevails: in a scene vibrant with emotion Strongheart decides to keep faith with his people, and despite his love, to obey the cruel law of the races. Yet, in renouncing human emotion and in breaking away he despairingly implores the superior force: " Oh, great spirit of my fathers, I call to you for help, for I am in the midst of a great desert, alone."

De Mille has been reasonably successful in steeping his play in the atmosphere of modern college life with its emphasis on athletic prowess and social diversion. That the eternal feminine along with jazz and racoon coats should play a part is simply an acknowledgment of existing conditions. The problem he presents is a real one, for only on the basis of social equality will the native reap all the advantages of civilization. One has good reason to suspect though that the barrier is more easily hurdled by the agile red man than by the admiring but still somewhat reluctant co-ed.

CHAPTER IX

JAMES FENIMORE COOPER

The writer who more than anyone else impressed his conception of the Indian upon America and the world at large is James Fenimore Cooper (1789-1851), in eleven of whose books the red man plays a prominent part. In addition to the well known Leatherstocking Tales, *Satanstoe, The Chainbearer, The Redskins, The Wept of Wish-ton-Wish, Wyandotté,* and *The Oak Openings* furnish the stage on which the native of the forest contends with the invader of the clearings. Cooper was vitally interested in this dramatic and picturesque conflict between the static man of primeval nature and the representative of an advancing civilization that swept all before it. With poignant regret he watched a race endowed with not a few of mankind's noblest qualities fall before the superior knowledge and the cunning of a ruthless and grasping people. The colors of the ever changing pageant vary between somber and bright, with the former unquestionably predominating. For a simple reading of all the available material will at once refute the claim of excessive idealization advanced by critics either limited in their viewpoint or only slightly acquainted with the great novelist. The candid observer will readily admit that, taken all in all, Cooper has given the world a remarkably complete and faithful picture of the character and life of the aborigines of primitive America.

Although his knowledge of the native was much more extensive than that of many writers dealing with aboriginal life, Cooper had, contrary to general opinion, little first hand acquaintance with the American Indian. When late in 1790 the fourteen months old James was brought to Cooperstown, the red man had left that part of the state. For as early as 1768 by the treaty of Fort Stanwix the Iroquois relinquished the Lake Otsego region, and during Cooper's life only roving bands of degenerate half-breed Indians frequented the neighborhood. He himself told an acquaintance: " You have the advantage of me, for I never was among the Indians. All that I know of them is from reading and hearing my father speak of them," and his daughter Susan also admitted that his own opportunities of intercourse with the red men had been few.

This does not mean, however, that the novelist was ignorant of Indian life and character. Indian relics abounded in the neighborhood of Cooperstown, and, as a matter of fact, Cooper used every opportunity of becoming acquainted with the natives short of studying them in their savage grandeur and state of wildness. In *Notions of the Americans,* 1828, he tells us that in the more interior parts of the country he had frequently met Indian families, either travelling, or proceeding to some village, with their wares. To him they seemed stunted, dirty, and degraded descendants of the ancient warlike possessors of the country. Those near the coast appeared to be in civilization, comforts, and character, about on a level with the lowest classes of European peasantry. Some of these Indians he characterizes as thieves, " though in common they are rigidly honest; nearly always so, unless corrupted by much intercourse with the whites." At one time he visited on Long Island King Peter, who claimed to be a descendant of the ancient sachems and was holding his court in the woods. He found the Indian dwelling with his family in a wigwam of a most primitive construction, which he proceeds to describe in detail. " The man himself was a full-blooded Indian, but his manner had that species of sullen deportment that betrays the disposition without the boldness of the savage. He complained that ' basket stuff ' was getting scarce, and spoke of an intention of removing his wigwam shortly to some other estate."

According to his daughter Susan, " occasionally some small party of the Oneidas, or other representatives of the Five Nations, had crossed his path in the valley of the Susquehanna, or on the shores of Lake Ontario, where he served when a midshipman in the navy. And more recently, since the idea of introducing these wild people into his books had occurred to him, he had been at no little pains to seize every opportunity offered for observation. Fortunately for his purpose, deputations to Washington from the

Western tribes were quite frequent at that moment; he visited these different parties as they passed through Albany and New York, following them in several instances to Washington, and with a view also to gathering information from the officers and interpreters who accompanied them." While in *The Pioneers* Cooper could largely rely upon his own observations, in the other books the results of his studies are evident on many pages.

It is clear that Cooper carefully gathered all available material from what he considered the most authentic sources. His daughter Susan testifies that he was at pains to obtain accurate details regarding Indian life and character by studying such earlier writers as Heckewelder, Charlevoix, Penn, Smith, Eliot, and Colden, and by examining likewise the narratives of Long, of Mackenzie, and of Lewis and Clark. Combined with his own observations this formed a respectable body of valuable material.

There can be no doubt that the works of Rev. John Heckewelder (1743–1825), a Moravian missionary among the Delaware and Mohegan Indians, were the mine from which Cooper drew much of his precious ore. Especially important is the former's *An Account of the History, Manners, and Customs of the Indian Nations who once Inhabited Pennsylvania and the Neighboring States*, 1819. With other Moravian missionaries Heckewelder had succeeded in converting a goodly number of Delawares and Mohegans, who for a time lived upon the Muskingum River west of Pittsburgh and later near Detroit. Among these praying Indians the kind and zealous missionary spent the better part of his life and became their greatest historian, though some would have us believe that credulity and partiality color many of his pages. The fact is that his beloved Delawares nearly always appear in a favorable light, while their enemies, the Iroquois, are pictured as little short of diabolical.

It was but natural that Cooper should have been drawn to the rich material which Heckewelder offered in his *History, Manners, and Customs of the Indian Nations* and in two other publications appearing in the same year, all of which evoked immediate and enthusiastic praise. For instance, the critic Nathan Hale claimed that Heckewelder had described in the most authentic and satisfactory manner the character and condition of the Indians, and that no work could compare with it as far as correct information and copiousness of details were concerned. J. Pickering likewise spoke highly of the favorable picture Heckewelder had drawn of an unfortunate race. He himself believed it to be essentially true, and he was persuaded that in spite of some undeniable faults and vices, the candid reader " will be surprised to perceive how much their blemishes of character have been exaggerated, and how little we have known of their virtues."

Already in his review of *The Spy* in 1822 W. H. Gardiner had pointed to the Indians as a highly poetical people, whose superstitions might be successfully employed by some future wizard of the West to light up a new train of glowing visions. He was confident that the savage warrior with his figurative diction, his attitude toward death, his implacable hatred and cunning would serve as " no mean instrument of the sublime and terrible of human agency. And if we may credit the flattering pictures of their best historian, the indefatigable Heckewelder, not a little of softer interest might be extracted from their domestic life."

No wonder that Cooper eagerly utilized the material so highly praised by what appeared to be competent critics. But *The Last of the Mohicans* upon its appearance in 1826 immediately drew the criticism of General Lewis Cass, Governor of Michigan Territory, who speaks of Heckewelder, " a worthy, zealous Moravian missionary," as " a man of moderate intellect, and of still more moderate attainments; of great credulity, and of strong personal attachments to the Indians." Condescendingly he refers to the amusing naïveté and the unreasoning partisanship for the Delawares of this otherwise lovable man. In a mood of irritation Cass maintains that " the effect of Mr. Heckewelder's work, upon the prevailing notions respecting Indian history, is every day more and more visible. It has furnished materials for the writers of periodical works, and even of *history;* and in one of those beautiful delineations of American scenery, incidents, and manners, for which we are indebted to the taste and talent of an eminent novelist, 'the last of the Mohegans' is an Indian of the school of Mr. Heckewelder, and not of the school of nature."

Only a few months later Gardiner in his review of *The Last of the Mohicans* executed what can be considered only a curious right-about-face. In pointing out that the main design of the work was manifestly to exhibit the characteristics of savage rather than of civilized life, he gratefully acknowledged Cooper's superiority over his predecessors, whose red men " had not been copies from nature; but mere creations of the poet's brain, the half-formed dreams of a disturbed imagination." But he claimed that Cooper's Indians were also somewhat of the visionary order, even though his dream was somewhat more consistent, and he had interwoven in his vision more of what really belongs to the aboriginal character than any other writer of poetry or romance. In particular he deplored that the novelist should have " relied exclusively upon the narrations of the enthusiastic and visionary Heckewelder, whose work is a mere eulogium upon the virtues of his favorite tribe, and contains, mixed with many interesting facts, a world of pure imagination." Since he regards the missionary a victim of an easy credulity, " it is therefore with great regret, that we have seen his wild traditions adopted by an author so generally read, and so deservedly popular, for the sober voice of history, and the whole fable of superior virtues and glories of the Lenni Lenape, incorporated into this table, and made the basis of its Indian mythology for such it must be called." In a work of fiction this might be of trifling moment, but by his minute descriptions and his assertion that he is not painting a romantic and imaginary picture of things, Cooper presents an altogether false and ideal view of the Indian character. Though he readily admits that in general the customs and manners of the Indians are very well depicted, the Delawares are beautified beyond aboriginal nature and the portrait of Uncas is especially objectionable.

In 1828 General Cass returned to the attack. He claimed that Heckewelder had " surveyed the character and manner and former situation of our aboriginal inhabitants under a bright and glowing light. His account is a pure, unmixed panegyric. The most idle traditions of the Indians with him become sober history; their superstition is religion; their indolence philosophic indifference or pious resignation; their astonishing improvidence, hospitality;

and many other defects in their character are converted into the corresponding virtues." He is furthermore charged with ignorance of the character of the most important Indian tribes, his knowledge having been confined to a small band of the Delawares. The critic therefore deeply regrets that Cooper instead of following the unreliable Heckewelder " did not cross the Allegheny, instead of the Atlantic, and survey the red man in the forests and prairies, which yet remain to him." If the popular novelist would only adopt such a course, he might give to the world a series of great works and incidentally discover " how far he has wandered from nature in following the path marked out by Mr. Heckewelder." In a rather detailed manner the distinguished military man points out that in both *The Last of the Mohicans* and *The Prairie* Cooper consulted " the book of Mr. Heckewelder, instead of the book of nature." In spite of the great pleasure he has derived from the reading of Cooper's works, he is forced to admit that " his Uncas and his Pawnee Hardheart, for they are both of the same family, have no living prototype in our forests." They are civilized men and not Indians, or rather " the Indians of Mr. Heckewelder, and not the fierce and crafty warriors and hunters that roam through our forests."

Strictures so severe the sensitive novelist did not leave unanswered. In the Preface to a new edition of the Leatherstocking Tales, without directly admitting his debt, Cooper vigorously defended Heckewelder's view, and boldly asserted his own right to point out the more elevating characteristics of the red man. " It has been objected to these books that they give a more favorable picture of the redman than he deserves. The writer apprehends that much of this objection arises from the habits of those who have made it. One of his critics, on the appearance of the first work in which Indian character was portrayed, objected that its ' characters were Indians of the school of Heckewelder, rather than of the school of nature.' These words quite probably contain the substance of the true answer to the objection. Heckewelder was an ardent, benevolent missionary, bent on the good of the redman, and seeing in him one who had the soul, reason, and characteristics of a fellow-being. The critic is understood to have been a very distinguished agent of the government, one very familiar with Indians, as they are seen at the councils to treat for the sale of their lands, where little or none of their domestic qualities come into play, and where indeed, their evil passions are known to have had their fullest scope. As just would it be to draw conclusions of the general state of American society from the scenes of the capital, as to suppose that the negotiating of one of these treaties is a fair picture of Indian life."

Cooper insisted that " it is the privilege of all writers of fiction, more particularly when their works aspire to the elevation of romances, to present the *beau idéal* of their characters to the reader. This is which constitutes poetry, and to suppose that the redman is to be represented only in the squalid misery or in the degraded moral state that certainly more or less belongs to his condition, is, we apprehend, taking a very narrow view of an author's privileges. Such criticism would have deprived the world of even Homer." And to this view Cooper clung throughout life.

Of the thirteen novels of Cooper in which the Indian plays any considerable part, two offer little of interest and need not detain us long. In the sea tale *Afloat and Ashore,* 1844, degenerate Indians of the Northwest Coast gain temporary possession of the ship Crisis, but they are soon swept from the deck by the superior cunning of the white sailors. Although these natives of an unknown tribal affiliation are not entirely devoid of intelligence, they are a degraded and wretched lot, and the author never had beheld any beings so low in the scale of the human race as the Northwestern savages appeared to be. The other work, a historical novel entitled *Mercedes of Castile,* 1840, and dealing primarily with the first American voyage of Columbus, devotes some space to the beautiful Ozema, sister of a Haytian cassique. The chivalrous Don Luis de Bobadilla, fiancé of Mercedes, rescues her from the unwelcome attentions of a fierce carib chief. Between the nobleman and the " princess," who bears a remarkable similarity to Mercedes, a tender affection springs up, which is deepened when on the return voyage to Spain Don Luis during a terrific storm bestows upon her a cross, an act interpreted by the simple child of nature as a marriage ceremony. This belief, nurtured in secret and later made known to the Spanish queen, leads to an estrangement and a near rupture between the Spanish lovers. After the misunderstanding has been cleared up, Don Luis and Mercedes are united, and Ozema is baptized. But she suddenly dies when her offer to become the second wife of Don Luis is rudely rejected by the officiating archbishop. Though Ozema's sweet innocence and native grace are appealing, it can hardly be claimed that, especially with her almost miraculous gift of acquiring the Spanish language, she is a convincing figure.

The eleven works dealing with the native of the forests and the prairies of America were written over a period of twenty-five years, and even *The Pioneers* and *The Deerslayer*, which mark the extreme limits of Chingachgook's career, are fully eighteen years apart. The five so-called Leatherstocking Tales are with one exception in reality Indian romances that give a fairly complete portrait of the red man in his native habitat. Their discussion as a group may appropriately be postponed until the reader has become acquainted with some other less known but not necessarily unimportant delineations of the American native which the prolific pen of the novelist gave to the world.

After laying the scene of *The Pioneers* and *The Last of the Mohicans* in New York, and that of *The Prairie* in the Far West, Cooper turned to another section of the country in order to reap the advantages that a new background naturally offered. Following in the path of several of his imitators such as Miss Francis (Child), Mrs. Cheney, and Miss Sedgwick, he utilized in 1829 the rich material awaiting exploitation in New England. The accounts of the unhappy fate of King Philip and descriptions of Indian captivities, especially the classic example of Martha Dunstan, had prepared the soil for the favorable reception of a work of romantic realism. But Cooper's attempt to recreate Puritan frontier life proved to be as disappointing as his failure to depict the thrilling racial conflict in the form of a stirring narrative. At the start, the outlandish title *The Wept of Wish-ton-Wish,* in no way indicating that here we have a tale of King Philip's War, formed an unnecessary handicap. The *Wept* in the title naturally draws attention to the kidnapping of little Ruth from the valley designated as Wish-ton-Wish, which Cooper thought was Indian for "whippoorwill," while as a matter of fact it turns out to be the term for "prairie dog." Neither did the English title *The Borderers* nor the French *The Puritan Family* prove to be more illuminating. If anything, this curious vacillation foreshadows a lack of emphasis and of logical progress which the bewildered reader might rightfully expect. In spite of honest intentions, the delineation of Puritan life was patently beyond the powers of a man who himself in old age ruefully confessed: " Nothing Yankee agrees with me." And as for the Indian tribes and their leaders, it would be too much to claim that the novelist had given them imaginative life.

The story, which opens in 1666, or ten years before the outbreak of King Philip's War, in the valley of Wish-ton-Wish in Connecticut, is replete with action. After an uneventful opening, we see the members of the Heathcote household capture a fine looking young savage, who is later identified as the son of the famous Narragansett chief Miantonimoh. Soon an attack on the Puritan stronghold follows, in which the details of Indian warfare are given with considerable skill, although the descriptions are less thrilling than in several other of the author's novels. In the confusion of the attack the young savage kidnaps Ruth, the small daughter of Constant Heathcote, and makes good his escape. For a time it seems as if the whole household of the stern Puritan had perished under the burning and falling timbers of the blockhouse, but lo and behold, most of the members escape unharmed in the dry well of the stronghold, and the otherwise cunning savages leave under the impression that the palefaces have been wiped out.

In the rest of the book the author labors to restore the Wept of Wish-ton-Wish to her family. A strenuous effort to find the kidnapped daughter among a distant tribe proves futile, and not till ten years have elapsed does the issue come to a crisis. The attack on what has now become the village of Wish-ton-Wish under Metacom or King Philip with his Wampanoags and Conanchet with his Narragansetts leads to the capture of the Heathcotes. To his amazement the young chief Conanchet, who is none other than the kidnapper and now the husband of the Wept of Wish-ton-Wish, realizes that his captives are members of the family he had believed wiped out in the conflagration. But though the mother recognizes the daughter now restored to her, the latter is unable to recall her childhood and, to the horror of her kinsmen, takes pleasure in scalping.

Metacom or King Philip is not the principal figure, but defers to his younger confederate and ally Conanchet, both of whom the author describes in a detailed manner. The great chief of the Narragansetts dominates the action, and his downfall and execution through treachery of his own people furnish the high point of the plot. During a surprise attack of the Puritans on the Indians the wily Metacom escapes, while Conanchet in shielding his old friend Submission or the regicide Goffe falls into the hands of the whites and his implacable Mohegan enemy Uncas. In the final extremity the great Narragansett leader upholds the best traditions of his race. As a man of his word who keeps his appointment at the place of execution after he has brought his wife from the whites, he is yet unwilling to be adopted by the Mohegans or be reconciled even at the price of his life. He dies as he had lived, noble, proud, and inflexible, devoted to his faithful wife but true to his conception of duty, " the last Sachem of the broken and dispersed tribe of the Narragansetts."

The delineation of the red man adds little to what had been given by the author in other novels. The bringing together of three of the greatest New England chiefs, Metacom, Uncas, and Conanchet, is a happy device, but the more heroic figure of the latter dwarfs the less noble and more fierce chiefs. The Indians exhibit the same tribal characteristics formerly ascribed to the Hurons, love of scalps being one of their chief traits. In depicting scalping as an old custom about ten years before 1675, Cooper probably is in error, as it is very doubtful that at this time scalping had become an ingrained habit of the New England Indians.

The Puritan attitude toward the natives shows on the whole commendable moderation. As a mysterious stranger, the regicide Goffe masquerades under the name of Submission, dubious in his friendship for the Indians and in his loyalty to his white kinsmen alike. The Wept of Wish-ton-Wish has lost the attributes of civilization, and desperately clings to her savage mate. While the Puritan authorities may not tolerate torture of the enemies, they are perfectly willing to profit from treachery and from internecine strife among the natives of the woods. Most despicable and hypocritical appears Meek Wolfe, the pastor of the Puritan flock, who embodies all the traits and animosities which history and tradition have assigned to the stern New Englander of earlier days.

A fine psychological study of the Indian's contradictory character is found in *Wyandotté*, 1843, in which Cooper aimed to sketch " several distinct varieties of the human race, as true to the governing impulses of their educations, habits, modes of thinking, and natures. The red man had his morality as much as his white brother . . ." The story roughly covers the thirty years between 1765 and 1795, the main events falling into the period of the Revolutionary War. Fierce assaults by Mohawks and Onondagoes are made on the Hutted Knoll or the country estate of Major Willoughby in Tryon County, New York. The stratagems and warfare of the savages fill many pages of the book, but they furnish little that is not found in other works of Cooper.

Of chief interest is the realistically drawn Wyandotté or Saucy Nick, the former name designating the proud Tuscarora chief, while the latter was used by the whites as an indication of his less noble traits. For many years the semi-savage had been an outcast from his tribe on account of ungovernable passions, and even members of the Willoughby family he served suspected him of rascality. The desire for scalps, the propensity for drink, and last but not least, an extreme aversion to flogging governed his actions. Major Willoughby had made the fatal mistake of subjecting the proud nature of the savage to this personal humiliation, and in the end he paid for it with his life. Thirty long years had passed since the first flogging, years filled with kindness on the part of the major, who at one time had even saved the life of the Indian from the bayonet of one of his grenadiers; but the gratitude had been flogged out and fierce resentment was wont to take its place. Though he was attached to the Willoughby family, and even risked his life for them, his wavering purpose of thirty long years suddenly revived at the favorable opportunity. While contemplating the murder, his back feels well, as he expresses it, and even in viewing the corpse later, he remains unmoved, in the belief that, by " curing the sores on his back in this particular manner, he had done what became a Tuscarora warrior and chief." So deep-seated is his hatred that in passing the grave later he would throw a flower on the side where Mrs. Willoughby rested, but shake a menacing finger at the other which hid the person of his enemy. In that " he was true to his nature, which taught him never to forget a favor, or forgive an injury," the typically Indian attitude. Only when Wyandotté becomes a Christian, does this struggle between his good and bad qualities partly subside. It once more revives in a dramatic scene at the grave of his victim many years later, after the son had been informed of the facts. Nick was deeply agitated. " His youthful and former opinions maintained a fearful struggle with those who had come late in life; the result being a wild admixture of his sense of Indian justice, and submission to the tenets of his new and imperfectly comprehended faith. For a moment, the first prevailed. Advancing with a firm step to the general, he put his own bright and keen tomahawk into the other's hands, folded his arms on his bosom, bowed his head a little, and said, firmly, —

' Strike! Nick kill cap'n — major kill Nick.' "

When the son forgives him, he is reconciled and falls dead on the grave of his victim. But Christianity had so little affected his basic character and changed his course of life that there were drawn from his pockets strings of strange-looking hideous objects, human scalps which he had collected " in the course of many campaigns, and brought, as a species of hecatomb, to the graves of the fallen."

During 1845 and 1846 there appeared three novels which are practically forgotten to-day, overtaken by a deserved oblivion like the question of Anti-rentism which bulks so large in the last. In *Satanstoe*, 1845, *The Chainbearer*, 1845, and *The Redskins*, 1846, Cooper discusses the economic questions of the day in the form of narratives which trace the history of the Littlepage family from the French-Indian War of 1758 to about eighty years later.

Heavily freighted with the discussions of efforts on the part of tenants to overthrow the patroon system in New York, the stories founder on account of this mass of material inserted with an ulterior purpose. The three books may do honor to Cooper as a citizen and a patriot who wants justice to prevail, but the artist in him almost completely vanishes. The red man is obviously introduced in order that the noble traits of the native may serve as a contrast to the vulgar greed and the disgusting manners of the settler.

Satanstoe, deriving its name from a peculiarly shaped tract of land in the county of Westchester, the family estate of Cornelius Littlepage, is largely occupied with family affairs before the Indians enter. General Abercrombie's assault on Ticonderoga in 1758 fails. Indians accompany the armies, and as both the French and the English pay a snug sum for human scalps, there is a manifest eagerness on the part of the savage allies to make the most of the opportunity. Susquesus or Trackless, an honest Onondago who lives outside of his tribe and who as a representative of the native appears in a favorable light, shares the desire of his people for glory and gain. Throughout, gory scalps and unspeakable atrocities play a large part. The hostile Hurons especially commit frightful cruelties, suspending, scalping, and mutilating their victims. Susquesus' party retaliates, and succeeds in reaching the fortified seat of Ravensnest. Presently an attacking party of Hurons under the leadership of chief Musquerusque, whom Susquesus' negro companion Jaap had flogged, tries to destroy the stronghold by means of setting it afire. Unfortunately, the negro falls into their hands, and his release is out of the question, since the Hurons want his scalp to serve as "a plaster to this warrior's back." In vain had Susquesus warned the negro, when lack of room in the boat made the release of the chief advisable, not to flog him, for the Huron chief " got tender back; never forget rope." But the negro escapes his fate by getting away and by smashing the head of his opponent, and the Hurons are thrown into a panic by a sudden charge of the besieged and dispersed.

The attitude of not a few of the whites is best expressed by the Rev. Mr. Worden's belief that Christianity is essentially a civilized religion. Henceforth he will not be so rash and imprudent as to push duty to exaggeration, but will confine himself to preaching the gospel in the colonies, " letting alone these scalping devils the Indians, who, I greatly fear, were never born to be saved."

Susquesus, the sober and honest Onondago, even though at first under a cloud of suspicion on account of living outside of his tribe, is easily the outstanding figure among the Indians. Cooper evidently takes undisguised delight in the portrait he paints of the noble savage: " There he stood, straight as the trunk of a pine, light and agile in person, with nothing but his breech-cloth, moccasins, and a blue calico shirt belted to his loins with a scarlet band, through which was thrust the handle of his tomahawk, and to which were attached his shotpouch and horn, while his rifle rested against his body, butt downward. Trackless was a singularly handsome Indian, the unpleasant peculiarities of his people being but faintly portrayed in his face and form; while their nobler and finer qualities came out in strong relief. His nose was almost aquiline; his eye, dark as night, was restless and piercing; his limbs Apollo-like; and his front and bearing had all the fearless dignity of a warrior, blended with the grace of nature. The only obvious defects were in his walk, which was Indian, or in-toed or bending at the knee; but, to counterbalance these, his movements were light, springy and swift. I fancied him, in figure, the very *beau-idéal* of a runner." It is detailed descriptions such as these that have according to some critics helped to make Cooper's Indian a permanent figure in literature.

The same Susquesus or Trackless plays an equally prominent part in *The Chainbearer,* which falls in the year 1784. The story contrasts an Indian's loyalty to a white friend and the vulgar ruthlessness of the squatter. Mordaunt Littlepage and " Chainbearer," a former captain in his regiment and now a surveyor, come in violent conflict with Aaron Thousandacres, who held that if there were no surveyors, there would be no boundaries to farms but the rifle, which to him was the best lawmaker that man ever invented. Accordingly he simply takes possession of the country, and assisted by his numerous brood carries on his lumbering operations. As a type of the reckless borderer so disgusting to

Cooper, he disregards all law and property rights, which to the author was the basis of all civilization.

In order that he may unmolested float his boards down the river, the unscrupulous squatter secures the persons of his potential enemies, the Indian included. The latter's release after certain promises on his part gives rise to the following remark as to the character of the native: " I had heard that the faith of an Indian of any character, in all such cases, was considered sacred, and could not but ask myself, as Susquesus walked quietly out of prison, how many potentates and powers there were in Christendom who, under circumstances similarly involving their most important interests, could be found to place a similar confidence in their fellows! "

The development of the plot with its bloodshed and various escapes need not detain us here. Suffice it to say that the Indian revenges the fatal shooting of his friend the Chainbearer, whom Thousandacres in his callousness had even denied medical aid. At least it was suspected that the Trackless sacrificed the squatter to the manes of his friend, dealing out Indian justice without hesitation or compunction, although self-respect and pride of character sealed his lips. The coroner's verdict was that Thousandacres had met accidental death, but there was probably " as little ' accident ' as ever occurred, when a man was shot through the body by a steady hand, and an unerring eye." In a ravine near the marked grave of his friend the aging Trackless makes his abode, averse to manual labor, but maintaining his elastic step, upright movement, and former vigor.

Much more than in the preceding works does Anti-rentism, or the relation between landlord and tenant, raise its head in *The Redskins* to spoil any joy that the narrative might otherwise have given. Since the economic questions are constantly kept in the foreground, it would have been almost miraculous had the story been a success. The book exposes the loose ideas about property rights and the semi-barbarous conditions of a new settlement. At all times the author keeps painfully before the reader what is already indicated in the subtitle *Indian* and *Injin,* the latter " a white man, who, bent on an unworthy and illegal purpose, is obliged to hide his face, and perform his task in disguise. The Indian is a redman, neither afraid nor ashamed to show his countenance, equally to friend or enemy."

The two groups are constantly contrasted: the one, disguised and shirking the duties of civilization, nay, an enemy of the established order and using force to break contracts legally and morally binding; the other, descendants of the fierce but lofty-minded aboriginal inhabitants of this continent, among them the hoary, honest Susquesus, a magnificent sight, with his fiery eyes, composed features, and impressive air, honored by representatives of the tribes whom the white man had forced like the bears, the elk, and the moose, out of the forest of America, upon the vast plains. Representatives of the latter actually appear in the story, a party of famous chiefs on their way to Washington, with their medals, their fine appearance, and their quiet, dignified, not to say lofty bearing. They easily rout the Injins bent upon mischief. Time and again the differences between these two groups are brought out. "The one is natural, dignified, polished in his own way — nay, gentlemen-like; while the other is a sneaking scoundrel, and as vulgar as his own appellation," not above firing buildings and hay-barns whenever an opportunity presents itself.

The history and fine qualities of the aged Susquesus, the upright Onondago whose fame had spread through many tribes, are at last revealed. While still a young man, he had fallen in love with Quickwith, a captive girl of the Delawares brought in by Waterfowl. "Their eyes were never off each other. He was the noblest moose of the woods, in her eyes; she was the spotted fawn in his." But their union is vetoed by Waterfowl, who claims the prize himself. Susquesus respects the law of the red men, leaves never to return, and for a time associates with the Mohawks. Chief Eagleflight tells the anti-renters to be honest like "the Upright of the Onondagoes." The latter himself points out that a promise of a red man is law under any and all circumstances; he makes few professions, but lets his acts speak for him. Various invidious comparisons between the red men and the palefaces are made, all with a definite point in regard to the controversy raging in New York state, in which the aristocratic

Cooper sided with the landlords. The novelist thus prostitutes the reserved, courteous, and reliable Indians for the purpose of putting to public shame the vulgar, low, and shifty paleface tenants.

Susquesus or Trackless is carried through three novels and over a period of time covering eighty years, which makes him a man more than a century old. We see him at the age of twenty-six, engaged in war, after his disappointment in love; we witness him later revenging his white friend; and in the end we find him berating the whites for breaking their pledged work. His own people he admonishes to be honest in their conduct, which will make them richer than white men. In some respects he is even superior to Chingachgook. In him there is no deterioration as in the great Mohegan, for at no period in his life does he touch intoxicating liquor, but grows old and white in possession of his powers of mind and body.

Though written last, *The Deerslayer,* 1841, opens the Leatherstocking Series, and strange as it may seem, the story composed during Cooper's " most turbulent period of controversy," is one of the best, if not the best, of his Indian tales. It enjoys the advantage of a natural setting in the wilderness, far away from the corruption of white settlements. Over it there is thrown the poetic glamour of the young warrior in love, willing to risk his life for his betrothed and for his friend Deerslayer. Thus interwoven with the dread danger and the thrilling rescues is a romantic passion surmounting all obstacles and well on its way to consummation.

The center of aboriginal interest is Chingachgook or the " Big Sarpent — so called for his wisdom and cunning," a name that Cooper found in Heckewelder as " Chingachgook — a large snake." He is " a brave and just minded Delaware," belonging to a fallen people, who nevertheless upholds the best traditions and the ancient greatness and power of the Mohicans. At times called a Delaware in the confusing terminology of the book, he is a Mohican or Mohegan by blood and of the family of the great chiefs, none other than the renowned and far-famed Uncas being his father. The dispersal of his own tribe had thrown the young chief with the Delawares, where his tall, handsome, and athletic figure and manly qualities had won him the fairest of the maidens, the lovely Wah-ta!-Wah or Hist. Through treachery of Briarthorn fallen into the clutches of a raiding party of Hurons, she is now anxiously waiting for the rescue at the hands of her lover. Except in the appealing figure of Hist, the Delawares under the leadership of the wise and just Tamenund play no direct part in the story, but they are said to be as manful as any other tribe when the proper time to strike comes. In direct opposition to the " Mingoes " or Iroquois in the wider sense, their moral standards are high, and even the white Deerslayer scrupulously redeems his pledged word, in order that on his first warpath he might not disgrace himself in the eyes of his tutors. Such a eulogy of the Delawares to the disparagement of the Iroquois, generally conceded as among the finest representatives of the red race, plainly shows the influence of the partisan missionary Heckewelder.

Chingachgook embodies the best traits of the red man. Though his good qualities are strongly emphasized after the manner of Heckewelder, yet he has the distinctive aboriginal characteristics and never denies the peculiar " gifts " of his people. With hereditary bravery and cunning he has hung on the flanks of his enemies for an opportunity to meet his mistress and incidentally to secure a scalp on his first warpath. The desire for the lovely girl has mastered him, and his flight with her from the Huron camp to the canoe has all the elements of romantic adventure. Yet he hardly ever forgets the necessary precautions, or his position as head of the household, for like other women his wife will carry her own papoose and perform the duties ordinarily incumbent upon the squaw. Agreeable to Indian custom, his self-restraint is admirable, only occasionally broken through by curiosity and surprise, as when the ivory chessmen are revealed. Love of woman does not dampen the strong affection for his friend, for at the critical moment he boldly steps into the circle of the Hurons, if necessary to die at the side of his white companion.

The teachings of the Moravian missionaries seem to have affected the young chief but little, especially in regard to scalping. Like Deerslayer they conceded the validity of peculiar " gifts " to each race, but disapproved of scalp bounties. Chingachgook's interest in and desire for scalps, seconded by Hist, is but natural, since they represented glory and profit. The thought of securing the trophy from the head of the first Iroquois killed by Hawkeye throws Chingachgook's whole being into excitement. And this desire on the part of the red man is approved by the hunter, who tells his young friend: " As for your looking for scalps, it belongs to your gifts, and I see no harm in it." In fact, he would consider it sinful to withstand such natural gifts, especially that of scalping, which was considered a signal virtue in a native, the Indian prizing the scalp more than the life of the enemy. " To slay, and not to bring off the proof of victory, indeed, was scarcely deemed honorable." The Hurons share this feeling. When they find their kinsman who was killed by Deerslayer still in possession of his scalp, there are " shouts of delight ": the enemy had been unable to secure the " trophy, without which a victory was never considered complete." Time and again they deeply regret that so far they have secured only a single scalp, that of Hutter — their desire powerfully stimulated by the rich reward of the French government for any number they might bring in.

The attitude of the ex-pirate and Hurry Harry undoubtedly expressed the sentiment of the borderer. Both considered the Mingoes as more than half devils, and to be dealt with as such. The rich bounty offered by the colonial government gave the whole a commercial tinge, and consequently they made no difference between warriors and helpless women and children. Hurry looked upon the redskins as animals, with nothing human about them but cunning. Cooper aptly characterizes the general feeling when he says: " Like most vulgar-minded men, he had only regarded the Indians through the medium of their coarser and fiercer characteristics. It had never struck him that the affections are human; that even high principles — modified by habits and prejudices, but not the less elevated within their circle — can exist in the savage state; and that the warrior who is most ruthless in the field, can submit to the softest and gentlest influences, in the moments of domestic quiet. In a word, it was the habit of his mind to regard all Indians as beings only a slight degree removed from the wild beasts that roamed the woods, and to feel disposed to treat them accordingly, whenever interest or caprice supplied a motive, or an impulse." Deerslayer's refusal to take scalps must be considered very exceptional and idealistic. Among rough borderers he would have been looked upon as a freak, for scalping, according to contemporary testimony, was an honorable practice, even among refined gentlemen and ladies.

The Hurons exhibit all the traits ascribed to them by Heckewelder. They are treacherous, cruel, even fiendish. The Iroquois killed by Deerslayer in his first memorable encounter with a human enemy had sought the white man's life after they had shaken hands as a pledge of friendship. The Mingoes vainly try to induce Deerslayer to sacrifice Hutter and to share in the spoils. Their enemies they submit to the most refined cruelties in torture, which is, however, only an application of the " religious principle never to forget a benefit, or to forgive an injury."

On the other hand, they are not without their better qualities. Like most Indians they respect those who are afflicted by the Great Spirit with mental troubles. They admire bravery and stoical endurance in friend and foe alike. There is a certain dignity and loftiness of bearing, upset only now and then by some extraordinary cause. They are not even devoid of a certain delicacy and refinement. Deerslayer's first victim, when witnessing the generous attitude of his enemy, " with the high, innate courtesy that so often distinguishes the Indian warrior, before he becomes corrupted by too much intercourse with the worst class of the white men," tried to express his gratitude. Rivenoak, with all his native fierceness, is not without mercy, even if largely motivated by the desire to gain the famous hunter as a member of his tribe. It is true, The Panther is less generous and noble, but that does not alter the fact that humane feelings were not foreign to the heart of the native.

The Indian women appear in a two-fold light. The mild and submissive girls with their low and musical voices are, on the whole, appealing, though harsh treatment seldom evokes their sympathy. Hist is the embodiment of true loveliness. But Cooper has evidently little use for the hardened hags like Sumach, who can never satisfy their vituperative and hateful spirit. They are hideous, repulsive, and fiendish.

Tribute, both direct and indirect, is paid to the cunning and power of observation in a savage, who follows a scent like a hound. But after all, he is not the equal of one who like Chingachgook has benefited from white association, and in many respects he is inferior to the white man. He is by no means remarkable for his skill or force in athletic exercises; witness the mighty Hurry without difficulty meeting the onsets of several savages. Deerslayer likewise leaves them behind in the race, for as in " the case with vigorous border-men, he could outrun any single Indian among his pursuers." The superiority of the white man in the handling of the rifle is marked. The hunter had found that it was not their gift to be as certain with powder and ball as the paleface. Even Chingachgook, trained as he had been in the arts of the settlements, in this respect cuts but a sorry figure beside his white friend, an inferiority emphasized in more than one novel.

On the whole, though the woodcraft is comparatively slight and the theme of flight and pursuit secondary, Cooper has written a thrilling narrative. The strength of the novel lies, apart from its setting, in the picturesque encounters between brave and resourceful warriors, with not a little of the romantic thrown in. There is a certain unity, with the scene definitely localized, an absence of distractingly boresome or humorous characters, and a poetic glamour that welds all into one whole. The ending, focussing as it does practically all characters in one picture, with the swift destruction of the bloodthirsty Mingoes, is especially effective.

In 1826 Cooper published *The Last of the Mohicans*, the most famous and most popular of all his works. The subtitle " a Narrative of 1757 " indicates that it follows *The Deerslayer* by about fourteen years. Instead of glorifying like the first of the Leatherstocking Tales one lake and its environs, it celebrates the American forest, with the one significant exception of the thrilling boat race on Lake George. When during the summer of 1825 Cooper with a party of friends visited that region of New York state, the Honorable Mr. Stanley, later Lord Derby and Prime Minister of England, pronounced the caverns at Glens Falls " the very scene for a romance," which the author obligingly promised to write.

More than any other of Cooper's works *The Last of the Mohicans* makes the Indian the central point of interest, and the popularity of the romance is in a large measure due to its action, the series of breathless adventures built chiefly around the device of flight and pursuit. The first part deals with the adventures of Heyward, Munro's daughters, and their companions on the dangerous journey to Fort William Henry, the frightful massacre on the part of Montcalm's savages forming the historical climax. The second part concerns itself with the rescue of the captive girls and its complicating adventures. Aside from the interest that naturally attaches to the experienced Hawkeye, the core of the story is made up by the tragic race-conflict and its actors, in the main red men. The title itself clearly indicates where in the eyes of the author the chief emphasis was to lie. That interest, powerfully aroused and kept alive by extraordinary happenings, is what makes the tale a success in spite of the many and serious shortcomings of the book as a work of art.

Looked at historically, the title is patently a misnomer. Authors dealing with the vanishing race of the red men have a peculiar fondness for heroes that represent the last of a proud line of chiefs, a temptation which Cooper likewise could not resist. Almost in the beginning he has Chingachgook declare: " I am on the hilltop and must go down into the valley; and when Uncas follows in my footsteps, there will no longer be any of the blood of the Sagamores, for my boy is the last of the Mohicans." And the century-old Tamenund closes the tale with the lament: " In the morning I saw the sons of Unamis happy and strong; and yet, before the night has come, have I lived to see the last warrior of the wise race of the Mohicans." As a matter of fact, Uncas was by no means the last of the Mohicans, for as late as 1932 chief Uhm-Pa-Tuth of the Lutheran Stockbridge Indians in Wisconsin could claim that proud distinction. Like Heckewelder in his *History, Manners, and Customs of the Indian Nations,* Cooper is guilty of a confusing ignorance of the real facts. The Mahicans were an Algonquin tribe that occupied both banks of the upper

Hudson River, extending north almost to Lake Champlain. During the 18th century many of them were dispersed; only those that gathered at Stockbridge and in 1833 migrated to Wisconsin have preserved their identity. The Mohegans, on the other hand, to which Cooper's Uncas evidently belongs, at the time of the first English settlements were a group forming one tribe with the Pequots and resided chiefly in Connecticut. During the difficulties with the colonists the treacherous subordinate chief Uncas broke away, helped to destroy the Pequots, and as a consequence of their downfall gained considerable power. Needless to say, he has given nothing but his name to Cooper's hero. Later large numbers of the Mohegans removed to other states, but the rest of the tribe still resides in the vicinity of Mohegan or Norwich in Connecticut. Thus the title of Cooper's book in reality should have been " The Last of the Mohegans." But he rolls Mahicans, Mohegans, and Delawares all into one, although Heckewelder had made a distinction between the Delawares and the Mahicanni.

Cooper likewise betrays a curious uncertainty when speaking of the divided allegiance of the Delawares during the French and Indian War, who according to Heckewelder fought on the side of the French in consequence of the ill treatment received by the English after William Penn's influence had waned. In *The Last of the Mohicans* a band of the Delawares had followed Montcalm's army, but at the crucial moment it remained idle and offered the rather lame excuse that their hatchets were dull and needed sharpening. Chingachgook and Uncas, with their friend Hawkeye, are deadly enemies of the French and her allies, especially the Mingoes, the hereditary foes of the just Delawares. Cooper is conscious of the difficulty and offers the explanation: " It is true that white cunning has managed to throw the tribes into great confusion, as respects friends and enemies, so that the Hurons and Oneidas, who speak the same tongue, or what may be called the same, take each other's scalps, and the Delawares are divided among themselves; a few hanging about their great council fire on their own river, and fighting on the same side with the Mingoes, while the greater part are in the Canadas, out of natural enmity to the Maquas — thus throwing everything into disorder, and destroying all the harmony of warfare." It was essential that Leatherstocking as an English subject and patriotic American fight against the French, while Chingachgook's sympathies as a Delaware should have caused him to side with the French against the hated Mingoes. But as life-long friends Leatherstocking and Chingachgook must fight side by side, and so we find them enlisted with the English, the Delaware chief indiscriminately trying to root out as enemies all red men not belonging to his tribe.

The mature Chingachgook is naturally more experienced than in *The Deerslayer,* and accordingly assumes the position of leader instead of the youthful Uncas, who looks to him for guidance. In the prime of manhood, he exhibits warlike qualities at their height. In all that pertains to woodcraft, the scout readily defers to him, and he relinquishes the command of the attacking Delawares when their chief appears. The Indian code of scalping is also his. When surrounded by enemies on the island, he resignedly takes the eagle's plume from his head, and smooths the solitary tuft of hair, in order that the scalp-lock may be in readiness to perform its last and revolting office. At the successful surprise attack on Magua's band in the forest a little later, he quickly and business-like gathers the scalps while Uncas goes to the help of the distressed females. So great is his zest for scalps that after the party has safely passed the French sentinel at the " bloody pond," he slips back and scalps the hapless Frenchman, a revolting act that draws from Hawkeye the scarcely half-approving remark: " 'Twould have been a cruel and inhuman act for a whiteskin; but 'tis the gift and natur' of an Indian, and I suppose it should not be denied," but he wishes that it had befallen an accursed Mingo.

The relations of Chingachgook to his son are those of an affectionate father. Once Cooper shows us how late at night he speaks to Uncas in soft and playful tones of affection, giving expression to gentle and natural feelings for fully an hour. The death of his son stuns him, and he is so overcome with grief as to be unable to pronounce the monody of the father at the public funeral. Only later does he sufficiently recover to speak of his good, brave, and dutiful son, and the last act shows him grasping the outstretched hand of Hawkeye, and then those two sturdy and intrepid woodsmen bow their heads together, " while scalding tears fell to their feet, watering the grave of Uncas like drops of falling rain."

The titular hero of the book is probably the most idealized red man in the works of Cooper, the fine qualities of the youth as yet largely unmodified by the grim experiences of later life. In physique Uncas is nature's nobleman, an upright, flexible figure, graceful and unrestrained in the attitudes and movements of nature. There are revealed the " dark, glancing and fearless eye, alike terrible and calm; the bold outline of his high, haughty features, pure in their native red; or the dignified elevation of his receding forehead, together with all the finest proportions of a noble head, bared to the generous scalping tuft." Throughout the story, and particularly during his captivity in the Huron camp, his physical qualities are emphasized. Carefully trained in the art of woodcraft, he at all times gives a good account of himself, though his inexperience in warfare and his high mettle draw him into an ambush and lead to his capture. But his warlike qualities including the awakening zest for scalps and his proud bearing under difficult circumstances win the admiration of experienced hunters and warriors. In fact, he embodies all that is good and best in the renowned line of the hereditary chieftains of the Mohicans.

Toward his father, Uncas displays a deference and filial affection in perfect keeping with the Indian code. His innate courtesy and delicacy is pronounced, and the chivalric attitude toward women so obvious that it has drawn the sneers of unsympathetic critics. A growing love for Cora and the sacred rights of hospitality might partly account for his extraordinary behavior. However, it is hardly an aboriginal trait, and Cooper himself is careful to indicate the exceptional nature of these attentions when he speaks of Uncas " performing all the little offices within his power, with a mixture of dignity and anxious grace, that served to amuse Heyward, who knew well that it was an utter innovation on the Indian customs, which forbid the warriors to descend to any menial employment, especially in favor of their women." And at the rescue of the sisters from Magua's band his interest in their welfare transcends that of the warrior.

Uncas' love for Cora has been considered strange by some critics, but it is not at all unnatural that an Indian should be drawn to the mulatto, witness Magua's fondness for the dark and luxuriant beauty. This attitude of the young chief toward negro blood serves as an effective barrier between him and most of his white admirers. The tragedy of it is that this affection and rivalry on the part of those two dusky savages should lead to his early death, but then he was spared the temptations which his once also noble father could not withstand.

The villain of the story, almost diabolical in his scheming enmity and hatred, is the Huron Magua or Le Renard Subtil. Yet in spite of all his deviltries, one cannot help but accord him some measure of sympathy and admiration. The fire-water of the white men had led to his downfall, and the proud chief had tasted the humiliation of a public flogging at the hands of Munro's men. Brave, cunning, and resourceful, and withal a consummate orator and skilful diplomat, he possessed all the qualities that would have made him a commanding figure among the natives had not moral delinquencies rendered such a position untenable. To him the author attributes all the qualities and concomitants of villainy. His outward appearance arouses shuddering horror, and the manifestations of anger such as the grating of teeth and hellish exultation reach the limits of the permissible. His mode of revenge by filling the heart of the parent with unspeakable anguish at the thought of her enforced squawhood is repugnant to human feeling and hardly would seem to be a realistic touch. Moral principles, however, this traitor to his own people had none, and the four fatal wounds inflicted upon Uncas are nothing less than the expression of wanton bloodlust and malice. His eagerness to have Cora enter his lodge as a squaw is not inconsistent with Indian character, as has sometimes been claimed. The love of the aborigines for white women and children is well known, and as Francis Parkman has pointed out, " The coldest warrior would gladly have received her into his lodge, and promoted her to be his favorite wife, wholly dispensing, in honor of her charms, with flagellation or any of the severer marks of conjugal displeasure."

Magua plays a vital part in the horrible massacre of the helpless after the surrender of the fort, this butchery by the dark cloud of savages in the army of Montcalm constituting the historical climax of the story. The description is vivid, made more terribly picturesque by particular instances of inhuman cruelty as when the savage snatches the child from a mother in order to secure the shawl. " The savage spurned the worthless rags, and perceiving that the shawl had already become a prize to another, his bantering but sullen smile changed to a gleam of ferocity, he dashed the head of the infant against a rock, and cast its quivering remains at her very feet," and then tomahawked the mother. Acts such as these would go far toward making inevitable the destruction of a race whose " gifts " precluded that consideration for the helpless which has always been one of the attributes of civilization. The revolting horrors and the drinking of human blood would seem to call for the uprooting of such a race, the application of a law at least as stern as the Mosaic code of an eye for an eye and a tooth for a tooth.

Other aspects of Indian conduct and warfare, though dark, appear less horrible. The attack on the island is managed with all the adroitness of a policy calculated to reduce the losses to a minimum and to overcome the enemy by strategy. Failure in this case is met with angry howls and fierce denunciation. Short, furious onsets with hand to hand encounters and discreet retreats when the enemy proved too strong were part of the warrior's code. Indian discipline and battle strategy are revealed in the camp of the Hurons and by Uncas' attack of Magua and his band just before the end. Rifles play an important part in the fighting, but even here the Indian strategy of ambush, of sufficient cover, and of overwhelming a weaker party is never forgotten. The traditional bravery of the red man is, however, not universal, for cowardice led Uncas into a snare. It finds its reward according to what seems to have been the usual procedure judging from the conduct of the accused. The chief upbraids him: " Your tongue is loud in the village, but in battle it is still. None of my young men strike the tomahawk deeper into the war-post — none of them so lightly on the Yengeese. The enemy know the shape of your back, but they have never seen the color of your eyes." His name never to be mentioned again, in fact, already forgotten, the convicted yet stoic coward has the keen, glittering knife of the chief thrust into his bosom. Even the father repudiates such a son, putting the blame on Chippewas cheating his squaw. Thus cowardice is stamped out, just as merit, whether of the living or the dead, is duly exalted.

Indian beliefs, customs, and practices Cooper describes with more than ordinary skill. Such are the worship of the tortoise, the beaver and the bear, reverence for the burial places of the dead, the sympathetic treatment of the feeble-minded, chaste attitude toward female prisoners, and a number of other characteristics that impress the reader. As in other of his works, high tribute is paid to the woodcraft of the native, though some of the exploits strain belief. In other respects, as in the handling of firearms, the red man is inferior to the white. The funeral rites of the Delawares receive detailed treatment that speaks well for the author's descriptive skill. The scenes in which the aged and feeble Tamenund appears are also extremely well handled. They are an expression of the Indian's reverence for old age exemplified in the patriarch who upholds the Delaware's proverbial reputation for justice. It is barbaric splendor which he displays, clothed in the finest skins, covered with hieroglyphics, his bosom loaded with medals of silver and gold, armlets and ornaments adorning his figure, a diadem encircling his brow and covering the snow-white hair with the glossy hues of three drooping ostrich feathers dyed in a deep black — this is indeed a figure that ought to satisfy the eyes of the picturesquely inclined. All the sadder that principles which he and the Mohegan chief embodied were destined to pass from the face of the earth in the death of these wise and just Delawares.

The Pathfinder, 1840, marks an ambitious attempt on Cooper's part to combine in one story two types of fiction, that of the forest and of the sea, in both of which he excelled. Like *The Deerslayer* and *The Prairie,* it takes high rank as a work of art, but its popularity has been less than that of *The Last of the Mohicans,* probably on account of its amphibious character and its comparative lack of thrilling adventures. In comparison with the central core of Hawkeye's love for Mabel Duncan, the Indian material, after the thrilling opening, is of secondary importance. Even Chingachgook sinks into the background for dozens of chapters, to emerge only toward the end in a fitting close. But though not plainly visible, the red men of the forest, especially in the form of the ferocious and dreaded Mingoes, are constantly hovering near Lake Ontario to exact a terrible toll of their English enemies in the stirring year of 1760.

As in other books of the series, Cooper pays enthusiastic tribute to the boundless woods bordering the lake, with the atmosphere profoundly affecting the imagination. They are peopled by treacherous Mingoes to whom are applied all the epithets appearing in the earlier works with a few additional ones thrown in. The characterizations of both the Delaware and his enemies are those of Leatherstocking or the Pathfinder, gleaned from the pages of Heckewelder with his partiality for the peaceloving Mohicans and his antipathy to their ruthless destroyers. " Big Sarpent " has most of the qualities of the younger man, with possibly a little more of caution and of deliberation which time and experience had meanwhile taught him. He is as fond of scalping as ever, collecting the scalps of all who have fallen by his own hand or those of his white friends. This passionate desire may have been stimulated by the attempt of a foe whose endeavor as shown by a knife mark all along his left ear just fell short of success through the timely intervention of Hawkeye's deadly rifle. This aboriginal weakness is readily excused by his white brother here as elsewhere as " a gift " of the red man, to be enjoyed like any harmless pleasure. Wise and cunning he is, and not " treacherous, beyond what is lawful in a redskin." For all that, had it not been for the timely support given him at crucial moments, he would have gone on the long trail to the happy hunting-grounds, because at times he is a little rash, and his eye and arm have been unable to develop that precision and steadiness of aim which sends the bullet to its fatal mark.

The Mingoes encountered while the party is approaching the lake have all the cunning and diabolical ferocity of the red man at his best or worst. The keen observation of the young savage who is at the point of detecting the camouflage employed by Hawkeye's party does honor to his woodcraft, and with a little less pride and fear of derision would have proved the undoing of the concealed. These Mingoes, however, are not quite cunning enough to detect the presence of their Delaware nemesis, who, after the struggle for the canoe in the rapids, fearlessly mingles with them and even carries off three scalps. Of romance and interest there is enough at first, but that episode comes to an end all too soon at the fort, and it is rather long before the action at the Thousand Islands brings us another good view of the redskins. Incidentally, this perilous journey to the fort draws attention to a similar episode in *The Last of the Mohicans*, in comparison with which it suffers from the lack of breathless action.

The savages in the pay of the French at the Thousand Islands are scoundrels, bloodthirsty, cruel, and treacherous, veritable fiends in human form. Indulgence in liquor loosens their fury, and even the French leader takes the precaution of putting out the fire, for in their mad orgies the worst is to be feared. The corporal and his soldiers are shot down in cold blood and scalped, and then seated on the grass, with one holding a fishing rod, in order that the whites might be lured to a certain death. As Dew-of-June so characteristically remarks, the Indians now make the bodies of the slain work. However, these Mingoes are only indifferent shots, as Cap has no difficulty in avoiding their fire. When real danger appears, they prudently flee for shelter.

Among individuals, even more than Chingachgook does the Tuscarora Arrowhead attract the attention of the reader. Ostensibly in the service of the English, he is really a traitor, accepting also pay from the French. This noble-looking warrior has all the wild grandeur and nobility of a chief. When caught on the lake he submits with the calm and reserved dignity with which, in the author's eyes, the American aborigines are known to yield to fate; but just as soon as a chance to escape presents itself, he avails himself of it without a moment's hesitation. As leader of a band he shows real ability and not a little of sagacity in keeping out of brawls. But his cunning is matched by his callous ferocity; it is he who plans the massacre of the various groups on the island, and who tomahawks the defenseless wife of soldier Sandy, whose reeking hair was hanging at his girdle as a trophy within less than two minutes. Harsh and brutal in word and action, he treats his own wife in a condescending manner. Like Le Renard Subtil, he has an eye for paleface beauties and gives an unpleasant degree of attention to Mabel as a desirable addition to his domestic establishment. In this and other respects he is akin to that great Huron, but somehow his villainy is less deep-dyed.

Evidently taking pride in her great warrior and sharing his view of the palefaces as invaders, his true-hearted and submissive little wife Dew-of-June looks upon the tyrant with mingled dread, respect, and love. She exhibits all the subdued mildness and the degraded condition of the wife of a savage, and only when he is away does her feminine charm exert itself. Although scenting in Mabel a rival, she enshrines her in her bosom, and with true feminine feeling shields her, without in any way playing the traitor to her husband and the designs he harbored. In danger she exhibits some of the resoluteness of her courageous mother, and in lighter moments her sweet infantile laugh bares a kind and sympathetic heart. To her stern husband she is true even in death, for in him she had lost her only racial friend. At his grave she lingers a month, and when necessity compels a sad farewell, she prays in the manner of her people for Arrowhead's success on the endless path he had so lately gone, and for their reunion in the land of the just. Meek, resigned but sorrowful, she takes up her abode with Mabel and Jasper, but soon grief breaks her heart, and beside Arrowhead she finds her last resting place. Truly, loyalty could go no further.

The rôle played by the Indians in *The Pioneers*, 1823, which is a description of the frontier as Cooper himself knew it from actual observation at Cooperstown, is in keeping with the facts. Degenerate savages not seldom had met the author's eyes, and after these rather than after the noble red men of Heckewelder, Chingachgook or " Indian John " is patterned, although the missionary's influence is not entirely absent. Whether the "Great Snake" derived any characteristics from a particular Indian said to have lived with his son near Cooperstown is of course doubtful. But so much is certain, hardly a trace of idealization may be detected in "Indian John," who exhibits all the qualities of the degraded red man of the settlements.

Chingachgook appears in our realistic novel as an old man of seventy years, and, like his companion Natty Bumppo, has fallen upon evil days. He is now the sole representative of a once renowned family, and his earlier more glorious life is only alluded to, a portrait which Cooper was to fill out later with an increasing idealization derived from the benevolent Heckewelder. During the French-Indian War he is said to have been a fierce fighter, who one day after a battle appeared with thirteen scalps on his pole, an impressive record when one remembers that he never scalped any he had not killed with his own hand. At times he still harbors the wild resentment and the brutal ferocity with which he had once tracked the Mingoes and never allowed an injury to pass unrevenged. The silver medallion of Washington suspended from his neck by a thong of buckskin would indicate that he had won laurels also in the Revolutionary War.

But now he is practically helpless, unable even to make baskets. Long since he had been christianized by the Moravians, who always appear in Cooper's novels as intimate with the Delawares. Sad to say, their influence had not been able to transform his life. Though deeply attentive at services, the love of the firewater had mastered him and proved his downfall. In spite of the realization that rum is the tomahawk of the whites, and that the evil spirit is in their jugs, the chief is wholly conquered by this master weapon of the palefaces. It is a disgusting scene when the tipsy old man imagines himself on the track of his enemies and makes a fruitless effort to release his tomahawk. But when the cup beckoned, a grin of idiocy spread over his face, and seizing "the vessel with both hands, [he] sank backward on the bench and drank until satiated, when he made an effort to lay aside the mug with the helplessness of total inebriety."

Cooper in no way spares the feelings of his readers when he

portrays the last representative of a once powerful tribe in all his disgusting reality. Even the teachings of his Moravian friends "Indian John" repudiates at the end, for he dies a heathen, trusting only in the Great Spirit of the savages, and in his own good deeds. There is little of consolation when Effingham in a charitable mood lowers the curtain before the fallen chief with the remark: "His faults were those of an Indian, and his virtues those of a man."

As the last of the Leatherstocking Tales, *The Prairie*, 1827, may appropriately close our discussion of the group, with its scene entirely different from that of the preceding four. Since the Pawnees and the Sioux have supplanted the Delawares and the Hurons, Heckewelder's book could no longer serve as the convenient source, except that general characteristics were easily transferred. The author is said to have carefully studied the boundless plains which the narrative glorifies, and acquainted himself with representatives of the tribes that were to play the chief part. Tuckerman states that in the spring of 1826 "Cooper followed a deputation of Pawnee and Sioux Indians from New York to Washington, in order to make a close study of them for future use. He was much interested in the chief's stories of their wild powers, dignity, endurance, grace, cunning wiles, and fierce passions. The great buffalo hunts across the prairies he had never seen; the fights of mounted tribes and the sweeping fires over these boundless plains all claimed his eager interest and sympathy with the resultant desire to place 'these mounted tribes' and their desert plains beyond the Mississippi in another Indian story. One of the chiefs of this party — a very fine specimen of a warrior, a remarkable man in every way — is credited with being the original Hard-Heart of 'The Prairie.'"

Cooper himself tells us in *Notions of the Americans* that, as one recedes from the Mississippi, the finer traits of savage life become visible; "and, although most of the natives of the Prairies, even there, are far from being the interesting and romantic heroes that poets love to paint, there are specimens of loftiness of spirit, of bearing, and of savage heroism, to be found among the chiefs, that might embarrass the fertility of the richest invention to equal. I met one of these heroes of the desert, and a finer physical and moral man, allowing for peculiarity of condition, it has rarely been my good fortune to encounter.

"Peterlasharroo, or the young knife chief of the Pawnees, when I saw him, was a man of some six or seven-and-twenty years. He had already gained renown as a warrior, and he had won the confidence of his tribe by repeated exhibitions of wisdom and moderation. He had been signally useful in destroying a baneful superstition, which would have made a sacrifice of a female prisoner whose life he saved by admirable energy, and a fearless exposure of his own. The reputation of even this remote and savage hero had spread beyond the narrow limits of his own country; and when we met, I was prepared to yield him esteem and admiration. But the impression produced by his grave and haughty, though still courteous mien, the restless, but often steady, and bold glance of his dark, keen eye, and the quiet dignity of his air, are still present to my recollection."

Him Cooper presented a gift of peacock feathers, which the savage received with a quiet smile as evidence of a wish to be grateful rather than as a sign of any selfish gratification. Actually he was highly pleased, for the present was worth thirty horses. "But, notwithstanding my unintentional liberality, no sign of pleasure, beyond that which I have related, was suffered to escape him, in the presence of a white man."

The Indian material as also the magnificent setting so fascinated the author that he spent more time in writing *The Prairie* than in writing any other novel, and the book was always a favorite with him.

It was a happy thought to shift the scene west of the Mississippi among the picturesque and colorful tribes of the plains with their more joyous abandon and moving landscape. As a convenient connecting link the aged trapper is made to serve, who speaks of the Pawnees as a valiant and honest tribe, and "second only do I take them to be to that once mighty but now scattered people, the Delawares of the Hills." The place of the Hurons is evidently filled by the "Siouxes" or Sioux, the "Ishmaelites of the American deserts," whose hands from time immemorial had been turned against their neighbors of the prairies, and who are just now engaged in a raid against the Pawnees. The Pawnee Hard-Heart is a counterpart of Chingachgook at his best, while the Sioux Weucha and Mahtoree are duplicates of Arrowhead and Le Renard Subtil. The chiefs with their followers go about the stealing of cattle and horses with all the cunning one might expect from criminals long schooled in the arts of villainy.

Chief Mahtoree by his daring skill would excite no little admiration were it not for the fact that cunning and duplicity had for so long obscured the better and nobler traits of his character. Triumphs he accepts with seeming self-restraint, but belied by a single gleam of fierce joy breaking through his frown. To have captured the hitherto invincible Pawnee warrior Hard-Heart, who had slain eighteen of his people, constituted no mean achievement even for such a renowned chief. With his enemy once in his clutches, he skilfully appeals to the Indian's passion of revenge, and is beside himself when his rival in glory escapes. A warrior he is, but a cruel and treacherous one, whose swarthy visage is lit up by a gleam of secret joy when he believes that his generous and confiding enemy will fall under his sudden strokes. That single combat on the island in the surging stream has something epic to commend it. When, however, Mahtoree's deep-laid treachery avails him nothing, but ends in a mortal wound, the never-dying sentiment of pride imbibed from early youth gains the upper hand, and with his last expiring strength the warrior throws himself into the river, lest the scalp of a mighty Dakotah dry in a Pawnee tent.

Most of the other Sioux are worthy companions and followers of their cruel and treacherous chief. Weucha represents the understudy who wants to excel his greater tribesman by threatening attitudes, but like his prototype the Weasel he falls under his own tomahawk in the hands of the man he had endangered. Especially hateful is the superannuated warrior who, moved by a deep-seated love of vengeance and ruthless savagery, prepares to distribute knives to the women in order that the hags may butcher the prisoners. These withered and remorseless old crones live up to their reputation of harboring fiendish designs.

For all that, Cooper does not ignore the fame of the "Iroquois of the Plains," whose fierce bravery would have carried the day had not Ishmael Bush and his brood at the crucial moment intervened in behalf of the Pawnees. The action of Swooping Eagle in saving at least the glory of the tribe stands out in bold relief even if the episode has its lurid aspects. When a fatally wounded friend of Mahtoree begs him that he "carry the white hairs of an old warrior into the burnt wood village," he readily complies in order to save the old man and his scalp from falling into the hands of the enemy. And when it appears certain that both cannot escape the approaching Pawnees, these brave warriors, governed by the same feelings of glory and united in the principles of their honor, dismount, the head of the old man is cut off, and the Swooping Eagle flourishes the grim and bloody visage in the sight of the approaching enemies as he darts away from the spot with a shout of triumph.

While Mahtoree and his people play the part of consummate villains, Cooper evidently approves when Hard-Heart was unanimously "proclaimed and reproclaimed the worthiest chief and the stoutest brave that the Wacondah had ever bestowed on his most favored children, the Pawnees of the Loops." The chief is kind, noble, and generous, though his feelings are at times veiled behind the cold mask of Indian self-denial. Those qualities are complemented by watchfulness, cunning, and bravery, with a dash of the picturesque and the cavalierly thrown in. His leggins, for instance, are fearfully fringed, from the gartered knee to the bottom of the moccasin, with the hair of human scalps. When in that last single combat his mortally wounded enemy has thrown himself into the turbulent stream, he follows as a matter of course and does not emerge until he can flourish the scalp of the great Sioux. Unafraid and determined to live and die as a Pawnee, he refuses adoption by the hostile tribe. One boon only had he asked of his enemies, namely that his horse be killed on his grave, so that he might ride him to the blessed prairies and come before the Master of Life like a chief. In delicacy, reserve, and dignity he is an example to his people, who are such apt pupils that many a diplomatist of the most polished court, according to Cooper, might have striven in vain to imitate their courtesy.

The author incidentally alludes to various customs, among which the sacred rite of adoption appears more prominently than in any other of his works. To fill the place of a son, the aged Le Balafré, father-in-law of Mahtoree, claims as his own the young man, whose faultless form, unchanging eye, and lofty mien had evidently impressed him. The moving speech of the kindhearted man, though it proved to be futile, expresses a truly aboriginal trait. " My son opened his eyes on the ' waters of the wolves,' " said Le Balafré, in the language of that nation, " but he will shut them in the bend of the ' river with a troubled stream.' He was born a Pawnee, but he will die a Dakotah. Look at me. I am a sycamore that once covered many with my shadow. The leaves are fallen and the branches begin to drop. But a single sucker is springing from my roots; it is a little vine, and it winds itself about a tree that is green. I have long looked for one to grow by my side. Now have I found him. Le Balafré is no longer without a son; his name will not be forgotten when he is gone! Men of the Tetons, I take this youth into my lodge."

Another form of substitution or adoption, though of a different kind, pertains to wedlock. As is well known, matrimony among the red man was somewhat of a flexible institution. Mahtoree's morals were rather accommodating, influenced, as Cooper indicates, by the whites. He had provided himself with a most charming companion in Tachechana, " the Skipping Fawn," with a clear and healthy complexion and other attractions. " Her hazel eye had the sweetness and playfulness of the antelope's; her voice was soft and joyous as the song of the wren, and her happy laugh was the very melody of the forest." But when Mahtoree has found in Inez a more gorgeous flower of the prairie, he unceremoniously proposes to install the new favorite as his mistress and turn over his own wife to his temporary confederate, the squatter Ishmael Bush. In a moving scene the young squaw with her babe in her arms appeals to her lord, but when the latter unfeelingly but nevertheless convincingly demonstrates to her that the white woman is the more attractive, the simple child of nature unhesitatingly turns over to her supposed rival all her ornaments and even her child. Toward the end of the story she is found in the lodge of Hard-Heart, who by his victory over Mahtoree had incidentally delivered her from a domineering yet fickle husband. That such an arrangement was in no way considered extraordinary, may be gathered from the fact that the squaw of the Winnebago killed by Pigeonswing soon entered as wife the lodge of his slayer.

Taken all in all, *The Prairie* is a well-constructed story, nothing short of a masterpiece in the opinion of able critics, though the lack of the ' piled and rapid incidents of *The Last of the Mohicans* ' has made it less of a favorite with the general public.

In 1848, only three years before his death, Cooper brought his Indian tales to a close with *The Oak Openings,* the scene of which is laid in the still unpeopled forests of Michigan near the site of the present city of Kalamazoo, and in which the religious element plays a prominent part. The outbreak of the war of 1812 throws its ominous shadows across the life of the bee-hunter Ben Boden or " le Bourdon," who in the oak openings, that is the irregular spaces or grassy glades between the bur-oaks, is following his interesting and profitable occupation. By the twists of chance he finds himself in the company of the besotted Gershom Waring, whose attractive sister Margery links his fate with that of the family of the daring and improvident adventurer. But with the help of the friendly Chippewa runner Pigeonswing and of " Scalping Peter," whose bloodthirsty designs are turned to thoughts of peace by the prayers of a dying missionary for his destroyers, they succeed in escaping the clutches of the hostile Indians, and their dangerous journey down the Kalamazoo River and across the lakes ends at last in the harbor of Erie, safe under American protection.

From the first chapter to the last the red man plays an important part in the narrative. After an enthusiastic description of the Michigan forest, Cooper lets the renowned Pottawattamie warrior Elksfoot and the young Chippewa runner Pigeonswing meet, the former an ally of Great Britain, while the latter firmly adheres to the American cause. Almost immediately the author adroitly reveals through the bee-hunter that the English, like the French, never had scruples about employing the savages in their conflicts. These highly polished and humane nations " would carry on their *American* wars by the agency of the tomahawk, the scalping knife, and the brand," though at all times fully aware that the savage spared neither sex nor age, defiling the door-post of the frontier cabin by the blood of the infant and covering the remains of the tenants with the smouldering ruins of the log-houses.

Spurred on by the twin motives of honor and monetary reward, the savage desire for scalps is particularly avid and darkens the atmosphere of the tale. While the enemies of America are assiduously cultivating that barbarous taste, even the noble Pigeonswing never denies the aboriginal trait. In the very beginning he succeeds in scalping his renowned antagonist and later is willing to risk his life in order to secure the trophy so much valued according to the Indian code. The Pottawattamies and their confederates prize scalps beyond their earthly possessions, and their admiration for Scalping Peter, who " had already forty notches on his pole, to note the number of scalps taken from the hated whites," knows no bounds. His pole, artistically decorated with seven fresh human scalps, serves like a magic password to facilitate his approach to the Pottawattamies and to deepen their respect. The corporal and the missionary he had left with the bee-hunter and his companions he looks upon simply as so many bearers of the coveted prize, and in his talk he adds the remaining whites to the number of his victims. This all-pervading passion Cooper duly notes, and though he does not excuse the practice, yet he claims that civilized life had, and still has, very many customs little less excusable than that of scalping.

The mysterious " Tribeless," called also Onoah by the Indians and Scalping Peter by the whites, is the dominating personality among the red men. The author attributes to him nothing less than the grand scheme of rallying all the Indians of the Northwest in an endeavor to recover the possessions they had yielded to the palefaces. Inspiring universal respect and fear, all his actions are bent toward that one purpose, which he seeks to reach by any means at hand. Like Tecumseh and others, his horizon was limited, and he did not even perceive what the much younger Pigeonswing surmised, namely, that the whites were too numerous and too strong to be brushed aside. At the midnight council at

Prairie Round attended by the fifty chiefs and at a later meeting he pleads for harmony among all the tribes and develops his plans. He is powerfully seconded by others, all of them speaking in the figurative language which the Indian in Cooper so much affects. The report of the fall of Detroit adds zest to their deliberations. Only when Onoah advocates that they spare the bee-hunter and his newly married wife, does his influence wane, and henceforth Bear's Meat assumes the leadership, though Scalping Peter for the sake of gaining his own ends remains on cordial terms with the parties. The eloquent, but misshapen, contemptible drunkard and coward Weasel fittingly finds his reward when just before his own execution Corporal Flint succeeds in braining him with the tomahawk snatched from his side.

The noble Parson Amen accompanying Peter represents the power of the Holy Spirit among savage tribes, a matter upon which Cooper lays much stress. To the modern reader it seems a grievous mistake to let him expound on any and all occasions his pet theory that the American Indians are the lost tribes of Israel, now looked upon as the fantastic conception of a few visionaries that becomes nauseating by constant repetition, but at that time still widely held. Aside from this apparent defect of artistry, the missionary upholds the best traditions of those courageous and unselfish men who braved hardships and the very jaws of death in order to bring to the heathen of North America the saving truths of the Gospel. It was he who changed the whole course of Peter's life and incidentally became the instrument of saving the whites. Already Margery's conviction that the rights of the natives should be respected had disposed him favorably toward her and the bee-hunter; but it was the dying prayer of the missionary for his enemies that brought about in the heart of the fierce warrior and zealous prophet a change akin to conversion. The upright and altruistic life of the missionary had gained for him a death without torture and a decent burial without barbarous mutilations. The tribute Cooper pays to the influence of the soldier of the cross is as realistic as it is well deserved.

While actual drinking plays no part in *The Oak Openings*, we note besides the casual reference to the Weasel as a drunkard the delightful description of the Indians' boundless enthusiasm over the supposed discovery of a whiskey spring. The remnants of liquor contained in the two kegs destroyed as a precautionary measure by the bee-hunter excite no end of interest on the part of the savages, and Cooper deliberately prolongs the description in order to emphasize the extent of the native's fondness for the fire-water. In this case, the inordinate desire coupled with superstitious notions saves the shrewd and resolute bee-hunter, who with his mummeries and ceremonies is able to gain the boat. The superstitious nature of his enemies again serves him in good stead when his simple mathematical superiority in the discovery of honey brings him the reputation as a great medicine man who is able to make the insects do his bidding. The white man's safety lies partly in his ability to play upon the superstitions and to benefit from the relative ignorance of the child of the forest.

The last part of the story even more than the very beginning is dominated by the theme of flight and pursuit, one of the stock devices so dear to the author's heart. Only that here native cunning and deception are pitted against each other, for the bee-hunter and his companions are really in the hands of their two redskin friends, who mingle among their enemies and by every device try to throw them off the track. Hiding their charges during the day in swamps and out of the way places, and under the cover of darkness floating them down the Kalamazoo River, with an exceptionally daring and adroit bit of deception at the most critical point, Peter and Pigeonswing succeed in getting them out into Lake Michigan, where they are temporarily safe from the savages, who are inferior navigators. And at critical moments they re-appear to facilitate the passage of the fugitives into Lake Huron and Lake Erie. Strange that their plans should not have been detected and frustrated, for at least twice Scalping Peter had given Bear's Meat and his band grounds for suspicion, and Pigeonswing was known to be the friend of the hostile Yankees. Be that as it may, both live unharmed to a ripe old age, for thirty-six years later the author meets them at the scene of the story, with Peter's heart overflowing with universal love, proof sufficient that the Indian was not beyond the benevolent influence of Christian civilization.

With not a little of regret, Cooper saw the red man disappear before the superior moral and physical influence of the white, a fate that seemed inexorable. As pointed out in *Notions of the Americans*, probably no land was ever taken without a treaty or purchase, but how far an equivalent was given, is another question, " though I fancy that these bargains are quite as just as any that are ever driven between the weak and the strong, the intelligent and the ignorant." He believed that the government was honestly trying to carry out the stipulations of the treaties, although " certain borderers, who possess the power of the white man with the disposition of the savage, do sometimes violate their conditions." The nation has not committed any unprovoked wrongs against people like the savages. As a matter of fact, " the inroad of the whites of the United States has never been marked by the gross injustice and brutality that have distinguished similar inroads elsewhere."

The attempts to establish an Indian territory in the West interested Cooper greatly, for he believed that, were such a plan carried into effect, it would check the constant diminution in the number of the Indians, " and that a race, about whom there is so much that is poetic and fine in recollection, will be preserved."

With that last thought we have again touched upon a controversial point, namely Cooper's alleged idealization of the Indian. Some of the more important critics voiced their opinions in the preceding pages. After the death of Cooper these were powerfully reenforced by Francis Parkman, who on the issue of a revised edition of Cooper's Works in 1851 took occasion to point out defects in what he considered otherwise the most original and the most thoroughly national of American writers. He charges that the Indian characters " are for the most part either superficially or falsely drawn; while the long conversations which he puts into their mouths are as truthless as they are tiresome. Such as they are, however, they have been eagerly copied by a legion of the smaller poets and novel writers; so that, jointly with Thomas Campbell, Cooper is responsible for the fathering of those aboriginal heroes, lovers, and sages, who have long formed a petty nuisance in our literature." In his opinion Uncas " does not at all resemble a genuine Indian. Magua, the villain of the story, is a less untruthful portrait."

These strictures of Parkman, who is a historian of national and racial conflicts, are at least in part answered by Cooper's retort to General Cass. And in their sweeping nature they have been sustained by few competent critics. Catlin, a great deal of whose life was spent on the plains, had a high regard for the qualities of the aborigines. And George Bird Grinnell, whose knowledge of the plains Indian was both comprehensive and minute, rushes to the defense of the novelist with this observation: " The Indian of Cooper — with his bravery, his endurance, his acuteness, his high qualities of honesty, generosity, courtesy, and hospitality — has been laughed at for half a century. Yet every man who has mingled much with the Indians in their homes has known individuals who might have sat for the portraits which Cooper drew of some of his aboriginal heroes." And others like the ethnologist Ten Kate believe that, although Cooper appreciated the good qualities of the Indians, he did not on the whole try to idealize them. It is a strange twist of fate that the much more idealized Leatherstocking should have escaped censure and even have been exalted as the most original and faithful delineation of the American frontiersman.

The truth of the matter is that in Uncas, Hard-Heart, the younger Chingachgook, Conanchet, Susquesus, and in a few others the novelist heightened the noble qualities within the bounds permissible in romances. Some good Indians there always have been, and Cooper did not hesitate to superimpose upon the basic foundation of aboriginal traits a few of the brighter colors of the imagination. But these figures are few and far between, and it would be a serious mistake to crowd out of the picture the cruel, bloodthirsty, treacherous, and fiendish savages with which practically all his Indian stories are peopled. The general truthfulness of Cooper's Indian portraits has been accepted by posterity and has not been successfully challenged.

CHAPTER X

STARK REALISM ON KENTUCKY'S DARK AND
BLOODY GROUND

It is no mere coincidence that the least favorable portrait of the red man is set off by the " bloody ground " of Kentucky. Early associations and a specialized interest in this region with the settler's attitude uppermost undoubtedly had their share in inducing Dr. Robert Montgomery Bird (1805–1854) to paint such a dark picture unrelieved by brighter hues. He early had been impressed by the literary possibilities inherent in the Indian material, and his unpublished drama *King Philip or the Sagamore*, written in 1829, is said to have furnished John Augustus Stone with ideas for his prize play *Metamora,* which the actor Edwin Forrest made popular throughout the country. Later his unfortunate experience in furnishing plays to the singularly ungenerous Forrest persuaded Bird to forsake the drama for other more remunerative employment.

Unquestionably Bird's most successful story and also one of the outstanding novels of the century is *Nick of the Woods, or the Jibbenainosay,* 1837, which in popularity ranks second only to Cooper's Leatherstocking Tales. An English edition appeared in the same year, and the German version ten years later ran to more than ten thousand copies. In 1877 the novel was translated into Dutch, and as recently as 1905 into Polish. In America it struck the popular fancy to such an extent that one year after its publication Louisa Medina could base upon it one of the most successful melodramas of the time. Here as well as in England edition followed edition, and the fact that the story is available in popular form to-day testifies to its unfailing interest.

The germ of *Nick of the Woods* was implanted in the medical student of Philadelphia by a young Kentuckian named Black, who introduced him to his fellow countryman John Grimes, then an enthusiastic student of art. On one of their occasional walks along the Wissahickon, Bird was impressed by a story Mr. Black told about his native state. He noted the facts and, when in June 1833 he accompanied his friend Grimes to Kentucky, visited the scene of the tale. On a subsequent visit in the fall of 1835 he made further inquiries and collected additional material. Some of the white characters, as the immensely interesting scape-gallows Ralph Stackpole, are largely drawn from life, while the story of Wandering Nathan or the Nick of the Woods, important for the Indian element, "has a similar foundation in truth; but its origin belongs to one of the western counties of Pennsylvania."

The Indian warfare on the Kentucky border forms the principal theme of the novel, with a romantic story of young love hindered by dark intrigues closely interwoven. The viewpoint is that of the settler who wrested from the savage the garden land of his domain, and his frontier exploits are glorified at the expense of the native who is looked upon as a wild beast, to be exterminated like the wolf, the bear, and the panther. So dark is the picture that in the Preface to the first edition, which appeared anonymously, the author felt called upon to defend himself against the anticipated accusations of injustice: "We owe, perhaps, some apology for the hues we have thrown around the Indian portraits in our pictures — hues darker than are usually employed by the painters of such figures. But, we confess, the North American savage has never appeared to us the gallant and heroic personage he seems to others. The single fact that he wages war — systematic war — upon beings incapable of resistance or defense — upon women and children, whom all other races in the world, no matter how barbarous, consent to spare, — has hitherto been, and we suppose to the end of our days will remain, a stumbling block to our imagination: we look into the woods for the mighty warrior, 'the feather-cinctured chief,' rushing to meet his foe, and behold him retiring, laden with scalps of miserable squaws and their babes: Heroical? *Hoc verbum quid valeat, non vident.*"

Bird opens his story in 1782 during the closing period of the Revolutionary War, when the Shawnee and the Wyandot were still hunting the bear and the buffalo in the canebrake, and the cruel and wily enemy waylaid the settler at the gate of his solitary home. It is significant of prevailing conditions that Colonel Bruce's son Big Tom was the third of that name, the first two Toms having been killed by savages, whom the Colonel designates as " red niggurs," several of which he had been fortunate enough to dispatch. Even squaws and children had beaten to death white prisoners, and men like Colonel Crawford were put to the double torture and roasted alive.

Those are grim scenes indeed which Bird paints before our eyes in Captain Roland Forrester and his beloved Edith's progress through the wilderness. In trying to avoid the enemies in the forest, the party chances upon the body of a " savage of vast and noble proportions, lying on its face across the roots of a tree, and glued, it might almost be said, to the earth by a mass of coagulated blood, that had issued from the scalp and axe-cloven skull." Terror-struck, Roland observed " a shudder to creep over the apparent lifeless frame; the fingers relaxed their grasp of the earth, and then clutched it again with violence; a broken, strangling rattle came from the throat; and a spasm of convulsion seizing upon every limb, it was suddenly raised a little upon one arm, so as to display the countenance, covered with blood, the eyes retroverted in their orbits, and glaring with the sightless whites . . . The spasm was the last, and but momentary; yet it sufficed to raise the body of the mangled barbarian, so far that, when the pang that excited it suddenly ceased, and, with it, the life of the sufferer, the body rolled over on the back, and thus lay, exposing to the eyes of the lookers-on two gashes, wide and gory, on the breast, traced by a sharp knife and a powerful hand, and, as it seemed, in the mere wantonness of a malice and lust of blood which even death could not satisfy." The gashes in the form of a cross clearly indicate that it is the work of the Jibbenainosay, the spirit or the Nick of the Woods, of whom the natives are in mortal fear.

At this point a Quaker, derisively called Bloody Nathan because he is the only man in Kentucky who won't fight, joins the party and leads the frightened group to the abandoned cabin of the Ashburns, whose home had been fired and every one of the nine occupants, down to the last baby, had been massacred. But so efficient had been the vengeance of the settlers that only one of the murderers had succeeded in reaching his home.

Next follows a vivid and picturesque description of a battle against terrific odds, as every one, even the peaceful Nathan, fights for dear life. Involuntarily we are reminded of Cooper, whose acquaintance may have benefited Bird not a little. With breathless interest we watch the varying fortunes of the conflict, often changing with bewildering rapidity. While Nathan goes for help, the party escapes across the dark stream only to fall into an ambush. Tom Bruce's attack is skilfully met by savage strategy, and old Piankeshaw and his warriors end the affray by striking the corpses repeatedly with their knives and hatchets, " each seeking to surpass his fellow in the savage work of mutilation." Dr. Bird cannot restrain his indignation and inserts the scorching comment: " Such is the red-man of America, whom courage, — an attribute of all lovers of blood, whether man or animal; misfortune, — the destiny, in every quarter of the globe, of every barbarous race which contact with a civilized one cannot civilize; and the dreams of poets and sentimentalists have invested with a character wholly incompatible with his condition. Individual virtues may be, and indeed frequently are, found among men in a natural state; but honor, justice, and generosity, as characteristics of the mass, are refinements belonging only to an advanced stage of civilization."

Rather artfully the author has woven not a few Indian characteristics into the very fabric of subsequent events. Brooding over the loss of a son, Old Piankeshaw puts Roland in imminent and repeated danger of being murdered, and the latter's discomfiture during the homeward journey of the Indians is not a little increased by the insulting mirth of the savages, a trait properly scored by Bird. The tipsy old man more and more turns out to be a funny creature, as he tries to empty a whiskey keg and in his senseless rage shoots his own horse. To check his approaching madness, the two young savages are finally forced to spill the liquor, with a fierce quarrel as the natural result. The unfortunate captive is to pay for it all; the half-crazy warrior threatens to have him run the gauntlet through every village of the nation, and then to burn him alive for the edification of the women and children. But the ever watchful Nathan without any apparent difficulty surprises the Indians during the night, and after dispatching them, frees our hero.

Further adventures in the Indian country would now seem unnecessary, were it not for the fact that Edith has been carried off by another division of the war party. This brings us at last to the village of Wenonga or Black Vulture, located in a beautiful valley watered by a tributary of the Miami. This old chief incidentally furnishes the author an opportunity to paint one of his unforgettable portraits. As supreme commander of the raiding party it was he who had supervised the division of the spoils, an old man of exceedingly fierce and malign aspect, wasted and withered into the semblance of a consumptive wolf. He is tall and raw-boned, with a scar disfiguring his nose and cheek, his gait halting, his left middle-finger short of a joint, and a buzzard's beak and talons tied to his hair. In a speech of great fury he had boasted before Roland of his numerous murders of white people whose scalps for thirty or more years had been hanging in the smoke of his Shawnee lodge, and he gloried in the fact that he loved white man's blood better than whiskey, never spared it out of pity, since he " had no heart," his interior being framed of stone as hard as the flinty rock.

We now learn that it was also this redoubtable warrior who ten years before had loosened all the fierce passions in Nathan's breast. When the peaceful Quaker as a sign of friendship had put his gun and knife into the hands of the Shawnee chief, which were red with the blood of his neighbors, that same knife had struck down his oldest boy, and that same gun had slain the mother of his children. Too late Nathan had arrived to save any of his five offspring; his wife's blood spouted up his bosom, and his aged mother called for help in her death struggle. Even the unhappy man himself had stood on the threshold of eternity, for during the epileptic fit which the recital of the outrage brings on, his cap falls off and Roland notices that " a horrible scar disfigured the top of his head, which seemed to have been, many years before, crushed by the blows of a heavy weapon; and it was equally manifest that a savage scalping-knife had done its work on the mangled head."

Ever since, Nathan had retaliated in kind. Near Black Vulture's town both he and Ralph Stackpole, who is rescued from Indians flogging him, without any compunction whatsoever scalp their enemies, and Bird puts his seal of approval upon this act: " Such is the practice of the border, and such it has been ever since the mortal feud, never destined to be really ended but with the annihilation, or civilization, of the American race, first began between the savage and the white intruder. It was, and is, essentially, a measure of retaliation, compelled, if not justified by the ferocious example of the red-man. Brutality ever begets brutality; and magnanimity of arms can be only exercised in the case of a magnanimous foe. With such, the wildest and fiercest rover of the frontier becomes a generous and even humane enemy."

With bold yet deft strokes the further developments are clearly sketched. Disguised as an Indian, the ferocious Nathan without any untoward incident explores the town which is bereft of the chief fighting men. He confronts the drunken Wenonga, the evidences of whose hideous crimes served as an ornament of his person. For the time being he defers sweet revenge in order to listen to the captive Edith in the chief's wigwam, among whose articles appears conspicuously a " bundle of scalps, some of them with long female tresses — the proofs of the prowess of a great warrior, who, like the other fighting-men of his race, accounted the golden ringlets of a girl as noble a trophy of valor as the grizzled locks of a veteran soldier." Bird's comment upon the women is fully as cutting. The hag guarding Edith is a specimen of fierce and unappeasable malice visited upon the unlucky captive who had more to fear from the squaws of the tribe than from its warriors; examples abounded where their cries for vengeance had consigned to torture men whom even the cruel husbands had intended to spare.

Stackpole's daring plan of stealing the Indians' horses having gone awry, even the cautious Nathan with his precious burden Edith cannot avoid capture, and stark tragedy threatens to overwhelm the would-be rescuers. However, in accord with Indian custom, his epileptic fit exempts the Quaker for the time being from any violence, or at least till he can tell the withered chief in his wigwam where may be found the Jibbenainosay or the Nick of the Woods, who had destroyed all of the old man's children. In a scene of tense emotion the hideously bedaubed warrior tells Nathan that in his love for white man's blood he killed his brother " the Quakel "; that in spite of the pleas of his own comrades for mercy he destroyed the whole family, and then with savage triumph he points to the shrivelled scalps, once crowning the heads of childhood and innocence, now adorning his fire-post.

This is too much for the bereft man, who sinks senseless to the floor, followed almost immediately by a bloodcurdling event. For when the vengeance-crazed chief, upon promise that the Jibbenainosay be brought to him, cuts his fetters, the old Quaker springs into action, bears the savage to the earth and sinks the iron tomahawk into his brain, " and Wenonga trode the path to the spirit-land, bearing the same gory evidence of the unrelenting and successful vengeance of the white-man that his children and grand-children had borne before him." With the words " Ay, dog, thee dies at last! at last I have caught thee! " Nathan left the scattered hull, " dashed the tomahawk into the Indian's chest, snatched the scalping knife from the belt, and with one grinding sweep of the blade, and one fierce jerk of his arm, the gray scalp-lock of the warrior was torn from the dishonored head. The last proof of the slayer's ferocity was not given until he had twice, with his utmost strength, drawn the knife over the dead man's breast, dividing skin, cartilage, and even bone, before it, so sharp was the blade and so powerful the hand that urged it.

" Then, leaping to his feet, and snatching from the post the bundle of withered scalps — the locks and ringlets of his own murdered family, — which he spread a moment before his eyes with one hand, while the other extended, as if to contrast the two prizes together, the reeking scalp-lock of the murderer, he sprang through the door of the lodge, and fled from the village; but not until he had, in the insane fury of the moment, given forth a wild, earpiercing yell, that spoke the triumph, the exulting transport, of long-baffled but never-dying revenge."

The impending death of Stackpole and Roland at the stake furnishes Bird once more an opportunity to utter his uncompromising hostility to Indian character. Edith's heartrending shriek is without effect upon the human fiends engaged in the delight of torturing prisoners. The pity which under different circumstances might be deeply felt has entirely vanished, and the mind is voluntarily given up to the drunkenness of passion and cruelty in its most atrocious and fiendish forms. An official of the Spanish Inquisition might moisten the lips of a heretic stretched upon the rack, and a pirate relent over the form gasping to death under his lashes and heated pincers; but the author recalls no instance where an Indian torturing his captive at the stake has ever looked upon the agonies of the wretched victim with any feelings but those of exultation and joy. But that joy is not vouchsafed to the savages this time, for at the crucial moment the army of General George Rogers Clark arrives and the intended victims are saved, while vengeance in accord with frontier fashion is visited upon all within reach of the white arm, and the means of livelihood of the Indians are destroyed. Then the inevitable marriage of Roland and Edith as well as of other couples takes place, and having satisfied his revenge, the shadowy but terrible Nick of the Woods, Nathan Slaughter, disappears, to haunt the forests no more.

Nick of the Woods, or the Jibbenainosay, is one of the most powerful novels America has ever produced. On a romantic background, the darkest and stormiest period in the annals of the Indian border is traced with a vividness and picturesqueness little short of astounding. The portraits of Piankeshaw and of Wenonga rival in color and distinctness those of Stackpole, Roland, and Nathan. The latter, the Jibbenainosay, under the guise of a peaceful Quaker moves like a mysterious figure through the gloom of the forest, his trail marked by the slaughtered corpses of savages until he succeeds in tracking down the destroyer of his hearth and home. In vindictive cruelty and merciless savagery his terrible figure is fully matched by the bloodthirsty fiends of the forest who on their part strive to the utmost to make Kentucky deserve its reputation as the Bloody Ground. It is stark realism without a vestige of the romantic, devoid of poetry and sentiment.

Not that Bird's delineation remained unchallenged, even

though in the Preface to the first edition the author had anticipated and met any probable criticism. At the issuance of a revised edition in 1853 he seized the opportunity to turn on his critics. There he speaks with approbation of the bold spirits who with a natural vengeance retaliated in the shadow of the Indian's wigwam some few of the cruel acts of butchery with which he so often stained the hearthstone of the settler. The sole reason for drawing his Indian portraits with Indian ink and rejecting the brighter pigments with their more brilliant effects, even adding an " Indian-hater " to the group, was his aim to give, " not the appearance of truth, but truth itself — or what he held to be truth — to the picture."

Bird claims that, at the period *Nick of the Woods* was written, the genius of Chateaubriand and Cooper had thrown a poetic illusion over the Indian character, so that the red man appeared as the embodiment of grand and tender sentiment, a new style of the beau-idéal so to speak, " brave, gentle, loving, refined, honorable, romantic personages, nature's nobles, the chivalry of the forest." He maintains that such are not the lineaments of a race existing in an uncivilized state, and " that such conceptions as *Atala* and *Uncas* are beautiful unrealities and fictions merely, as imaginary and contrary to nature as the shepherd swains of the old pastoral school of rhyme and romance," and that among the tribes now known no beings resembling them in the slightest degree are found. " The Indian is doubtless a gentleman; but he is a gentleman who wears a very dirty shirt and lives a very miserable life, having nothing to employ him or to keep him alive except the pleasures of the chase and the scalp-hunt — which we dignify with the name of war." Bird believes the Indian capable of civilization under restraint and friendly instruction, but in his natural barbaric state he is a barbarian. His intention was to give real Indians as they existed and still exist, ignorant, violent, debased, and brutal, with the worst deformities of the savage temperament receiving their strongest and fiercest development in war or in the scalp-hunt.

The author is surprised that his attempt to give a correct and true picture of the native has been misinterpreted as a design to influence the passions of his countrymen against the remnant of an unfortunate race, to excuse the wrongs of the whites, or to hasten the period of his extermination, which he believes improbable or even impossible. He equally denies the insinuation of Mr. Ainsworth, editor of the English version, that his views were " colored by national antipathy, and a desire to justify the encroachments of his countrymen upon the persecuted natives, rather than by a reasonable estimate of the subject." Such charges he declares to be devoid of any foundation in truth. Thus sixteen years after the first publication of the work the author stoutly maintained the correctness of his unchanging opinion in regard to the native and brushed aside all insinuations and attacks as having no basis in fact.

When looked at in the light of Bird's purpose to portray the savage in his natural state, especially when engaged in war or in the scalp-hunt during the fierce struggle along the Kentucky border, one can understand the absence of more humane and gentler traits. The natural tendency of the savage is guided but not softened by renegades who in such alliances further their own dark designs. But even at the best, the conflict between white and red assumes a fierce aspect, and both settler and savage appear bereft of humane and almost human instincts. The frontiersman strikes at his implacable enemy as at a rattlesnake, while the ghastly career of Bloody Nathan is invited by that fiend in human form, Black Vulture, whose dark portrait remains unrivalled in the literature of the Indian.

CHAPTER XI

SIMMS' ROMANTIC NATURALISM

One of the most faithful portraits of the American native is painted by William Gilmore Simms (1806–1870), the greatest story-teller the Old South produced. Circumstances and environment had admirably equipped him for such a task. Ordinarily, one could hardly expect that in his native Charleston he would acquire the lore of a race that had passed from the seaboard, and yet, some of the stories told him by his grandmother, who had experienced the pioneer days, dealt with the native who formerly haunted the environs of that quaint settlement. And then, there came curious tales from the western wilderness about his father's adventurous life among the natives, transmitted to him with all the embellishments of that imaginative grandmother of his. And when at about the age of ten William heard from the lips of his visiting father the particulars of his fighting the Creeks under Jackson, romantic as well as realistic details must have impressed themselves upon the plastic mind of the gifted boy. Nine years later Simms gained a first-hand acquaintance with the natives during a protracted visit with his father in Mississippi and a sojourn among the Creek and Cherokee nations. In the drunken and naked Creeks thronging the streets of Mobile and the life of the wilderness tribes in their freedom he saw both sides of Indian character. While only a few shorter poems were the immediate result of this lengthy trip, the accumulated experiences stood Simms in good stead when later he began to write the books in which the Indian plays such a large part. Throughout his life he availed himself of every opportunity to study the native, whether by personal observation or through the eyes of the most reliable authorities.

Simms' delineation of the Indian is found in several essays and poems, in short stories, and in two novels. The poems, including one in praise of The Last of the Yemassee, need not detain us long, for they are in no sense remarkable. Among them, a longer tale entitled *The Cassique of Accabee* describes how a stalwart Indian chief, in spite of his love for a fair-haired white girl he had saved as a child, generously allowed the white suitor to marry her; but how later he unhesitatingly stabbed the husband who had deserted the trusting wife. Although Simms' biographer cautiously characterizes the poem as " even now not unreadable," it has little merit and as a consequence has deservedly sunk into oblivion.

Little or no purpose would be served were we to discuss the short stories and the two outstanding Indian novels in the order of their production. The former as of less significance may be taken up first, while the popular story of the heroic struggle and tragic end of the Yemassee will bring the chapter to a fitting close.

The volume of short stories entitled *The Wigwam and the Cabin* utilizes the most varied romantic and realistic material. Rather skilfully the author describes the personal characteristics and the emotional life of the savage in *The Two Camps,* a legend of the Old North State. Like so many others of his kind, Daniel Nelson had formed a contemptuous estimate of the native, who in the form of a painted devil was believed to " sculp " every white head that came within convenient reach of his tomahawk. His belief in aboriginal depravity became somewhat modified when the wounded young Indian of a prominent family, named Lenatewá, whom he had saved, gratefully protected the isolated settler, and on coming to power established peace. However, in the general war between the Cherokees and the whites, made more gruesome by wholesale scalping, Nelson's daughter falls into the hands of hostile Indians. The wily Lenatewá succeeds in rescuing her by means of disturbing the hostile band's horses, for according to Simms a stolen horse and its welfare are just as precious to an Indian as a sweetheart to a white man.

As so often, a romantic element now enters in. For when finally peace has been re-established, the young chief pays court to the settler's daughter. Not unnaturally the mother opposes such a union, while the father favors the " monstrous fine-looking fellow," for " a young Indian warrior, when he don't drink, is about the noblest looking creature, as he carries himself in the woods, that God ever made." But the author, averse to miscegenation, at the crucial moment has fortune forsake the young chief, who in the very act of proposing is shot by his cousin and enemy Oloschottee, whose father had been killed as a result of his hostility to Lenatewá. However, poetic justice so far prevails that the affectionate daughter of the settler, impressed with the love of the noble red man, remains unmarried to the end of her days.

Next follow curiously romantic tales of a hen-pecked husband miraculously freed, of a love-lorn maiden throwing herself into a river upon seeing the scalp of her lover dangling from the neck of his conqueror, and the execution of stoic Sampson, whom tyrant Indian custom prompts to return voluntarily after having committed a murder.

As the natural virtues of the Southern Indians Simms emphasizes fierce valor and generous hospitality in *Lucas de Ayllon*. Captured through the treachery of the Spaniard de Ayllon, king Chiquola is resolved on suicide, not an uncommon occurrence in periods of great national calamity, and, as we learn incidentally, even resorted to when smallpox had disfigured a brave's visage, for " an Indian warrior is, of all human beings, one of the vainest, on the score of his personal appearance," thus uniting in himself the strange extremes of ferocity and frivolity. Meanwhile his queen Combahee is inconsolable, which furnishes Simms an opportunity to make a general observation. " We have heard so much of the inflexibility of the Indian character, that we are apt to forget that these people are human; having, though perhaps in a small degree, and in less activity, the same vital passions, the same susceptibilities — the hopes, the fears, the loves and the hates, which establish the humanities of the whites. They are colder and more sterile — more characterized by individuality and self-esteem than any more social people; and these characteristics are the natural and inevitable results of their habits of wandering. But to suppose that the Indian is ' a man without a tear,' is to indulge in a notion equally removed from poetry and truth. At all events, such an opinion is, to say the least of it, a gross exaggeration of the fact." The grief-stricken widow will marry her husband's brother only when de Ayllon, the object of her hate, shall blaze in the fire. Fortune favors her: for when in a shipwreck on the Florida coast two hundred of de Ayllon's companions perish, he himself is saved, only to be fastened to the palmetto under which the queen had grieved, and to be burnt in a fire lit by her arrow. But so overpowering are Combahee's emotions that during the act of becoming Edelano's bride a stroke of paralysis cuts the ceremony short.

Thus joy and sorrow, laughter and tears affect the Catawbas, the Choctaws, and the Cherokees as they do civilized peoples. The reputed impassibility of the Indian the author regards as a fiction, for fundamentally mankind is everywhere the same.

Although published twenty-four years later than *The Yemassee*, the colonial romance entitled *The Cassique of Kiawah*, 1859, depicts an earlier period of the Carolina settlement. The events take us back to 1684, when Charleston was still in its infancy, and the Indians were only just beginning to sense the dangerous nature of their white neighbors. Sharing the limelight with the seaport town and a gallant privateer, the Indians play a less prominent part than in the more famous earlier work. Nevertheless, this stirring tale has intrinsic value and derives added importance from the fact that the treatment of the Indian and the commencement of hostilities foreshadow the crucial struggle between the antagonistic races thirty years later.

From the first, Simms views the Indian in a sympathetic light, maintaining that, even though a savage, he is savage rather in his simplicity than in his corruption, with a brutality of barbarism rather than of vice. Not so the white man Jack Belcher, who on seeing three Indians with a chief fully armed, frankly confesses that he has no belief in the redskins and desires to keep his own skin sound; he doesn't want to be stuck full of arrows and to be fried alive in pitch-pine. If the three had surprised him, " Wouldn't they have been working in my wool, without saying, ' By your leave, brother? ' The red devils! call *them* human? I'd as soon trust a monkey, or a sucking tiger, in the matter of human bowels and affection! "

Practically the same opinion is held by Governor Robert Quarry, whose policy is one of gross selfishness. He tells Colonel Edward Berkeley, proprietor of twenty-four thousand acres of land on the Kiawah or Ashley River and consequently the cassique or lord of that precinct, that his ideas of human perfectibility and of humanizing the Indians are all wrong. The latter employs the son of the neighboring chief as hunter in order to detach him from the life in the woods with the ultimate purpose of the gradual diversion of the tribes from barbarism to the civilizing tasks of culture. But his plan draws from the governor only the scorning reply: " Ah, my dear cassique, you are nursing philanthropy in defiance of all experience. You might as well warm the frozen snake at your fireside, and hope that its gratitude will take the venom out of its fang. There is but one safe course with these savages. It is that which the New-Englanders employed. Buy up the scalps of the warriors, and sell the women and children to the West Indies. This is our proper policy."

It seems that the immensely profitable Indian trade attracted the shrewdest white men, who were far more competent to deal with the savages than the blundering authorities, although the latter were not above sharing in that trade whenever an opportunity presented itself. The former secured their own safety by such diplomatic means as maintaining a wife in each tribe instead of intimidating the natives by whipping, as advocated by a scout. The Cassique held that ill treatment had made the Indians what they are; kind treatment, on the other hand, would transform " Nature's Noblemen " into good fellows and good Christians. But the motive behind the suggestion of King Cussaboe that the Cassique employ his son Iswattee as a hunter and subsequent events hardly reveal any benevolent intentions on the part of the savages. The ulterior designs of the chief are indicated when the Cassique's brother Calvert watches him hiding in the presence of the boy and with solemn ceremonies a sheaf of arrows tied in the skin of a rattlesnake. The experienced pirate adds one to their number, so as to confuse the Indians in regard to the time of the attack. Incidentally, the sense of dignity, the reserved air, the lofty carriage, the imposing manner, and the grand speeches delivered on the formal occasion of embassies, and the effective training the Indian boy received in hunting, are all commented upon.

Some of the shrewd whites rightly infer that chief Cussaboe is only awaiting the predetermined night when his son will turn over to him the keys to the buildings of the Cassique, and thus open the way to plunder and slaughter. And the governor in one sense welcomes the inevitable war as a means of securing slaves and scalps. On the other hand, the chief's son dislikes his rôle of treachery with its havoc and murder, and his nature revolts at the work assigned him. " He does not fear death or strife. But his moods are naturally gentle; his fancies are lively; his susceptibilities large; his imagination lofty; he would better make the orator or the poet of his people, than their sanguinary warrior! The red men make their mistakes, even as the whites, in *willing* a pursuit for their sons which is inconsistent with natural endowment."

In his struggle to find a way to escape and to save the whites, the emotional side of the Indian boy finds expression in hot and scalding tears, great sobs shaking his bosom and bursting from his parted lips. For contrary to common opinion, the red man can weep, moan, and laugh like the men of another race, *if he be alone*. But his self-esteem, which is always nursed by solitude, will never suffer a witness of his tears, and hardly of his laughter. He is not adamant, even though he may hide from the sight of the white man as from a mocking superior his passionate emotions, his agonies, his fears, and his tears.

Meanwhile the whites did not remain idle. By dexterously striking down stragglers, the Indian guide Ligon enlarged his private collection of scalps. And the Cassique's brother Calvert had taken care to lock and to make secure on the fated night all the three buildings which the philanthropist in his " amiable insanity " had left wide open. But on account of the addition of that one arrow the boy Iswattee naturally did not expect the attack until the following night and accordingly had not appropriated the keys to the buildings. Upon discovering the embarrassing mistake he attributes to the negligence of the boy, the chief becomes a raging tiger and vents his wrath upon the innocent son. Nevertheless, the assault is to be made at the customary time of dawn, when human sleep is deepest. But for once the moment is ill-chosen, as evidenced by the warm and totally unexpected reception which the sneaking attackers receive.

The description of the assault and defense ranks with the best found in American literature. We note especially the natural caution of the savage and his fear of loss, while a " wild woman," frenzied by the bloody death of her son, exhorts the combatants to havoc and revenge. Supremely picturesque appears one of the Iawas, a priest or magician who, gashing himself with a huge ocean-shell and drawing the woefullest sounds from a great conch, invoked upon his people the terrors of all their savage gods if they did not wreak vengeance upon their white enemies. " The appearance of this Iawa was frightful in the extreme. He was of immense size and stature, nearly seven feet in height, muscular and well limbed, but of little flesh, and he wore a head-dress of buffalo-horns in a fillet of feathers. His age was greater than that of any of his people, but not one exhibited such wonderful agility, was so lithe, rapid, and powerful of limb and movement. His contortions, savagely frantic and fantastic, as he threw his hands up in air, and whirled through the masses, gashing his breast till the blood issued from every part of it, struck awe and terror even into the souls of those who had been wont to behold his previous displays, and who had long been familiar with such savage rites. With the woman as a Fury, such as haunted the footsteps of Orestes, and the Iawa as a terrible necromancer, calling up the dead and dismal inhabitants of the infernal abodes," the warriors rallied, but the headlong rush of the savages was checked by a raking fire that threw them into disorder in spite of all the fierce chief could do.

The decisive moment is near when Calvert on account of the danger from fire determines upon a sally to come to grips with the enemy under the leadership of the savage conjurer, the great Iawa of his tribe, howling and practicing those grotesque and almost demonic contortions which usually excited his people to madness. That redoubtable person, seemingly endowed with a charmed life, leads the horde himself, armed with an enormous macana or warclub — a huge mace, five feet long, of the hardest wood, into the sides of which were let, nearly its whole length, double rows of sharp flint stones, like arrowheads, but thrice as large and quite as keen. In the ensuing fight Calvert keeps close to the Iawa who at such a short range finds it difficult to manage the mace, while his own sharp, sudden blows of the tomahawk are very effective. After the old chief Cussaboe has been hewn down, the conflict narrows down to a single combat between the two champions as the closing scene of the contest. The Indian magician fought fiercely, and his mighty macana was whirled about in the air, the whizzing sound of its motion being heard for thirty feet or more. Growing more feeble from his unwonted exertions, he began to stagger several times. " But he made a final and powerful effort. He felt that it was probably the last he could make; and, with a wild cry, uttering certain guttural words in his own language — doubtless addressed to his false gods — he whirled the *macana* about his head, and it sung fearfully in the air as it descended! It required all of Calvert's dexterity to elude the blow, which grazed him narrowly, smiting the cap from his head! The force thrown into the stroke bore the Iawa completely about, while the heavy end of his mace sank in the ground. Before he could recover himself, lift his weapon, or again meet the *eye* of his enemy, the tomahawk had descended once, twice — the first blow stunningly, the last fatally; the heavy steel crunching deeply into the brain! The conjurer sank forward, with a single yell, which found many a fearful echo among his people. Down he went, like a great tower, and in his fall his conflict ceased. The red warriors had no leader left. Subsequently it was found that he had three musket-balls in his body. Yet he had not faltered once! "

The eager Ligon in his passion for scalps and captives found it hard to show even decent restraint in the sight of his more humane white companions. " This business was an old one, practiced pretty generally from the Plymouth rock to the capes of Florida; by the Pilgrim Fathers as by the Cavaliers; and indeed, the example of setting the red men at loggerheads, slaughtering the warriors, and selling their wives and children into slavery, was set by the virtuous people of Massachusetts Bay, who justified it from Scripture, in numerous delectable texts, at the cost of the heathen." Overwhelmed by the events, the unfortunate Iswattee dies a madman within a week. And the experienced Calvert tells his philanthropic brother that he will never reform or refine the savage, who must be subdued. He clearly foresees that the colonial government will need to follow up the present war to the extermination or utter expulsion of these miserable tribes. A sad prophecy indeed, which was to come true only thirty short years later!

Greater and more definitely focused on the native is *The Yemassee,* a Romance of Carolina, which appeared in 1835. It immediately became, and still continues to be, Simms' most popular work. Within three days the large first edition was completely sold out, and before the end of the year the book was already in the third edition. In the Preface to the revised edition of 1853 Simms insists that his portrait of the red man, however it may differ from the opinion of readers, is correct. " I had seen the red men of the south in their own homes, on frequent occasions, and had arrived at conclusions in respect to them, and their habits and moral nature, which seem to me to remove much of that air of mystery which was supposed to disguise most of their ordinary actions. These corrections of the vulgar opinions will be found unobtrusively given in the body of the work." He maintains that obviously the picture of the Indian in his degraded attitude and humiliating relation with the whites must not be taken as a just delineation of the same being in his native woods, unsubdued, a fearless hunter, and without any degrading consciousness of inferiority, and still more degrading habits, to make him wretched and ashamed. " My portraits, I contend, are true to the Indian as our ancestors knew him at early periods, and as our people, in certain situations, may know him still." The only liberties taken are in the realm of mythology, while all the rest — the general peculiarities of the Indians in their undegraded condition — are based upon his own observations and the numerous authorities who had written from their own experience.

The Yemassee has a definite historical basis. It was in 1715 that the exasperated Indian tribes of the Carolinas planned a wholesale massacre of the white settlers. As told in the story, this uprising was partly instigated by the Spaniards and partly due to the fears of the natives that they would be dispossessed by the newcomers. Their plans succeeded in a frightful manner on the borders, but their march toward Charleston was cut short by a disastrous defeat at the hands of Governor Charles Craven, so that the scattered remains were forced to seek refuge among the Spaniards in Florida.

To the more general facts of history and of geography Simms adhered with great fidelity. The descriptions of the scenery are definite, accurate, and original, uninfluenced by Cooper, his great rival romancer in the North. Governor Craven, ordinarily masquerading as Gabriel Harrison, represents the type of Southern gentleman then in vogue. But his personal activities in the story, especially those of a military character, are highly improbable and often absurd, and in real life would inevitably have led to disaster. As already pointed out, the Indian portraits are painted from life after the best authorities and from personal observation. Unlike those of Cooper, the natives appear mainly on the dark background of frontier conditions, subjected to the stress of a life and death struggle with the superior white invader. The canvas is larger than usual, with considerable space devoted to the home life of the native. Also, the savage is less of a superman, and unendowed with those qualities that at times make Cooper's Indians far from realistic. The dubious " woodcraft " so irritating to a Mark Twain is practically absent. All in all, Simms' Indians are more like ordinary human beings, with the picturesque, however, set off in bold relief.

There can be no question that Simms follows from afar in the footsteps of Cooper, whose Indian tales he praised. It probably would have been difficult to avoid such influences altogether, although this lack of originality will always detract from his fame or even popularity. But Simms is much more than a mere imitator; in fact, he is a story-teller and portrait painter in his own right. In structure and sustained power he is inferior to Cooper, complicating his plot with diverse elements which his fellow romancer studiously avoided. However, this greater complexity has a compensating value in the greater richness of material which the more restrained and economic writer did not possess. On the whole, it would seem that Cooper by means of laying his scene, with the significant exception of *The Pioneers,* beyond the settlements, greatly simplified his task in writing romance, but it is idle to censure Simms for not following in his footsteps when the environment he chose admirably fits his picturesque realism. Personal observation and study had prepared him to portray the native in historic surroundings, and this he has done without allowing the sensational and sordid to play too large a part. In fact, by sparing the reader the gruesome details of drunken debauches and wholesale scalping he has earned the gratitude of a discriminating public.

Naturally only part of the material need concern us here. The love story of Gabriel Harrison and Bess Matthews, who is the object of more than one suitor and of the lust of the pirate Chorley, lies outside of our province. Suffice it to say that the greatness of the work does not lie in those love scenes, nor in the portrayal of Parson Matthews, the stern Puritan father, nor in the tiresome vauntings of the pseudo-humorist Dr. Constantine Maximilian Nichols. Like the Indians they are involved in those numerous and highly improbable hair-breadth escapes in which the pages of the book abound. As Simms allows his characters to run into danger with the recklessness of a maniac, so he also rescues them in the very nick of time with the benevolence of an omniscient and omnipotent god.

The tragedy of The Yemassee overwhelming the native is an all-embracing one. It is personal, domestic, and national, as disaster overtakes those unable to adapt themselves to the relentless march of civilization. And on the other hand, those who weakly accommodate themselves to the characteristics of the whites and sell their birthright for a mess of pottage are likewise swallowed up when an able and determined minority succeeds in putting its ideal to the test. By letting the young and the selfishly base succumb to the corruption of the invader, while a few patriots under the able leadership of Sanutee once more marshal the strength of the nation against the engulfing tides of white dominion, Simms succeeds in making the life and death struggle appear more plausible.

The tragic figure of the young chief Occonestoga, who under the influence of the poison drink of the whites does their bidding to the detriment of his own race, becomes all the more pathetic in view of the qualities of body and mind inherited from the gentle Matiwan and the proud and noble Sanutee. Endowed with all the attributes of the hunter, the warrior, and the leader, but for his failings he would have been the pride of his parents, one of whom even in his debasement is unable to cast him entirely adrift, and when all other means of redemption have failed, by a fatal stroke saves him for the Blessed Valley of the Good Manneyto. The besotted son shows a curious vacillation that marks the degenerate victim whom poison drink has robbed of the full possession of his faculties. Only now and then does he rise above the morass of unspeakable debasement and despair into which he had sunk. His character is finely and consistently drawn with a dénouement both relentless and satisfying.

In following the once glorious but latterly unworthy and miserable career of the young chief, the author allows us to catch glimpses of the emotional life of the savage not dedicated to the stern business of war. It is true, the red man observes " with something like scorn those evidences between the lovers of that nice and delicate affection which belongs only to the highest form of civilization," but he is not insensible to feminine charm and love. Even if the nocturnal amour is pursued by the Yemassees with a fastidious regard to secrecy, not because of any moral reserve, but that such a pursuit savors of a weakness unbecoming to manhood, yet it is present, and the wooing of Hiwassee by Occonestoga's rival Echotee and her acceptance by means of breaking the stick of Checkamoysee, the Yemassee Hymen, reveal a tender and not indelicate phase of Indian life.

The faults and weaknesses of Occonestoga, partly sustained by the poison drink Harrison supplies him, inevitably lead to his tragic end. Vanity, love, and defiance, with murder of his own father in his heart, all play a part in his downfall. The climax is reached in the great twenty-fifth chapter, when the executioner attempts to shear from his breast and arm the broad arrow, the badge of the Yemassee, a ceremony that would have made him like the other dishonored chiefs an expatriated man, homeless, nationless, and godless, an outcast who was barred even from the forest heaven. Simms spared no pains to make the gruesome event effective. The scene at the sacred burial mound of the forefathers ringed in by the sacred trees and lit up by the millions of fireflies from the neighboring swamp is heart-gripping. The weird music, the old women with their flaming torches, and the officiating priests and the executioner all help to create an atmosphere in harmony with the event. Even the sudden hurricane which the author conveniently lets pass over the assembly and which subsides when the prayer to the evil spirit is uttered adds to its effectiveness.

Sanutee himself, the father and "the well-beloved of the Yemassee," presides over the destinies of his son, while Enoree-Mattee, the great prophet or high priest, is master of ceremonies. The old crones, seconded by a crowd of women and children, demand that the sacred arrow be taken from the right arm of the dog, and then the huge, hideously bedaubed and ornamented Malatchie claims the prisoner as the slave of hell. The defense by Occonestoga's generous rival Echotee, made at the instance of the tender-hearted Hiwassee, once the young chief's favorite, is answered by the accusation of the executioner that "he hath drunk of the poison drink of the pale-faces — his feet are gone from the good path of the Yemassee — he would sell his people to the English for a painted bird." When the stern father affirms the doom of his offspring, the latter in a heartrending plea momentarily yields to his emotions, but is cut short by the derisive shout of the multitude; and when recovering himself he proudly begins the deathsong, his voice is drowned out by a tremendous clamor, for he is not to be granted the death of an honored brave. The ceremony of expatriation and outlawry follows: under the direction of the prophet the various castes and classes take final leave of one who could no longer be known among them. There are the marriageable women, the patriarchs of the nation, followed by the young warriors and his old associates. As Occonestoga cries out for death, the prophet in the name of the nation execrates and delivers him over to the Opitchi-Manneyto, the evil spirit of hell. Finally the old father in a scene of tense emotion disowns him. But when Malatchie begins to carry into effect the sentence imposed upon the victim, by now completely unnerved and convulsed with the spasm of the dreadful terror of the future, there comes wildly rushing into the area " Matiwan, his mother — the long black hair streaming — the features, an astonishing likeness to his own, convulsed like his; and her action that of one reckless of all things in the way of the forward progress she was making to the person of her child. She cried aloud as she came — with a voice that rang like a sudden death-bell through the ring —

'Would you keep the mother from her boy, and he to be lost to her for ever? Shall she have no parting with the young brave she bore in her bosom? Away, keep me not back — I will look upon, I will love him! He shall have the blessing of Matiwan, though the Yemassee and the Manneyto curse.'

The victim heard, and a momentary renovation of mental life, perhaps a renovation of hope, spoke out in the simple exclamation which fell from his lips —

'Oh, Matiwan — oh, mother!'

She rushed towards the spot where she heard his appeal, and thrusting the executioner aside, threw her arms desperately about his neck.

'Touch him not, Matiwan,' was the general cry from the crowd — 'Touch him not, Matiwan — Manneyto knows him no more.'

'But Matiwan knows him — the mother knows her child, though the Manneyto denies him. Oh, boy — oh, boy, boy, boy.' And she sobbed like an infant on his neck.

'Thou art come, Matiwan — thou art come, but wherefore? — to curse like the father — to curse like the Manneyto?' mournfully said the captive.

'No, no, no! Not to curse — not to curse. When did mother curse the child she bore? Not to curse, but to bless thee. — To bless thee and forgive.'

'Tear her away,' cried the prophet; 'let Opitchi-Manneyto have his slave.'

'Tear her away, Malatchie,' cried the crowd, now impatient for the execution. Malatchie approached.

'Not yet — not yet,' appealed the woman. 'Shall not the mother say farewell to the child she shall see no more?' and she waved Malatchie back, and in the next instant drew hastily from the drapery of her dress a small hatchet, which she had there carefully concealed.

'What wouldst thou do, Matiwan?' asked Occonestoga, as his eye caught the glare of the weapon.

'Save thee, my boy — save thee for thy mother, Occonestoga — save thee for the happy valley.'

'Wouldst thou slay me, mother — wouldst strike the heart of thy son?' he asked, with something of reluctance to receive death from the hands of a parent.

'I strike thee but to save thee, my son: — since they cannot take the totem from thee after the life is gone. Turn away from me thy head — let me not look upon thine eyes as I strike, lest my hands grow weak and tremble. Turn thine eyes away — I will not lose thee.'

His eyes closed, and the fatal instrument, lifted above her head, was now visible in the sight of all. The executioner rushed forward to interpose, but he came too late. The tomahawk was driven deep into the skull, and but a single sentence from his lips preceded the final insensibility of the victim.

'It is good, Matiwan, it is good — thou hast saved me — the death is in my heart.' And back he sank as he spoke, while a shriek of mingled joy and horror from the lips of the mother announced the success of her effort to defeat the doom, the most dreadful in the imagination of the Yemassee.

'He is not lost — he is not lost. They may not take the child from his mother. They may not keep him from the valley of Manneyto. He is free — he is free.' And she fell back in a deep swoon into the arms of Sanutee, who by this time had approached. She had defrauded Opitchi-Manneyto of his victim, for they may not remove the badge of the nation from any but the living victim."

In the whole range of American literature it would be hard to find a more noble and attractive woman than Matiwan, the mother of Occonestoga and the wife of Sanutee. Her fine qualities are many; but outstanding among them is the mother's undying love for an errant son. Her solicitude for the degraded knows no bounds: it does not even stop at murder in order to save the child of her bosom from the terrible punishment of eternal disgrace. Heart-rending are the scenes that reveal the tender relation between mother and son and the efforts to reclaim and save from harm the erring one. The same motherly solicitude extends to the enemy of her nation, for it embraces Harrison and his mother beyond the seas. Though seemingly disloyal in shielding and rescuing an enemy of her race, an act which strangely enough is not visited upon her head, she is a good wife to the great chief. Him she saves from the fatal blow aimed by a recreant son, and him she visits in camp before the last battle, in order to bear him the ominous tidings of the vision revealed as to the result of the final struggle. Beside the love for her son there is in the heart of this Roman mother and wife a place for her husband and lord whom she sustains in his pride even as life is ebbing away. This much is certain, in Matiwan Simms has created a character probably without a peer in the annals of Indian womanhood.

Outstanding among the Yemassee leaders, and really the head of the nation in spite of old Huspah's official position, is Sanutee, the husband of Matiwan and the father of Occonestoga. Though a kind husband and a good father with something of the sternness and austerity of the Roman, in the situation confronting him the more tender and domestic qualities are subordinated to the demands of the state, with which he is so much pre-occupied that he even forgets his hunting knife. Proud and impulsive, he is also fearless and brave. In the beginning his attitude toward the newcomers had been friendly, until the prospect of ruin to his race at the hands of the invaders forced upon him a policy of implacable hostility. Yet even then he gives the whites a fair warning to withdraw, and in his efforts to save the commissioners reveals humane qualities. His schemes of war and violence, as well as the alliance with the Spaniards, serve the one supreme purpose to which all others are subordinated, namely freedom and liberty for his nation.

To accomplish that end he spurns personal profit, unhesitatingly employs deception to overthrow the chiefs friendly to the whites, and even sacrifices his own son. In war he is cunning and methodical, assuming the most dangerous task himself. And when it comes to the last crucial battle, he chooses his ground with consummate skill, though Simms foils the stratagem of the early morning attack by the counter-stratagem of the white commander, a trap into which the real Indian hardly would have fallen. Even when he knows that his doom is sounded in that desperate struggle after the surprise, as his people are " striking the last blow for the glory and the existence of their once mighty nation," he is exerting his utmost. In his dying moments he still retains the homage and the affection of his warriors and receives from his life companion the assurance that he passes as the great brave of the Yemassee. Softer qualities may recede into the background, but even among the war thoughts they are not entirely lacking, as when just before the battle he approves Matiwan's act of saving the boy for the forest heaven. However, the glory of his people and his own are uppermost as he sings his song of many victories, and with the battle cry " Sangarrah-me, Yemassee — Sangarrah-me — Sangarrah-me! " he expires, the last great chief of his tribe.

Beside the crafty and mighty Sanutee, the other chiefs assume a subordinate position and play a secondary rôle, such as the old and tottering Huspah and the stalwart Manneywanto. Degraded and disowned for selling the birthright of their nation for personal gain, they vanish with their companions into the night, with never another glimpse of their fate. Outstanding among Sanutee's associates is the dark Ishiagaska, a treacherous and bloodthirsty savage who eagerly looks forward to the time when the scalps of the whites shall shrivel around the long pole in the lodge of the warrior. Interesting but pathetic is the figure of Chinnabee, last chief of the Coosaw, subtle, bold, and brave, whose dark eye glared and whose teeth gnashed like those of the hungered wolf as he confronted in the governor the destroyer of his people.

In ascribing personal qualities to the Indians, Simms resisted the temptation of endowing them with the supernatural, and stayed well within the bounds of probability. Naturally the forest people possess those accomplishments which environment made inevitable. But their keenness and cunning are, on the whole, not any greater than those of the white man. In adjusting themselves to nature and to animal life they show remarkable aptitude, exemplified for instance by their directing the forces in the attack on the blockhouse through the purported cries of the whippoorwill and by Matiwan's skilful imitation of the sounds of the cricket, the mocking-bird, and the wood-pecker. But oftentimes the whites prove themselves superior: they listen undetected to the most important proceedings, they elude capture, and they employ more effective strategy. And when properly warned, the settler and the borderer are not afraid to confront the native. While the savage hunter through constant exercise may ordinarily be superior in the use of his legs, his strength is less than that of the white opponent. Even Sanutee is not the equal of Chorley, and " savages were no opponents, generally speaking, to be feared in a trial of respective muscular strength," the Indians usually despairing of success when required to oppose the white man hand to hand. They are easily discouraged and subject to sudden panics. Unable to use firearms to any good effect, they have to fall back upon stratagems, ambuscades, and cunning to cope with the armed and more resourceful opponent. Their hope is the midnight surprise, the sudden onslaught, the terror inspired by the fearful war-whoop — all very well if the white settler happened to be caught unawares, but of little avail when fully prepared.

Certain qualities of the native the author takes pains to point out and to emphasize. The most striking is perhaps the Indian's show of emotion, for he is not sternly and indifferently cold, the assumed habitual taciturnity of the native being a popular error. In the presence of whites he may be silent from his ignorance of the language and from a feeling of inferiority. " In his own habitation, uninfluenced by drink or any form of degradation, and unrestrained by the presence of superiors, he is sometimes even a jester — delights in a joke, practical or otherwise, and he is not scrupulous about its niceness or propriety. In his council he is fond of speaking; glories in long talks; and as he grows old, if you incline a willing ear, even becomes garrulous. Of course, all these habits are restrained by circumstances. He does not chatter when he fights or hunts, and when he goes to make a treaty, and never presumes to say more than he has been taught by his people." When Harrison was led captive into the village, there was little of taciturnity. " Hootings and howlings — shriekings and shoutings — confused cries — yells of laughter — hisses of scorn — here and there a fragment of song, either of battle or ridicule, gathering, as it were, by common instinct, into a chorus of fifty voices — most effectively banished silence from her usual night dominion in the sacred town of Pocota-ligo."

The public business transacted by the native, as well as his preparation for war, follows well established customs, which are described in great detail. For instance, " no assembly of the white man compares, in seeming solemnity at least, with that of the red." While uninterrupted by others, the speaker naturally would show whatever emotions agitated his soul. The council voting the English certain concessions and its sequel of the overthrow of the selfish chiefs instigated by the cunning Sanutee show to what lengths the aroused populace might go in expressing their outraged feelings over the sacrilegious appropriation of the old burial places. The conduct and horrible convulsions of the great prophet of the tribe are a terrible sight, calculated to influence the superstitious mind of the multitude. And the marshalling of the six thousand warriors for the decisive conflict is a spectacle at once lurid and imposing. We note how carefully the national pride or the great glory of the clan, that desperate passion among the Southern Indians, is safeguarded. Even the smallest tribe does not lose its identity, but is properly recognized by being allowed to strike the gigantic figure representing the enemy. And the torture of the unfortunate but unflinching Irishman, serving as a means to arouse the warriors to their greatest height of fury in their war-song, adds the final touch of reality.

The forest warfare follows the accepted modes of the savages. It is the well known night attack, with its war-whoops and scalpings and the stratagems used to gain entrance to the blockhouse by the window and by the firing of the logs. In their marauding tactics and systematic siege they show only ordinary cunning. In fact, it would appear that the raising of the siege of the blockhouse was somewhat premature, as a more skilful disposition of the forces might have secured the destruction of the hard-pressed imprisoned whites before the rescuing party could have arrived. The activities of the attacking parties are overshadowed by the blacksmith's daring, by the bravery and strategy of Harrison, and especially by the resoluteness of Granger's wife, who knows how to cope with the wily savages. Even the Puritan divine is no mean obstacle to the lustful desires of the forest brave. The author speaks with evident delight of the romance of Indian warfare, including the single combat, and of the highly ingenious art to which it had developed.

It is plain that Simms, while fully describing the treachery, cruelty, and bloodthirst of the native tribes, does not place the blame at their door, but rather at that of the scheming palefaces who often appear as thoroughly bad, or as Simms categorically declares: " To sum up all in little, our European ancestors were, in many respects, monstrous great rascals." For the Yemassees are said to have been originally a generous and gallant race, gentle and forbearing; but provoked by the repeated aggression and abuse of the newcomers, they chose strife and hostility in preference to becoming the slaves of a superior people. That they should have employed all available means in this their struggle for existence, whether treachery, deception, or savage vengeance, was only what might be expected of a proud and outraged people.

On the other hand, notwithstanding the latent sympathy which the author shows an inferior race, destiny evidently had to take its course. " It is in the nature of civilization to own an appetite for dominion and extended sway, which the world that is known will always fail to satisfy. It is for her, then, to seek out and to create, and not with the Macedonian madman, to weep for the triumph of the unknown. Conquest and sway are the great leading principles of her existence, and the savage must join in her train, or she rides over him relentlessly in her onward progress." In adaptation therefore, and not in stubborn defiance, lies the salvation of the savage.

CHAPTER XII

A PROMISE UNFULFILLED AND A MELANCHOLY FATE

During his early life John Greenleaf Whittier (1807-1892) belonged to that small group of enthusiastic men who believed that the history and traditions of the Indians furnished excellent material for poetic treatment. In his case such an attitude was all the more natural if we remember that his father when a young man had traversed the wilderness to Canada and would relate his adventures with the Indians to the eagerly listening group on those long winter evenings so vividly described in *Snowbound*. And the mother, born in the Indian-haunted region of Somersworth, New Hampshire,

> Told how the Indian hordes came down
> At midnight on Cocheco town,
> And how her own great-uncle bore
> His cruel scalp-mark to fourscore.

Small wonder that a number of Whittier's earlier productions deal with a subject thought so promising. The poet's opinions, however, soon underwent a change, and toward the end of his life he relegated some of these efforts to the Appendix of his complete works. Among them is *Mount Agiochook* in the White Mountains, supposed by the Indians to be the residence of powerful spirits, and in consequence rarely ascended by them. But now even the slopes know the native no more, only the caverns and summits serving the strange gods of heathendom as a dwelling place. Of greater interest is *Metacom,* which describes the last days of Philip, chief of the Wampanoags, at once the most powerful and sagacious sachem ever to make war upon the English. Like most of Whittier's poems dealing with the native, it contains a great deal of description, and in addition much talk by the wily chief.

Unquestionably of greatest importance among these early productions is *Mogg Megone,* covering in the Collected Works eleven closely printed pages. For five years beginning with 1830, Whittier tells us, he worked on this delineation of the border strife between the early settlers of eastern New England and their savage neighbors. Though the personages and incidents are mainly fictitious, the young poet strove valiantly to make them realistic. Mogg Megone is a chief in league with John Boniton, whom the English have outlawed. Provided the Indian also signs over to him large stretches of land, he promises his fair daughter Ruth to the chief who at their instigation had at last succeeded in scalping her white seducer. Thus white man's greed and an Indian's lust, with the inevitable firewater, are the twin motives of action. However, when the savage has fulfilled the agreement, the outlaw decides to kill the drunken lout who in his fitful slumbers attempted to rise and muttered:

> — Mogg will have the pale-face's hair,
> For his knife is sharp, and his fingers can help
> The hair to pull and the skin to peel, —
> Let him cry like a woman and twist like an eel,
> The great Captain Scamman must lose his scalp!
> And Ruth, when she sees it, shall dance with Mogg.

When in spite of these savage sentiments the remembrance of his rescue from a cold and wintry grave by the Indian chief causes the hand of the outlaw to falter, Ruth, less weak as the old love for her seducer returns, strikes the Indian dead. Later she confesses her deed to the Jesuit priest at Norridgewock, Maine, but he gives her scant comfort. In the third part are described the labors, trials, and disappointments of the Jesuit Father Râle, whom the English rangers put to the sword, sparing none of his flock. When much later Baron Castine and his French forces arrive at the deserted town, they find Ruth Boniton — but dead.

The superabundant descriptions and the crude execution of *Mogg Megone* stamp it as a work of Whittier's early youth, and as he himself confessed in 1857, " it is scarcely necessary to say that its subject is not such as the writer would have chosen at any subsequent period." And in the preface to the poem he frankly

A PROMISE UNFULFILLED

admits: " Looking at it, at the present time, it suggests the idea of a big Indian in his war paint strutting about in Sir Walter Scott's plaid."

Among the poems dealing with Indian subjects not relegated to the Appendix three may be singled out for brief comment. *Pentucket* is a spirited description of the French-Indian attack on Haverhill on the Merrimac, during 1708, when

> — smote the Indian tomahawk
> On crashing door and shattering lock;
> Then rang the rifle-shot, and then
> The shrill death-scream of stricken men, —
> Sank the red axe in woman's brain,
> And childhood's cry arose in vain.

Interesting is *The Funeral Tree of the Sokokis,* describing the unusual burial of the Sokokis chief Polan, killed in 1756. " The surviving Indians ' swayed ' or bent down a young tree until its roots were upturned, placed the body of their chief beneath it, and then released the tree, which, in springing back to its old position, covered the grave, the Indian's fitting monument."

The longest and most important of these poems is *The Bridal of Pennacook,* dealing with the marriage of Weetamoo, the daughter of the great Pennacook chieftain, to Winnepurgit, Sachem of Saugus, with its subsequent developments. Indian customs and characteristics the poet was careful to incorporate in the tale. Though his young wife has just died, the proud chief sheds no tears, for

> The Indian's heart is hard and cold,
> It closes darkly o'er its care,
> And formed in nature's sternest mold,
> Is slow to feel and strong to bear.

He proceeds to woo and wed in royal style at Pennacook (Concord, N. H.) the winsome Weetamoo. The bride at first seems satisfied at her new but melancholy home, but later she expresses a wish to visit her father and people in the south, and is escorted by her husband's chief warriors. When at last she is ready to go home, and the father notifies the husband to take her back, the dark chief of Saugus demands that Pennacook return her with wampum gifts. This the haughty chief refuses to do —

> — may his scalp dry black
> In Mohawk smoke, before I send her back.

In turn the Sachem of Saugus soon places on the mat of the scorned wife a dusky rival. But woman's nature is everywhere the same, and the still faithful wife, unable to bear the separation any longer and heedless of the perils of the swollen Merrimac, launches her frail boat to seek the wigwam of her lord. But she is lost in the swirling waters of the river, and mourned in a beautiful farewell and funeral song of the Indian women.

Though *The Bridal of Pennacook* like the other Indian poems of Whittier is not particularly significant, it is noted for beautiful descriptions of New England scenery, the praise of the Merrimac river being especially fine. As in the case of similar productions, it reveals the eagerness of the youthful enthusiast to take advantage of whatever opportunity the native in his primitive setting seemed to offer to the poet.

The dozen or more poems of William Cullen Bryant (1794–1878) dealing with the Indian share the characteristics of his other verse. In the melancholy manner of the poet of dissolution and death they tell the story of a people vanishing from the face of the earth. *The Prairies* records the musings of the traveller who in 1832 had journeyed as far as Illinois and looked upon the remains of the mound builders, people he considered a race distinct from the warlike and roaming hunter tribes of the Indians. They possessed the rudiments of civilization, and cultivated the fields with the help of the bison. But disciplined only in the arts of peace, those swarming groups were unable to meet the fierce onslaughts of the red men. Only a solitary fugitive, overcome by a sense of desolation and fear bitterer than death, sought the mercy of his enemies. It was granted, and a bride from among the maidens adorned his wigwam. But even in the newly found domestic bliss there came to him the haunting memory of his first wife, her sweet little ones, with their death-shrieks stifled in the holocaust of his race.

However, the red man is fast sharing the melancholy fate of his victims. He has already passed from the eastern part of the United States, where, as depicted in *The Ages,* the Indian hamlet with the varying experiences of savage life has been displaced by the populous city of the whites. A representative of the vanishing people in *An Indian at the Burial Place of His Fathers* finds the ancestral burying ground cultivated and the paleface guiding his plow among the scattered bones. In his imagination he may recreate the original scene for a moment, but the bitter reality stares him in the face, as he sees his people pushed toward the setting sun and driven into the western sea. His fevered brain is only partly soothed by the fervent wish that their conquerors too may vanish without leaving so much as a trace behind. In *The Disinterred Warrior* the poet pleads that the mouldering relics of a noble race, or at least the graves of a people whom the whites have dispossessed, may be spared. For the choice spots of this earth, the crystal well and the clear rivulet, once resounding with aboriginal life, now re-echo with the bustle of white man's civilization.

Hardly less poignant than the lament over a vanishing people is the grief occasioned in that far-off time by disappointed love or the loss of a dear one. In *An Indian Story* the hunter Maquon finds on his return that his bride is gone, stolen by a ruffian; only after a lengthy pursuit does his grief turn to joy, for Indian girls recognize in a hillock of fresh dark mould in the pine-grove the ravisher's grave. No such earthly hope and rejoicing is destined to visit the heart of the tear-stained maiden in *The Indian Girl's Lament,* who has prepared her slain lover for the long journey to the happy hunting-grounds. Her one consolation is the wavering fancy that her departed lover's thought will stray earthward and drown her grief in her eagerness to join him in the leafen bower beneath the many-colored shade in the land of the blessed. Dark and foreboding is the atmosphere of *Monument Mountain,* where the fairest of the Indian beauties, with a gay heart, light form, and a wealth of raven tresses vainly struggles against the unlawful love for her cousin. Now her merry laugh is gone, and the pastimes and gayety of youth become strangers as she pines away. Even her confession to a bosom friend and playmate does not relieve corroding sorrow. So at last, decking her wasted form with flowers, she throws herself from the steep rock and perishes, to sleep beneath a mound and a cone of loose stones, which serve as a fitting monument of the hapless maid. Truly, life and destiny smote the individual as it crushed the race as a whole.

Of the real Indian, his customs and character, Bryant knew little or nothing, but the melancholy fate overwhelming him never failed to arouse the poet's interest. Such lore as this powerfully appealed to his fancy, as the sentimental aspect harmonized with his view of life. The scattered bones of a vanishing people found a fitting place in a landscape that served as a sepulcher of the ever changing life of the earth.

CHAPTER XIII

THE ATOTARHO OF THE IROQUOIS

The Iroquois Indians, by many looked upon and called the "Romans" among the natives of eastern North America, are brought to life in a spirited poem entitled *Frontenac: or the Atotarho of the Iroquois, a Metrical Romance,* published in 1849 by Alfred B. Street (1811-1881), state librarian at Albany, New York. His stay during early life in Sullivan County, then practically a wilderness, undoubtedly influenced him in his faithful description of natural scenery and in other respects. The poem of seven thousand octosyllabic lines is based upon the expedition undertaken in 1696 by Count Frontenac, Governor-general of Canada, against the powerful league or confederacy of the Iroquois, who, on his return, waylaid him and inflicted some losses.

The fierce Iroquois, mortal enemies of the French ever since the unfortunate encounter on Lake Champlain, lurk about Quebec; and one of their number has come on a very definite mission.

> A warrior he was, armed for strife,
> With tomahawk and scalping knife
>   Thrust through his wampum belt;
> The long lock crowned his shaven head;
> Bare, save the belt, his form of red,
> And where around his loins was spread
>   A stripe of shaggy felt.

On a grassy glade west of the city this stalwart brave tomahawks Sieur Lavergne and kidnaps little Lucille, daughter of Count Frontenac and his Indian wife Sa-ha-wee, whom he had wooed and won on her visit to France. But her brother is thought to have killed his erring sister later, and now the tribe reclaims its own.

Twenty-four years pass, and then Street shows us the Iroquois in all their strength in their native habitat, and among them

> The proudest of all the hostile array
> Was young Thurenserah, the Dawn of the Day,
> The League's Atotarho! the boldest in fight!
> The wisest in council! in form the most bright!
> The fleetest of foot, the most skilled in the chase!
> The glory and boast of the Iroquois race!

Besides this acknowledgment of the position of the Atotarho of the Onondagas as the first of the federal chiefs, the author introduces the Iroquois custom of feeding the sacred flame, in this case performed by none other than the mother of the chief. Strangely enough, this much beloved person dwells wifeless and is of delicate features; yet he has a haughty soul, and his slender form like a panther's is always ready for the spring. As becomes such a brave, there are constant reminders of war, for

> ... from the floor a sapling sprung
> With human scalps upon it strung;
> Age's gray locks, long woman's hair,
> Childhood's and manhood's blended there.

Another part of the poem introduces us to the Indian ball game, during which Frontenac's offer to plant the tree of peace arrives. The Atotarho, wearing a bristling scalp-lock, and as head sachem and war-chief of the confederacy also the white heron's plume, goes to Quebec. Reflecting the well known fear of the Iroquois on the part of the Frenchmen, his appearance and reputation arouse peculiar feelings, illustrated by the remark of a batteau-man who inquires of a comrade how the scalp feels upon his head. The loyalty of the Five Tribes to the English is well brought out by the fact that the Iroquois stubbornly refuse to conclude a peace unless their confederates are included. Fully upholding his tribe's reputation for bravery, the Atotarho in the ensuing fight makes his way through the throng and escapes.

In the third canto the author shows us the Indian on the war-path, exhibiting all the cunning and fierceness of which he was reputed to be capable. As usual, the bloodshed was not unprovoked by the whites, who reaped only what they had sown. A rousing war song prepares the warriors for the encounters that are soon to follow:

THE ATOTARHO OF THE IROQUOIS

Hooh! hooh! how the panther springs,
As flies the deer on affrighted wings!
Hooh! hooh! how he rends his prey!
So will the On-on-dah-gahs slay!

Hooh! hooh! how the eagle screams,
As the blood of the fawn from his talons streams!
Hooh! hooh! how the woods ring out!
So will the On-on-dah-gahs shout!

Hooh! hooh! how the sharpened knife
Will gleam again in the war-path's strife!
Hooh! hooh! how the lightning red,
The On-on-dah-gahs will flash in dread.

Hooh! hooh! how the hungry fire
Will wrap the French in its leaping ire!
Hooh! hooh! like the torrent's flood,
The On-on-dah-gahs will rush in blood!

Then at last
      Breaking the song, above his head
      The Atotarho flashed a sweep
      With his bright hatchet; down it sped
      And in the post was buried deep.
      The next one gave a piercing yell,
      And down his hatchet also fell.
      Another struck — another — shrill
      Whoop upon whoop resounding, till
      Blows rained upon the post so fast,
      In fragments round 'twas strown at last.

The stratagems of Indian warfare with their fearful results are depicted with considerable skill. The author with evident delight describes the enemies of the English outwitted and massacred by the cunning braves. French hunters, happy like children in their kill of moose and deer, are scalped in a surprise attack during the night, and the boatmen who find their bloody corpses experience a similar fate. Next a Carignan village, wrapt in slumber just before the dawn of day, is wiped out.

Especially picturesque and spirited is the attack on a French brigantine which dropped anchor near the shore of Lake Ontario, the crew being blissfully ignorant of the fact that three Indian war canoes had come to a halt under the sheltering cluster of spruce only a short distance away. Although the fearful destruction of the village forms the evening's talk, the blundering Frenchmen set only a single guard, and even he falls asleep as the night wears on. Only too soon all are to rue their careless slumber, for

> A haze has now spread a thick mantle of gray,
> The waters are hidden, the stars shrink away;
> From the roof of dark cedars quick movements begin,
> How silently, silently, onwards they win!
> Still silently, silently, every canoe
> Still urged the gray waters invisibly through,
> Like barks from the spirit-land, spectral and dim,
> So still fall their paddles, so light is their skim;
> Still silently, silently, onwards they glide,
> They reach without question the brigantine's side;
> Forms spring up the vessel — hush! hush! not a sound!
> They peer o'er the bulwarks, the sleepers are round:
> They grasp now their hatchets, all caution is past,
> To the deck, to the deck, they are bounding at last!
> Whoop! whoop! Thurenserah the foremost is there!
> Whoop! whoop! how their shouts ring abroad on the air!
> Upstart the pale sleepers, and wildered by fright,
> And with senses still swimming, they stand to the fight,
> Hand to hand is the battle, clash cutlass and knife!
> Clash steel-pike and hatchet; wild, wild is the strife!
> Ho, the young Atotarho! his eyeballs are flame,
> And the blood of his foes is splashed over his frame!
> At the sweep of his hatchet one plunges to death!
> At the dart of his knife gasps another for breath!
> God save the poor seamen! no succor is nigh!
> Christ save the poor seamen! they struggle to die!
> They are borne to the deck, o'er the sides they are cast;
> The water grows red round the brigantine fast,
> Till nothing remains of the crew but the dead,
> Then over the vessel deep silence is spread.
> Off dart the canoes, smoke the doomed bark surrounds,
> On the lines of the rigging flame flashes and bounds,
> Red pennons stream out from the red-circled mast,
> A glare all around on the vapor is cast,
> The waters blush crimson; but wildly and high
> The Iroquois war-song goes up to the sky.

> " Hooh! hooh! how the hungry fire
> Has wrapped the French in its leaping ire!
> Hooh! hooh! like the torrent's flood,
> The On-on-dah-gahs have rushed in blood!
> Hooh! whoop! like the torrents flood,
> The On-on-dah-gahs have rushed in blood! "

Naturally such victories demand that tribute be paid to the Great Spirit, and the dances of thanksgiving assume an especially lively character under the circumstances. Later, in order to exhibit the cunning of the Atotarho at its best, Street cannot refrain from sending the hero to Quebec, where the kidnapped Jiskoko, a beautiful half-breed maiden in love with the chief, is imprisoned. Disguised as an Indian girl, he demands of Frontenac his " sister's " release. In spite of the governor's refusal, he appears to succeed in his mission, for he is allowed to join Jiskoko in her cell, where he suddenly becomes warlike and kills the guard, whereupon both escape. Then, strange to say, the author lets the spirit of vengeance induce the chief to return in an assault on the life of the governor. But fate turns against such presumption, for Frontenac is saved, while during the pursuit of the Atotarho the lovely maiden Jiskoko, who instead of fleeing had waited for him in a canoe near by, is slain.

The five following cantos deal mainly with Frontenac's expedition into the Iroquois country, with the forest warfare and the final catastrophe as the high points. As often, the French have an ally and guide in We-an-dah, the pathetic figure of a chief whose proud spirit has been quenched by the all-potent fire-water:

> Ah, forest Chieftain! Noble Brave!
> Wert thou, indeed, so mean a thing!
> Better have filled a warrior's grave,
> Thou eagle with a broken wing!

The progress of the expedition is described in detail, though not without some misgivings. For, viewing one of the quiet and beautiful lakes, the author in a pious mood would have the whites pause lest the avenging rod of the Great Spirit strike them down for mistreating those who once had it in their power to destroy the early settlers.

But the march steadily goes on, and we view how the Iroquois tribes called by the war cry from their customary occupations assemble at the great council to devise means for meeting the invader. In order to further his preconceived plot and to show what contradictory motives and passions might rend such an assembly, Street makes the session a stormy one. On the one hand the traitor We-an-dah, claiming that he has beguiled Frontenac, advises a retreat, only to be met by the rallying cry of the Atotarho, who is ably seconded by the priestess with her final plea:

> " Braves! hear again the words of dread
> By bright To-gan-a-we-tah said
> A hundred hundred moons ago,
> ' When the White Throats shall come, if ye
> Shall separate, then yourselves will throw
> The Long House down, destroy the Tree
> Of Peace, and trample out the Flame! '
> Must now this doom our people claim? —
> Must ye with fierce and wicked will
> This awful prophesy fulfill? "

The result is a fierce fight, which leaves the war chief only a determined minority to oppose Frontenac in the forest. The resolute woman tending the sacred flame awaits the approach of the invaders with the French governor at their head, who recognizes in the priestess his Indian wife Sa-ha-wee.

Double dealing and forest warfare with all their gruesome results keep the reader in suspense as Chief We-an-dah repents of his treacherous designs and leads Frontenac into an ambush in " Wolf's Throat " glen, where

> All gaze round, but nought they see
> But rock, and bush, and bank, and tree,
> Whence shoots the flame of the fusee,
> And deadly balls shower fearfully;
> No mark for aim or blow
> Save now and then a plumaged head,
> A tawny arm, a legging red,
> A muzzle bend, an eye of dread,
> An instant seen, an instant fled,
> Ere gun or pike can bear.

THE ATOTARHO OF THE IROQUOIS

But suddenly the bewildered reader, as if he were viewing a heroic play of the Restoration, receives another jolt when Chief Ska-nux-heh turns traitor and delivers the Atotarho into the hands of the rejoicing Frenchmen.

As far as aboriginal interest is concerned, the poem ends in a lurid, melodramatic catastrophe at the burning stake, a scene the author might well have spared the reader, especially in view of its glaring improbability. As after the torture the Atotarho is led to the stake, the priestess confesses that he is Lucille, which is confirmed when Ska-nux-heh in baring his breast reveals a woman. When he shrinks to apply the torch, Lucille herself takes it from his hand and fires the pile, while in vain the fainting Frontenac whispers a plea to save his daughter. The mother alone is equal to the occasion: frantic with fear, she stabs the traitor, then

> Into the fire she dashes now,
> And nerved with all her mad despair,
> One flashing wreath around her brow,
> Around her form one blazing glare,
> She breaks from out the scattered flame,
> And forth she drags a blackened frame
> Which, staggering wildly to its knee,
> An arm throws proudly to the skies,
> Sounds a low war-whoop brokenly,
> Then drops, and, struggling faintly, dies.
> Turned into stone, with frenzied gaze,
> The talons of a ravenous blaze
> Keen in her flesh, the Priestess kneels
> Beside her child, a shriek then peals,
> A shriek of agony, so shrill,
> It made the hearts all round her thrill,
> Then swift as light, her knife she sheathed
> Within her breast, her blood gushed red,
> And as " I come, Lucille! " she breathed,
> She fell across her daughter, dead.

In common with not a few other Indian poems, the plot of Street's work is preposterous, for under the conditions of savage life it would have been impossible to hide the characteristics of sex. But once we overlook this outrageous imposture and a number of less serious improbabilities, not a few fine qualities appear.

As already mentioned, the descriptions of natural scenery of northern New York, especially in its primeval state, are faithful and happy. In addition, many picturesque scenes of Iroquois life bear the mark of authenticity. The daily occupations, the council, the dances, as well as the bloody encounters of a proud and gifted race, reveal to us the life story of the members of a confederacy that was emerging from savagery to barbarism, and presumably might have advanced to a civilized state. All in all, though falling perceptibly short of perfection in content, structure, and form, Street's metrical romance is a noble attempt to visualize the story of the " Romans " among the nations of eastern North America.

CHAPTER XIV

HIAWATHA — THE DAWN OF CULTURE

The name of Henry Wadsworth Longfellow (1807–1882) stands first and foremost among the poets dealing successfully with Indian material. This fame rests solely upon *The Song of Hiawatha,* his acknowledged masterpiece and perennial favorite. Though he early became interested in the native, the poems dealing with the subject he thought fit to be preserved are neither numerous nor significant. Among the juvenile efforts, relegated in the Complete Poetical Works to the Appendix, is *The Indian Hunter,* whose hero, discouraged by the encroachment of the whites, commits suicide by drowning. His skeleton, lying beneath the clear waters of the lake, with the hand still grasping the hunter's bow, is long after discovered by a fisherman. Another production even less in value is *Jeckayra,* written in honor of an Indian chief who accidentally died on a mountain now bearing his name.

Two short poems, each depicting an incident of Indian life, were accorded a place in the Collected Poetical Works. In the *Burial of the Minnisink* the body of the young warrior is solemnly conveyed to the grave, preceded by a dark-haired virgin train chanting the death dirge of the slain, and followed by the old men and famous chiefs leading the war-horse. After the burial of the young chief, his battle steed is freed and shot, in order that the dead rider may grasp again the accustomed rein in the happy hunting-grounds. The melancholy poem *To A Driving Cloud* deals with a dark and gloomy chief of the Omahas visiting the city named after his tribe. His demand for hunting-grounds clashes with the claim and the cry of Europe's downtrodden millions that they too have been created heirs of the earth. Not in the bustling city, but rather among his own people following the ordinary pursuits of life the solitary figure of the dark-skinned chief must seek whatever happiness fate still grants. And that is fast becoming a thing of the past. For as of old he is not now threatened by the Crows and the Foxes and the mighty Behemoth, but by the big thunder canoe and the caravan of the Saxons and Celts, whose breath drifts evermore to the west the scanty smokes of the wigwams.

Not a few critics agree that *The Song of Hiawatha,* 1855, is Longfellow's most original production, and that it likewise is America's most notable poem. Popular from the day of its publication when four thousand copies were sold, it has continued to hold the interest of millions, especially of the young, and there is probably no school child in the United States wholly unacquainted with the story of Hiawatha. It would seem that the author has succeeded in putting into the work whatever is poetic and appealing in the primitive man of America. In order to render the poem more acceptable to the white reader he had in view, Longfellow widely departed from the basic Indian material, without, however, eliminating the specifically Indian spirit.

The selection of material in the main favorable to the red man was largely determined by the kind and charitable nature of the poet. Rather early in life he had likewise received a powerful stimulus toward such an attitude. During his junior year in college he writes his mother under date of November 9, 1823, that he has read Heckewelder's *Account of the History, Manners, and Customs of the Indian Nations of Pennsylvania and the Neighboring States.* Henry remarks that this very interesting volume exhibits in a new and more agreeable light the character of these reviled and persecuted people. On the basis of Heckewelder's first hand study he believes, paradoxical as it may seem, that the Indians are " a race possessing magnanimity, generosity, benevolence, and pure religion without hypocrisy." His conclusion is that they have been most barbarously maltreated by the whites, both in word and deed, who render their cruelty more cruel, and their barbarity more vindictive, by publishing after the manner of the Pharisees the horrible crimes of their enemies.

This impression was probably deepened when at the Junior Exhibition in December he impersonated the character of King Philip in a " Dialogue between a North American Indian and a

European," his classmate Bradbury taking the part of Miles Standish. As the unfortunate chief he maintained against the claims of the white man that the continent had been given by the Great Spirit to the Indians, and that the English were wrongful intruders. In later years Longfellow carefully observed whatever Indians came into his way. On October 29, 1837, for instance, he writes to his father: "There is a grand display of Indians in Boston, — Black-Hawk [the famous leader in the Black Hawk War of 1832] and some dozen other bold fellows, all grease and red paint; war-clubs, bears-teeth, and buffalo scalps in profusion; hair cut close, like a brush, and powdered with vermillion; one cheek red, one black; forehead striped with bright yellow, with a sprinkling of flour between the eyes, — this will fit almost any of them. They are to have a *pow-wow* on the Common tomorrow." The interest he felt in the red man was increased by the Indians he observed in Maine and especially through his acquaintance with the Ojibway chief Kah-ge-ga-gah'-bowh, who in 1849 lectured in Boston on "The Religion, Poetry, and Eloquence of the Indian," and whom he entertained in his home.

However, even before 1849 Longfellow had carried the idea of a work on the Indians in his mind. His friend George Lowell Austin tells us how the subject was suggested to him. "A young gentleman who had graduated from Harvard College in one of those early classes which received so much attention from Professor Longfellow, just after his coming to Cambridge, had returned from the West with his memory well stocked with recent experiences among the Indians. While dining one day with the poet, he very much entertained the latter by a recital of what he had seen and heard during his rambles on the plains, and more especially by repeating some of the legends of campfire and lodge, which, as he claimed, were the 'folk-lore' of the red men. He very strongly suggested to Mr. Longfellow the pleasurable task of weaving these legends into a poem."

When, soon after, Longfellow began looking for material suitable for carrying out the suggestion of his former student, he was attracted by the *Algic Researches* of Henry Rowe Schoolcraft, an 1839 collection of Indian tales and legends both mythologic and allegoric, without which *Hiawatha* never would have been written. But he was slow to come to any decision. As he himself told Mr. Austin: " I pored over Mr. Schoolcraft's writings nearly three years before I resolved to appropriate something of them to my own use." Though various other books were naturally of material assistance, those of Schoolcraft remain the chief source.

In the journals and correspondence of the poet, given to the world by his brother Samuel in the *Life of Henry Wadsworth Longfellow,* we can follow in fair detail the genesis and composition of *The Song of Hiawatha.* On June 22, 1854, he writes: " I have at length hit upon a plan for a poem on the American Indians, which seems to me the right one, and the only. It is to weave together the beautiful traditions into a whole. I have hit upon a measure, too, which I think the right and only one for such a theme." Though he does not say so here, this measure, the rhymeless trochaic dimeter, was taken from the Finnish national epic *Kalevala,* which charming poem he had mentioned as reading with great delight on June 5, and which in 1842 he had enjoyed in German with the poet Ferdinand Freiligrath. On June 25 he makes the beginning of what he designates as "' Manabozho ' or whatever the poem is to be called," while after another three days he believes that he will name it "Hiawatha — that being another name for the same personage."

The composition of the poem made slow progress, various interruptions, sometimes of weeks, when Longfellow had lost the poetic mood, threatening to bring it to a complete standstill. Meanwhile he worked away with Schoolcraft, Tanner, Heckewelder, and sundry other books about the Indians, and tried to disentangle the legends. At times the subject delighted him and carried him away, at other times like sympathetic friends taken into his confidence he had serious misgivings, and found it difficult to put a live beating heart into it. Finally, on March 21, 1855, he finished the poem. " Of course the bells rang," he joyously records. Then came weary months of revising, re-copying, and reading of proof-sheets, with doubts as to whether certain cantos should be retained or suppressed. At last on November 10 the book came out, and the rejoicing author was told the same day by the publisher that more than four thousand copies of the first edition had been sold. A year and a half later the sale reached 50,000 copies.

The publication of *Hiawatha* created a literary sensation. Innumerable imitations and parodies, to which the meter readily invited, appeared, and newspapers and periodicals made fierce and furious charges of plagiarism. For instance, an article in the *Washington Intelligencer* accused Longfellow of having borrowed without acknowledgment not only the meter, but also " many of the most striking incidents of the Finnish Epic and transferred them to the American Indians." In England a similar war raged, with most of the critics on the poet's side. The author was keenly affected by these shafts, and hardly can be pictured in the mood attributed to him many years later by a Mr. F. A. Underwood, who claimed that being informed by his publisher of some particularly savage attack, Longfellow would ask in a casual way how the book was selling and being told, would say quietly: " Very well, then don't you think we had better let these critics go on advertising it? " Though he found some consolation in these sales and let the critics rage, he called the Washington newspaper attack by T. C. P. " truly one of the greatest literary outrages I ever heard of," and found it humiliating to think how many newspapers would give currency to the slander and not to the very good answer by Cowey. He himself never made an open reply to the charge of plagiarism, but he was exceedingly glad when the accusations were drowned out by the increasing volume of hearty praise.

The popularity of the poem was in no sense checked by these criticisms, as one edition followed another in rapid succession both in England and America. Within four months after the publication of *Hiawatha*, Boettger brought out a German translation, and a year later appeared the version of Freiligrath, whose work won high praise from the overjoyed poet. A Latin translation, " Carmen Hiawathae," was issued in 1862 by Professor Newman, and the following year saw the poem rendered into Russian.

The meter of *Hiawatha* proved to be a dividing point among the critics. As already pointed out, it is an imitation of the rhymeless trochaic dimeter of the Finnish epic *Kalevala*, with its parallelism or repetitions, though Longfellow contended that the parallelism is as much the characteristic of Indian as of Finnish song. Some critics scored him heavily for borrowing the form from another poem without acknowledging the fact. However, even the hostile reviewer in *Blackwood's Magazine* admitted that if Longfellow were the first to make the measure popular, it mattered very little who invented it; to talk of plagiarism would be absurd. Some found the measure monotonous, but as T. W. Parsons, the " poet " of *The Wayside Inn,* wrote the author: " The measure is monotonous, — admitted; but it is truly Indian. It is child-like, and suited to the savage ear. In your hands it does not weary so long as the interest of the narration is kept up. If that subsides, perhaps the ear becomes a little impatient. . . ." Others there were who, without shutting their eyes to the ever present danger of monotony, pointed out the peculiar felicity of the measure. Thus Dr. Oliver Wendell Holmes comments at length upon the form: " The eight-syllable trochaic verse of Hiawatha, like the eight-syllable iambic verse of the Lady of the Lake and others of Scott's poems, has a fatal facility, which I have elsewhere endeavored to explain on physiological principles. The recital of each line uses up the air of one natural expiration, so that we read, as we naturally do, eighteen or twenty lines in a minute without disturbing the normal rhythm of breathing, which is also eighteen to twenty breaths to the minute. The standing objection to this is, that it makes the octosyllabic verse too easy writing and too slipshod reading. Yet in this most frequently criticized piece of verse-work, the poet has shown a subtle sense of the requirements of his simple story of a primitive race, in choosing the most fluid of measures that lets the thought run through it in easy sing-song, such as oral tradition would be sure to find on the lips of the story-tellers of the wigwam." An English critic detects in the rise and fall of the verse something of forest music, expressing, as it were, the swaying of trees, the whirr of wings, the pattering of leaves, and the trickling of water. A French writer compares " the melody of the verse, rapid and monotonous, to the voice of nature, which never fatigues us, though continually repeating the same sound. Two or three notes compose the whole music of the poem, melodious and limited as the song of a bird." By another critic the verse is called sweet and simple and full of local and national color. Such simplicity of course renders the style attractive to children, with whom the poem has always been a great favorite.

The chief sources of *Hiawatha* Longfellow himself pointed out in the Notes to the poem, without, however, mentioning the *Kalevala*. The charge that he had imitated that poem, and borrowed its spirit and many of the most striking incidents he branded as absurd. Rather indignantly he writes Charles Sumner: " I can give chapter and verse for these legends. I know the *Kalevala* very well; and that some of its legends *resemble* the Indian stories preserved by Schoolcraft is very true. But the idea of making me responsible for that is too ludicrous." It can, of course, not be denied that the two poems contain quite a number of passages strikingly similar, even in expression, eloquent testimony to the fact that the Finnish epic furnished Longfellow with valuable suggestions, even for some of his finest and best known lines.

Thus, for instance, the warning of Hiawatha's grandmother and of Ahti's mother as to the rank and the tribal affiliation of the bride is similar, and in each case is disregarded by the suitor. The arrowmaker's daughter and the lovely maiden of Pohyola also bear a striking resemblance:

" Minnehaha, Laughing Water, Handsomest of all the women. I will bring her to your wigwam, She shall run upon your errands, Be your starlight, moonlight, firelight, Be the sunlight of my people! "	Fairest maiden of Pohyola, Daughter of the earth and ocean. From her temples beams the moonlight, From her breast, the gleam of sunshine, From her forehead shines the rainbow, On her neck, the seven starlets, And the Great Bear from her shoulder.

The wedding festival of both Hiawatha and of Ilmarinen have not a few features in common. And Chibiabos is evidently modelled after the Finnish minstrel with his harp of magic:

He the best of all musicians, He the sweetest of all singers. . . . . When he sang, the village listened; All the warriors gathered round him, All the women came to hear him; Now he stirred their souls to passion, Now he melted them to pity.	Wainamoinen, ancient minstrel, Played one day, and then a second, Played the third from morn till even. There was neither man nor hero, Neither ancient dame nor maiden, Not in Metsola a daughter, Whom he did not touch to weeping.

And finally, the reader who has been struck by the close resemblance in spirit and phrase of numerous passages, notes at the end similar elements:

Westward, westward Hiawatha
Sailed into the fiery sunset,
Sailed into the purple vapors,
Sailed into the dusk of evening.
....

Thus departed Hiawatha,
Hiawatha the Beloved,
In the glory of the sunset,
In the purple mists of evening,
To the regions of the home-wind,
Of the Northwest wind Keewaydin,
To the Islands of the Blessed.

Thus the ancient Wainamoinen,
In his copper-banded vessel,
Left his tribe in Kalevala,
Sailing o'er the rolling billows,
Sailing through the azure vapors,
Sailing through the dusk of evening,
Sailing to the fiery sunset,
To the higher-landed regions,
To the lower verge of heaven.

For his basic material, however, the poet is mainly indebted to Henry Rowe Schoolcraft's *Algic Researches, comprising Inquiries respecting the Mental Characteristics of the North American Indians,* with its tales and legends, to *Oneóta, or Characteristics of the Red Race of America,* and to his great work *History, Condition, and Prospects of the Indian Tribes of the United States,* volume III of which contains the Iroquois form of the Hiawatha tradition. The legendary matter dealing with the Algonquin hero Manabozho, Michabou, or the Great Hare, proved difficult to disentangle on account of inconsistent and contradictory details, as will be seen from the following serviceable summary given by Parkman: " As each species of animal has its archetype or king, so, among the Algonquins, Manabozho is king of all these animal kings. Tradition is diverse as to his origin. According to the most current belief, his father was the West Wind, and his mother a great-granddaughter of the Moon. His character is worthy of such a parentage. Sometimes he is a wolf, a bird, or a gigantic hare, surrounded by a court of quadrupeds; sometimes he appears in human shape, majestic in stature and wondrous in endowment, a mighty magician, a destroyer of serpents and evil manitous; sometimes he is a vain or treacherous imp, full of childish whims and petty trickery, the butt and victim of men, beasts, and spirits. His powers of transformation are without limit; his curiosity and malice are insatiable; and the numberless legends of which he is the hero the greater part are as trivial as they are incoherent. It does not appear that Manabozho was ever an object of worship; yet despite his absurdity, tradition declares him to be chief among Manitous; in short, the Great Spirit." According to Schoolcraft, " The conception of the character reveals rather a monstrosity than a deity, — displaying in strong colors far more of the dark and incoherent acts of a spirit of carnality than the benevolent deeds of a god. . . . Nothing was too low or trivial for him to engage in, nor too high or difficult for him to attempt."

To serve his artistic purpose of unity, the poet eliminated the trickster elements inconsistent with the dignity and seriousness of the culture hero. Such diverse and inharmonious qualities might not have struck the Indian as incongruous, but they almost certainly would have deeply offended the esthetic sensibilities of the white reader. Bayard Taylor, who had gone over the same material for a literary purpose, highly appreciated the artist's task and success in choosing from the mass in which the absurd and grotesque is mingled with the simple and characteristic, especially since few of the legends appeal to the sympathies of the white race. Longfellow likewise discarded all those incidents in which Manabozho appears as the Great Rabbit. In addition, he endowed Hiawatha with human attributes, and at times, as exhibited by his pathetic helplessness in the presence of the dying Minnehaha, reduced the heroic figure to that of a mere mortal.

After hesitating for some time between Manabozho and Hiawatha as the name of the hero, Longfellow at length settled upon the more euphonious Iroquoian term. Like Schoolcraft he committed the egregious blunder of believing the two to be identical, when according to more recent investigations they had no connection whatsoever. Hiawatha was the name of a noted reformer, statesman, legislator, magician, and according to tradition, also a prophet, who flourished about 1570, and with the help of Dekanawida, a Mohawk chief, succeeded in forming the celebrated League of the Iroquois, the Confederation of the Five Nations. By birth probably a Mohawk, he began his work of abolishing intra-tribal blood feuds and inaugurating other desirable reforms among the Onondagas, but was at first successfully opposed by their warlike chief and tyrant Atotarho. Only when most of the tribes had been won over, did the wily Atotarho deem it wise to join a confederacy which established law and convention for the common welfare. Since Hiawatha in the eyes of the masses had thus proved himself superior to the Onondaga chief reputed to be a great sorcerer, the deeds properly belonging to the chief gods of the Iroquois, particularly to Terahonhiwagon, an anthropomorphic deity, were in course of time attributed to him. This confusion in the minds of the Iroquois in New York finds a ready explanation in the fact that the tribes migrating to Canada after the Revolutionary War had taken the wampum records along, which left the remaining Iroquois without a fixed tradition. When Schoolcraft became acquainted with these mystic legends misapplied to Hiawatha, he confused him with Manabozho, the great Algonquin or Chippewa deity. While thus the basic material of the Algonquin cycle and the Iroquois cycle of legends contain some similar elements, Longfellow's poem dealing mainly with the Manabozho or Algonquin legends has not a single fact or fiction relating to the great historic Iroquoian reformer and statesman Hiawatha.

To an ethnologist this unwitting error of Longfellow's is distressing and nothing less than astounding, since the great Iroquois Hiawatha of Central New York is made to live and move among inveterate Algonquin enemies on the southern shore of Lake Superior. His mother also bears inappropriately the Dakotah or Sioux name Wenondah, while Manabozho's brother Chibiabos appears in the poem as a friendly bard. On the other hand, the arrowmaker's daughter of the Sioux is rightly named Minnehaha, " laughing water," in the Dakotah tongue.

As seems natural in view of the chief sources of the poem, the names with few exceptions are of Ojibway or Chippewa origin. Schoolcraft's own accomplished wife was a half-breed Chippewa, and the *Algic Researches,* which formed such a mine of material for the poet, is largely based upon her legendary Indian lore. Another source derived from the same tribe was laid under heavy contribution. Longfellow himself speaks of working away with

Tanner, whose *Narrative of the Captivity and Adventures of John Tanner During Thirty Years Residence among the Indians in the Interior of North America* had appeared in 1830. Pages 294–312 contain a " Catalogue of Plants and Animals Found in the Country of the Ojibbeways; with English names, as far as these could be ascertained." When one compares the names in Longfellow's poem with those appearing in the Catalogue, it is clear that many of them have been culled from this convenient list.

As already pointed out, *The Song of Hiawatha* always has been and continues to be a favorite with the children. The reasons for this are not far to seek. The ideas fall into convenient groups, and the form is simple enough for a child's mind to grasp. The human figures with their romantic interest are perennially fascinating. The hero with his miraculous powers and the heroine attractive as a princess in all her womanly loveliness cast a magic spell over an imagination not yet enthralled by sober reason. While the singer with his art charms the youthful mind, the mischief maker could not but appeal to the instinctive love of fun. Likewise the strong man Kwasind by his very presence and his deeds enhances the interest aroused in the susceptible nature of the young. No wonder that this biographical poem with its moving and lifelike figures enacting a story should make a strong appeal to the awakening imagination of our youth. And this appeal is measurably strengthened by the picture of nature, and the birds and animals, which are often shown in interesting and novel situations and not seldom endowed with the power of speech. Thus a combination of elements conspires to make the poem palatable to the child's taste.

Longfellow himself speaks of *The Song of Hiawatha* as an " Indian Edda," or the saga of a legendary hero sent as a benefactor to the American Indians. From his remark in a letter to Freiligrath that Hiawatha is " a kind of American Prometheus " we may reasonably infer that the so-called epic element interested the poet most, though it should of course be remembered that the whole " is purely in the realm of fancy," with authentic Indian history playing but an insignificant part. In the Introduction,

Nawadaha or Schoolcraft in the Vale of Tawasentha, that is, in his native village of Hamilton in Albany County, New York, sings of Hiawatha as a means

> " That the tribes of men might prosper,
> That he might advance his people,"

and those who love a nation's legends and the ballads of a people, which like voices from afar call to us to pause and listen, are urged to be attentive.

In the dramatic scene laid in the Pipestone peace country, which is based upon Catlin's account of the calumet quarry in Minnesota, the coming of the deliverer of the people is prophesied. This introduction of the hero at the very beginning through legendary material in no way connected with the Manabozho story is nothing short of masterly. Perhaps the suggestion was derived from Hiawatha's appeal for unity to the Iroquois tribes on the eve of his departure, and related in the third volume of Schoolcraft's great work. This appeal, artfully expanded and generalized, the poet skilfully put at the beginning instead of at the end of his poem. The various tribes, representative of the natives on the American continent, are grouped for the great council that is to stamp out the feud of the ages, the hereditary hatred, and the ancestral thirst of vengeance — a reflection of the chronic hostility and warfare that seems to have made peace and tranquillity among the Indians an unrealized dream. It is splendid advice the Master of Life imparts with his reminder,

> " All your strength is in your union,
> All your danger is in discord,"

which becomes an unheeded prophetic warning in connection with the announcement of the deliverer,

> " If you listen to his counsels,
> You will multiply and prosper;
> If his warnings pass unheeded,
> You will fade away and perish! "

The child of wonder quickly enters on his career of the Messiah. When his father, the fierce and ruthless Mudjekeewis, has outlined the work to be accomplished, he himself in fasting prays like king Solomon, not for personal favors,

> " But for profit of the people,
> For advantage of the nations,"

the object to be gained only by struggle and labor. In that very fasting and wrestling with Mondamin, the maize or corn, he secures from the Great Spirit as a new gift to the nations the food essential to the welfare of the people. With his two good friends, Chibiabos and Kwasind, he consults often,

> Pondering much and much contriving,
> How the tribes of men might prosper.

And his sailing of the birch bark canoe has no other purpose than that the strong man Kwasind help him to clear the river of the sunken logs and sandbars in order to make its passage safe and certain for the people. Hiawatha's fishing with its object of securing the much needed oil for the winter marks a step in his development as the nation's provider. Thus strengthened and encouraged he is enabled to slay the merciless and mightiest of magicians, Pearl-Feather,

> " Him, who sent the fiery fever,
> Sent the white fog from the fen-lands,
> Sent disease and death among us."

The wealth of the slain enemy and all the trophies of the battle the leader divides and shares with the people. Even his wooing and marriage, though also the result of personal affection and desire, is statesmanlike. He defends his choice of Minnehaha from among the once hostile Dakotahs for the very reason

> " That our tribes might be united,
> That old feuds may be forgotten,
> And old wounds be healed forever! "

Before the ancient arrowmaker and his lovely daughter he rejoices that after many years of strife and bloodshed peace at last prevails between the Ojibways and the Dakotahs. In his proposal the desire to cement that peace by the personal union is uppermost:

> "That this peace may last forever,
> And our hands be clasped more closely,
> And our hearts be more united,
> Give me as my wife this maiden,
> Minnehaha, Laughing Water,
> Loveliest of Dakotah women!"

Hiawatha's Wedding-Feast with its gayety and the Song of the Evening Star indicates that the bride from the late enemy tribe is well received, and an almost idyllic time follows, when

> Buried was the bloody hatchet,
> Buried was the dreadful war-club,
> Buried were all warlike weapons,
> And the war-cry was forgotten.
> There was peace among the nations;
> Unmolested roved the hunters,
> Built the birch canoe for sailing,
> Caught the fish in lake and river,
> Shot the deer and trapped the beaver;
> Unmolested worked the women,
> Made the sugar from the maple,
> Gathered wild rice in the meadows,
> Dressed the skins of deer and beaver.

And as Hiawatha had taught them, they cultivate the maize, which the blessing of the young bride is supposed to make more fruitful. The statesman is likewise interested in the preservation of the deeds of the fathers, pondering and musing in the forest on the welfare of his people, and to this end he instructs them in all the mysteries of painting and the art of picture writing.

With Hiawatha's Lamentation begin his earnest, but in the end ineffectual, efforts to protect his people from harm and danger. The personal grief over the death of his fellow worker and friend Chibiabos foreshadows the heavy clouds of adversity soon to darken the skies. Recovering from his grief, Hiawatha's thoughts return to his people, and everywhere he is teaching men the use of simples and of the antidotes for poisons, and as the cure of all diseases the sacred art of healing. The mischief maker Pau-Puk-Keewis, who had introduced the demoralizing game of hazard and even insulted his own person, he at length succeeds in destroying.

But disasters begin to arrive in troops. Kwasind is slain by the little people. The ominous ghosts of the departed ask that the lamentations for the dead cease, and that more appropriate provision be made for the journey to the spirit world. As a vague indication of what is to come, he is admonished not to fail in the greater trial and not to faint in the harder struggle still before him. Famine and fever arrive as unwelcome guests, and even the mighty Hiawatha, empty-handed, heavy-hearted, cries in vain to the Great Spirit that his beloved Minnehaha be saved. Broken in spirit, he vows to follow her departed soul as soon as his earthly task is completed. He need not wait long. With returning spring Iagoo brings his unbelievable stories of the white men. But Hiawatha affirms what the far-traveller has seen, asks that the messengers of the Great Spirit be welcomed as brothers, and prophetically speaks of the westward marches of the unknown crowded nations with their industrious thrift. But

> " Then a darker, drearier vision
> Passed before me, vague and cloud-like;
> I beheld our nations scattered,
> All forgetful of my counsels,
> Weakened, warring with each other;
> Saw the remnants of our people
> Sweeping westward, wild and woeful,
> Like the cloud-rack of a tempest,
> Like the withered leaves of autumn! "

Golden swarms of bees as forerunners of the whites soon make their appearance, followed by the Black-Robe chief, who in his capacity of priest and prophet offers them a new religion. Hiawatha asks that his guests be treated kindly, and after admonishing his people to listen to the words of wisdom and truth spoken by the strangers, departs on his long journey. Like one not of this earth and for this world, he sails into the fiery sunset in the West, to the land of the Here-after.

This epic element depicts the imagined history of the aborigines from hunting and fishing to the beginnings of agriculture and the development of art, medicine, religion, and literature. The subdued tragic element becomes stronger with the passing of time, the inexplicable departure of the Messiah, when his presence and guidance are needed most, foreshadowing the decline and fall of the red man. While in the main the poem is admirably conceived, the last part with its abruptness and weakness seriously mars it as a work of art. Longfellow himself felt this blemish when he admitted to Freiligrath: " The contact of Saga and History is too sudden. But how could I remedy it unless I made the poem very much longer? I felt the clash and the concussion, but could not prevent or escape it."

The allegorical significance of certain parts of the poem, such as the strife between night and day, summer and winter, appears generally on the surface and impresses even the casual reader. The element of anthropomorphic forces is skilfully introduced in conformity with the beliefs held by primitive man, and especially with the manito worship of the Indians. It is only with advancing civilization that these conceptions fade in the light of a more rational viewpoint. Thus there is maintained a consistent attitude reflecting the prevailing state of mind.

However, an element that changes the whole spirit of the original material and makes it particularly appealing to the younger mind is the introduction of the romantic. In the original this element is negligible. What Longfellow embodies in two lengthy cantos, the legend records in one short sentence: " Having accomplished his victories over the reptiles, Manabozho returned to his former place of dwelling and married the arrowmaker's daughter." But this inserted matter is precisely what interests the modern reader most. When we remember that Hiawatha's Wooing, a perfect gem, with the Blessing of the Cornfield's, the Ghosts, and the Famine, is one of the most successful and the most charming parts of the poem, it is clearly seen that not a little emphasis is placed upon sentiments dealing with the romantic and the domestic relations. While by these inventions Longfellow invested the poem with dignity and glamour, and made it palatable to the civilized reader, one cannot but agree with Stith Thompson that in this very way he has done violence both to the original myth and the spirit of the life which he depicts in *The Song of Hiawatha*.

On the whole, literary critics have given high praise to the charm of the poem, only comparatively few dismissing it in a condescending manner. Even ethnologists like Ten Kate, though shocked by the ethnographic errors and the many untenable details, testify to the spirit of the Song as being decidedly Indian. Bancroft says that " as a whole it represents wonderfully well the infantile character of Indian life when the inferior animals were half and half the equal companions of man, and external nature was his bosom friend." He tells the author that he has made everything of his subject which it permitted. T. W. Parsons admires the boldness with which the author walked lyre in hand among these poor painted children of the western forest and learned and taught us their simple melodies. The French critic previously cited for his admiration of the melody of the verse in his Gallic enthusiasm points to other qualities that give it a high rank among poetic productions, both ancient and modern: " The feeling for nature that pervades the poem is at once most refined and most familiar. The poet knows how to give, as a modern, voices to all the inanimate objects of nature; he knows the language of the birds, he understands the murmur of the wind amongst the leaves, he interprets the voices of the running streams; and yet, notwithstanding this poetic subtlety, he never turns aside to minute descriptions, nor attempts to prolong, by reflection, the emotion excited. His poem, made with exquisite art, has thus a double character: it is Homeric from the precision, simplicity, and familiarity of its images, and modern from the vivacity of its impressions, and from the lyrical spirit that breathes in every page."

Emerson's shrewd Yankee comment, while kind and in the main affirmative, is nevertheless a bit condescending and not without some misgivings: " I find this Indian poem very wholesome; sweet and wholesome as maize; very proper and pertinent for us to read, and showing a kind of manly sense of duty in the poet to write. The dangers of the Indians are, that they are really savage, have poor, small, sterile heads, — no thoughts; and you must deal very roundly with them, and find them in brains. And I blamed your tenderness now and then, as I read in accepting a legend or a song, when they had so little to give. I should hold you to your creative function on such occasions. But the costume and machinery, on the whole, is sweet and melancholy, and agrees with the American landscape."

In appraising Longfellow's poem as a contribution to American literature, Henry Rowe Schoolcraft, whose writings had furnished most of the material, places it high above previous productions. He claims that in spite of some cleverness and some successful passages in every attempt from the day of *Atala* and *Yamoyden* to Mr. Street's poem of Iroquois life, there had been general failure of popular attractiveness. According to him, one of the great faults of authors had been treating the Indian as a stoic through every scene, thus disconnecting him from human sympathies. People may admire fortitude, wisdom, and eloquence, but they can only love, or be deeply interested in, the bosom that has kind affections, whether the expression be simple and rude, or highly refined. " The Indian must be treated as he is. He is a warrior in war, a savage in revenge, a stoic in endurance, a wolverine in suppleness and cunning. But he is also a father at the head of his lodge, a patriot in the love of his country, a devotee to noble sports in his adherence to the chase, a humanitarian in his kindness and an object of noble grief at the grave of his friend or kindred. He is as simple as a child, yet with the dignity of a man in his wigwam." In his opinion, no attempt had been made before *Hiawatha* to show this. In order to avoid the direct issue with Indian character, the aim had been to excite interest by taking the hero or heroine from the half-breed class, with the result that we have had a half-breed class of poetry. He does not assert that success cannot be attained in this line, only it has not yet been demonstrated. It could not be supposed that Roderick Dhu, a Highlander, would in the hands of Sir Walter Scott have been made more attractive by taking from him the strong marks of full-blooded clanship. "If the Indian is ever to be made the material of popular poetry, it must be the full, free, wild Indian, — the independent rover of the forests and prairies, who loves the chase, loves liberty, and hates labor and the white man, under the impression that the latter symbolizes the advent of his curse and downfall."

Schoolcraft points to the fact that among the Indians some persons at burials recite the praises of the dead and cut the hieroglyphics on their wooden graveposts; others are skilled in religious, mystic, or elegiac songs or noted for reciting legends and stories. " To assemble these on grand occasions, with their rude instruments of music, appears to me the most eligible mode of procuring a correct and pleasing delineation of the picturesque and social scenes and beliefs of aboriginal life. For Hiawatha to collect together this poetic force on the occasion of his wedding, was certainly a most felicitous and eligible method of celebrating his nuptials." Viewing the production as a whole, Schoolcraft considers the thoughts highly poetical, and the rhythm most harmonious. By exhibiting those fresh tableaux of Indian life, the author has according to his opinion laid the reading world under great obligations, a criticism with which not a few discriminating readers will heartily agree.

Longfellow's *Song of Hiawatha* is unquestionably the longest successful poetic delineation of the American Indian thus far. Though unity in a measurable degree is achieved only by doing violence to the basic material, true art demanded the elimination of the incongruous. As indicated by Schoolcraft, we find depicted the free and independent native, just entering the dawn of civilization, and uncorrupted by contact with the whites. He is shown in his home and domestic relations, in his social and community life. His existence is not without the stress and strain which forest and prairie life imposes upon the savage, and which without farsighted leaders would end in disaster for large numbers.

In the main the picture is somewhat idyllic, for the rudimentary cultural elements fill the foreground, while the sterner and actually more prominent warlike elements are toned down or entirely omitted. If thus less realistic than many might have wished, the reason is to be found in the poet's kind and delicate nature, and in his desire to present the more lovable and appealing traits of savage life in a setting of story and song. Under such circumstances hate, brutality, and bloodshed are relegated to a past and a future that in their stark reality form the dark and ominous background from which the storm may suddenly burst upon a happy present which is nothing but a temporary lull from a tempest threatening misery and destruction. In spite of many bright and even gay colors, the somberer hues foreshadow the tragic end of a race whose intra-fratricidal strife rendered it incapable of beating off the impending attack of civilized man.

CHAPTER XV

THOREAU — FRIEND OF THE NATIVE

According to his intimate friend Channing, the last distinct utterance of the dying Henry David Thoreau (1817–1862) was the word " Indians." As that idea filled his soul to overflowing in the parting moments, so it directed many of his activities especially during the last twenty years of a life devoted to the study of nature and man. It may truly be said that the red man as the native American had become a master passion with one of America's greatest prose writers. He lighted up his morning, and he cast a ray of sunshine into the soul of the dying man. Even when pulmonary consumption sapped his strength, he worked " steadily at the completion of his papers to his last hours, or so long as he could hold the pencil in his trembling fingers," in order that he might get ready for publication *The Maine Woods,* in which the Indian plays such a large part.

In addition to *The Maine Woods,* 1864, and a few references in *Walden,* 1854, and *A Week on the Concord and Merrimac Rivers,* 1849, Thoreau's interest in the Indian is recorded in more than two hundred passages in his *Journal* and in eleven unpublished notebooks of about 2800 pages and approximately 540,000 words, filled with " Extracts relating to the Indians." During the last twelve years of his life he busied himself collecting material from all available sources for an elaborate work on the aborigines of America. So occupied was he with the collection of this Indian material, literary and otherwise, that he declined the appeal of Mrs. G. L. Stearns to write the life of his idol John Brown.

Already as a youth Thoreau had become imbued with the subject. With their heads full of the past and its remains, he and his brother John were accustomed to hunt for relics of the departed race in the neighborhood of Concord. He tells us for instance in the *Journal* that one Sunday evening nearing the brow of a hill which formed the bank of the Swamp Bridge Creek, inspired by his theme he broke forth into an extravagant eulogy of those savage times, using most violent gesticulations by way of illustration. " There on Nawshawtuct," said I, " was their lodge, the rendezvous of their tribe, and yonder, on Clamshell Hill, their feasting ground. There was, no doubt, a favorite haunt; here on this brow was an eligible lookout post. How often have they stood on this very spot, at this very hour, when the sun was sinking behind yonder woods and gilding with his last rays the waters of the Musketaquid, and pondered the day's success or the morrow's prospects, or communed with the spirit of the fathers gone before them to the land of the shades! "

It is characteristic of him that as a schoolmaster on the weekly excursions in the neighborhood he introduced his charges to the lore of the Indians. On these walks, his biographer Sanborn tells us, there was much instructive talk about the Indians who formerly lived or hunted there. During one of the expeditions Henry Warren noticed an instance of Henry's close observation in the matter of Indian antiquities, of which both brothers had become connoisseurs. He uncovered at what looked to him an appropriate setting one of the rude fireplaces of the Indians, but soon " he carefully covered up his find and replaced the turf, — not wishing to have the domestic altar of the aborigines profaned by mere curiosity." This reverent attitude toward the native American was a trait that clung to him to the end of his life.

Thoreau's interest in all that pertained to the vanishing race of America prompted longer trips which brought him nearer their hunting-grounds and in close contact with them. At that time the state of Maine was almost an undiscovered country, admirably suited for his investigations, for according to him, though the railroad and the telegraph had been established on the shores of Maine, " the Indian still looks out from her interior mountains over all these to the sea . . . a wilderness where the Indian still hunts and the moose runs wild." If we disallow the dubious claim that during his college vacation in 1835 he taught in Maine, his first visit to the state occurred in 1838. Then in August 1846 came a memorable trip to the Maine wilderness and Mount Ktaadn, the second highest mountain in New England. Another extended visit occurred in 1853 under the guidance of Joe Aitteon, son of an Indian governor, and finally in 1857 Thoreau made what he calls " a quite profitable journey, chiefly from associating with an intelligent Indian," Joe Polis, the chief man of the Penobscot tribe. During the interval there were numerous other trips which helped to give him a firmer grasp of the subject. The more extensive ones were a visit to Cape Cod in 1849, and to Canada in 1850. While the Cape Cod trip may not have been very profitable as regards the Indian, the passages in which he comments in *A Yankee in Canada* especially upon the differences in the treatment of the Indians by the French and the English testify to the value of that journey for his particular purpose. He probably also became acquainted with the St. Francis and Abenaki tribes, and went over some of the ground traversed by the Jesuit fathers, whose *Relations* he prized as an authentic source.

About 1850 Thoreau began the collection of material for a great work on the Indians, and continued the ingathering till his fatal sickness in November 1860, in all filling eleven notebooks. With a few exceptions the material consists of extracts from more than two hundred writers, and is drawn from the most diverse sources. As a rule he copies verbatim, using quotation marks, though at other times he gives the substance of the writer in a somewhat condensed form. The great majority of the works consulted are written in English. The few Latin authors utilized he translated without difficulty, while the large number of French books extracted he read with great facility, for he gives a good English rendition, here and there adding the original terms in parentheses.

The authors consulted were not uncritically copied, but scrutinized with great care. Baron Hontan's *Voyages* aroused Thoreau's suspicion; and in the case of not a few writers he successfully advances the charge of plagiarism. Fabulous accounts, whether written by Indians or whites, receive their proper evaluation. His unprejudiced mind doubted the affinities said to exist between the Indian and other languages, as the evidence presented seemed to him far from convincing. Omission of interesting material as well as indefinite statements were certain to draw his comment.

Thoreau's book evidently was to be a comprehensive one, judging from the list of " subjects " drawn up and the material dealing with most of the important tribes of the American continent, naturally more varied and abundant in regard to North America, and especially so for the present area of the United States. He quotes liberally from descriptions of the New England Indians from the earliest times down to the 19th century, drawing upon town histories as well as upon the more general and pretentious works. The Dutch writers and those dealing with the Virginia Indians are well represented, in the latter case Captain John Smith, Bartram's, Kalm's, and Lawson's travels and Jefferson's notes furnishing most of the material.

While the aborigines of the Atlantic Coast fascinated the investigator, those farther inland likewise proved to be of absorbing interest, for the Iroquois confederacy, the Delawares, and other tribes all receive detailed attention. The *Jesuit Relations*, Loskiel's and Heckewelder's works; and Schoolcraft's *Algic Researches* and *Oneóta, or Characteristics of the Red Race of America* were fruitful sources of information. For the tribes of the Great Lakes region and the Upper Mississippi especially Thoreau utilized Henry R. Schoolcraft's great work *History, Condition, and Prospects of the Indian Tribes of the United States* in six volumes, a publication under Congressional auspices, which he prized greatly on account of the abundant and apparently reliable material it furnished. From it he quoted more extensively than from any other single work, drawing upon the different volumes as they appeared and filling two hundred and twelve pages in his notebooks. If we take into consideration the extracts from the books mentioned above and the *Expedition Through the Upper Mississippi to Itaska Lake in 1832,* Henry R. Schoolcraft is for Thoreau as for Longfellow the most fruitful source, serving as a veritable mine of precious ore.

The mound builders with their ancient monuments time and again are represented in the extracts. While the Rocky Mountain region furnishes some exceedingly bright pages, the Pacific Coast tribes receive relatively meager attention. Just then the Southwest was being opened up by American explorations, and judging from newspaper clippings and reports of lectures embodied in the notes, Thoreau followed closely what seemed to be marvellous developments in the Pueblo region. The Southern tribes, especially those of the lower Mississippi valley, are well covered by extracts drawn chiefly from French books.

The Indians in the territory now mainly embodied in Canada were to Thoreau an object of extreme interest, the early French voyagers and explorers Cartier and Champlain, and the missionary Charlevoix being quoted at length. The most valuable material, however, he discovered in the *Relations* or reports of the Jesuits, clearly shown by the extensive extracts that fill three hundred and thirty pages of his notebooks. He covered fairly well the *Relations* from 1632–1690, using in practically every case the French original, which he translated into English, adding here and there a French word or phrase in parentheses. It is clear that he regarded these documents as reasonably authentic, and highly respected the writers and the whole order as benefactors of the Indians, for in the *Journal* under date of January 22, 1852, he pays their work this fine tribute: " That in the preaching or the mission of the Jesuits in Canada was their sincerity. The savages were not poor observers or reasoners. The priests were, therefore, sure of success, for they had paid the price of it."

Even the inhabitants of the Arctic North were drawn into the scope of Thoreau's investigations, likewise those nearest the South Pole, and in fact all the inhabitants of South America. The ancient Peruvians and the Toltecs with their civilization especially attracted his attention. And primitive people wherever found are mentioned for the sake of comparison, if for nothing else. The aborigines of the West Indies and of Australia, negro life in different parts of Africa, customs of the Egyptians, ancient and modern, the South Sea Islanders — all come under his scrutinizing gaze. Everywhere his comparative sense is alert in order that he may detect similarities between the relics of non-Indians and those of his beloved red men.

In his search for likely material Thoreau overlooked few

sources. Clippings from newspapers are found in all the notebooks. As he owned only a comparatively small number of the books utilized, a fact which may in part at least account for the copious extracts made, he noted carefully where certain works might be found, whether in the Harvard College Library, much used by him, in other libraries, in bookstores, or elsewhere. Lists of books appear on the last pages of his notebooks, the results of his inquiries and studies often being given later. He is anxious to work as faithfully and conscientiously as time and circumstances permitted, and in a particular case expresses satisfaction with the result achieved.

The question as to what Indian subjects interested Thoreau, and what kinds of extracts he made is partly answered by the fact that his range is extremely wide, covering practically the whole field. Not only sober histories, but stories of captivities and books on games such as Frederick Gerstaecker's *Wild Sports in the Far West* and Mayne Reid's works contributed their share toward piling up the material for a comprehensive and all-inclusive work. Descriptions of the customs, manners, and the mode of living of the natives fill many pages. Food, clothing, and shelter as well as what pertains to the mental and religious life receive careful attention. Although the table of contents drawn up for the proposed book points out what subjects he intended to present, it does not specifically indicate the fact that everywhere Thoreau looked at the red man with the eyes of the anthropologist, the naturalist, and the literary man. The picturesque and striking especially caught his eye. Illustrations in the books consulted he tried to reproduce, and though often crude, his efforts serve the purpose, with here and there some bordering on the artistic. Maps likewise appealed to him as a valuable means of description, and in numerous instances, as in the case of Schoolcraft's great work, he has drawn a copy on tissue paper.

As a rule the natives appear in their environment, the fauna and flora bulking large in the notebooks. Thoreau is unflagging in copying descriptions of the animals prevalent in the forests and on the prairies of North America, especially those that bear an intimate relation to the red man. The muskrat and the beaver;

the fox, the wolf, and the bear; the deer, the moose, and the buffalo enliven many pages. Delightfully he speculates about the ancestry of the dog, the early Indians' domesticated animal, his faithful companion and patient burden bearer. And then the description of plants! There are dozens of passages on tobacco, on the pumpkin, on the gourd, on all kinds of berries, blueberries and huckleberries as the author's favorites being especially prominent. These descriptions of plants are drawn from various sources, such as the *Jesuit Relations* and other incidental descriptions of Indian life and customs, with an occasional brief discussion by Thoreau himself thrown in. But he also turns to specific accounts, of which he has utilized a great many. Among them he valued especially Loudon's *Arboretum,* of which, after thinking of its purchase and saving up the money for years, he made himself a master.

In the two great literary controversies of that time, one raging about the source of Longfellow's *Hiawatha* and the other about the parentage of Cooper's Indians, Thoreau seems to have been a silent but interested spectator eagerly following developments. The chivalrous red men that enliven the pages of Cooper were criticized by Governor Cass and others as the product of the author's fertile imagination and as dream children that were total strangers to the forest. The same criticism, since Cooper had at least partly based his works upon him, was hurled against the Rev. John Heckewelder and his *History, Manners, and Customs of the Indian Nations Who Once Inhabited Pennsylvania and the Neighboring States,* in which the Moravian missionary had, a few years earlier, described the mission of his denomination among the Delawares. An article in the *North American Review* of January 1826, in the opinion of Thoreau composed by Cass, was especially trenchant. It is likely that Thoreau at least partly agreed with the sentiments in the article attributed to Cass, as he quotes at great length from it and previously had remarked about Heckewelder's work: " H. has the tone of a partisan of the Indians — esp. the Delawares — to some extent." But that he nevertheless put great store in him as also in another historian of the Moravian missions, George Henry Loskiel and his *History of the Mission of the United Brethren Among the Indians in North America* may be inferred from the fact that from the former he quotes one hundred and forty-four, and from the latter one hundred and forty-three pages, or two hundred and eighty-seven pages in all. Certain observations of his clearly indicate that he had read the venerable missionary's account with discrimination; and though he noticed Heckewelder's benevolent attitude toward and partisanship of the Delawares, views which color many pages of Cooper's Leatherstocking Tales, he hardly would join in the extremes of Cass's criticism.

Another controversy had flared up through the publication of Longfellow's *Song of Hiawatha* November 10, 1855, with its avowed indebtedness especially to Schoolcraft's *Algic Researches* and his *History, Condition, and Prospects of the Indian Tribes of the United States.* Thoreau quotes verbatim from Volume III of the history the long passage which admittedly formed partly the basis of Longfellow's charming poem. Not unnaturally he was also interested in the origin of the legend and Schoolcraft's account of securing and publishing it. A clipping from the *Detroit Advertiser* of January 25, 1856, found in one of the notebooks, completely demolishes Schoolcraft's claim to have been the first to publish the beautiful legend, as Mr. J. V. H. Clark makes out a good case for himself. Like Longfellow, Thoreau evidently did not even suspect that in *Hiawatha* " there is not a single fact or fiction relating to the great Iroquoian reformer and statesman," Schoolcraft having confused the historic Hiawatha with Manabozho, a Chippewa deity.

Compared with the quoted matter filling approximately 2800 pages, the original material found in the notebooks is negligible in quantity, consisting of some occasional remarks and six pages dealing with various subjects. The Indian, Thoreau claims, was not without guidance in moral matters, reason governing him in the absence of law. And in some respects the white man is not far above the Indian, since both are susceptible to certain psychological influences, the medicine man and the physician playing a similar rôle. The newcomer profited by what the native had done. As to roads, " the white man has but followed in the steps of the Indian. Where the Indian made his portages, the white man made his — or makes the stream more navigable. The New Englander goes to Wisconsin and Iowa by routes which the Indians discovered and used ages ago — and partly perchance the buffaloes used before the Indians. At the points of embarkation or debarkation on the route where was once an Indian is now in many instances no doubt a white man's city — with its wharves." White man's perversity and Indian shrewdness would vie with each other in barter and trade. The red man, of course, could not cope with the ingenuity of the European. Though he had, like the hardy, supple, and cold-tempered muskrat, a strong hold on life, both alike were at last exterminated by the white man's improvements.

It was unfortunate that when after twelve years of ingathering Thoreau had stored away in his eleven notebooks an abundance of varied materials covering practically every phase of a fascinating subject and was about to enrich literature by a work noted for unprejudiced accuracy, sympathetic treatment, and literary quality, a fatal malady should have begun to fasten itself upon him. That illness cut short further work on the Indian material except that the trip to Minnesota for the benefit of his health in the summer of 1861 brought him in contact with the Sioux. As mementos of the visit, the buckskin suit, snowshoes, and a saddle given him by an Indian friend may still be seen at Concord. When his biographer Sanborn remarks that "Thoreau does not seem to have been so much interested in these Indians as in those of Maine," it should be remembered that a man in failing health and exhausted by travel could not give the same attention to a subject that had drawn the robust man into the wilds of Maine four years before. Travel conditions naturally prevented him from keeping a regular journal, and later every available minute and every ounce of the waning strength went into the completion of *The Maine Woods,* with its central figure of Joe Polis. When we compare the rich materials of the eleven manuscript notebooks with the numerous and significant references to the Indians found scattered in the published writings, we cannot but believe that a cruel fate robbed the world of a great work dealing in a sanely realistic yet sympathetic and poetic manner with the child of nature on the American continent, which in the judicious combination of the essential, the striking, and the picturesque would have tended to satisfy alike the scholarly and the æsthetically inclined.

However, though Thoreau's efforts of a dozen years were not destined to be crowned by a finished literary production, the loss is considerably less severe than appears at first sight, for his main thoughts and ideas find expression in *The Maine Woods, Walden,* and *A Week,* and in the more than two hundred references of the *Journal.* The nature of the extracts in the notebooks and the passages in the published works combined furnish an almost complete picture of the deep interest, the thorough knowledge, and the sane attitude of the great poet-naturalist in regard to one of the most important race problems of the New World. As a comprehensive and well rounded treatment of an intriguing subject it deserves nothing less than the closest attention.

With his instinctive love of the native, Thoreau deplores that some poets and historians have spoken slightingly of the Indian as a race so low and brutish that it hardly deserved to be remembered. And in writing their histories of this country they have in a hostile manner disposed of what they looked upon as the refuse of humanity which littered and defiled the shore and the interior. Such a historian, though he may profess more humanity than the trapper, the mountain man, or the gold digger who shoots down a native as a wild beast, really exhibits and practices a similar inhumanity to him, the only difference being that he wields a pen instead of a rifle. Thereby he disregards the spirit of humanity animating both so-called savages and civilized nations, a feeling that should knit them together. As a matter of fact, " the thought of a so-called savage tribe is generally far more just than that of a single civilized man."

How unnatural is such an indifference to fellow beings! Even " the indigenous animals are inexhaustibly interesting to us! How much more then the indigenous man of America! " Granted that the natives are wild men, they are nevertheless much more like ourselves than unlike, and we wish to know what manner of men they were, their mode of life, customs, fancies, and superstitions. Certainly, their fancies and beliefs of the sea and the forest should concern us quite as much as the fables of Oriental nations, for they paddled over the waters and wandered in the woods which now are ours. And those historians who contemptuously assert that the Indian had no religion, might tell us how much more religion they themselves possess.

The marks of this race may be found on every hand, in spite of our poets and philosophers who regret that we have no antiquities in America, no ruins to remind us of the past. "Everywhere in the hills, in the corn and grain land, the earth is strewn with the relics of a race which has vanished as completely as if trodden in with the earth." Wherever one goes, he treads in the tracks of the Indian, and is reminded of his destiny. Now he picks up an arrow; again in scattering his hearthstones with the feet he finds in the embers the enduring implements of the wigwam and the chase. And in planting his corn in the same furrow, he displaces some memorial of his. As he walks the fields, he meditates on that vanished race, and sometimes in his fancy imagines that the crows representing dark-winged spirits rebuke his advance. Nature is the same as of old, but the human figures have changed, and the council house has been displaced by the legislative hall. New eyes give a new aspect to the land, for a country is but in the hearts of its inhabitants. And only so much of Indian America is left as there is of the American Indian in the character of this generation. A significant statement indeed, but only too often ignored.

A great number of the more than two hundred references to Indians in the *Journal* deal with finds of pestles, mortars, axes, shell remains, soapstone pots, and especially arrowheads and Thoreau's elucidating comments. Since the time in the fall of 1837, when he tells us that he found his first arrowheads, till near the close of his life he seems to have made a systematic search for these indications of the departed race. The references are most frequent and numerous during the last ten years, showing how much emphasis he placed upon the subject. He never tires of looking for them: "Many as I have found, methinks the last one gives me about the same delight that the first did."

Not only in corn and grain and potato and bean fields, but in pastures and woods, by woodchucks' holes and pigeon beds, and sometimes in a meadow where a restless cow has pawed the ground, arrowheads meet his searching eye. From ground cultivated for the first time, he, and not the farmer, gathers the first crop. As soon as the sun bares the sandy fields of snow, the hunt begins. " It is one of the regular pursuits of the spring," he tells us. " As much as sportsmen go in pursuit of ducks, and gunners of musquash, and scholars of rare books, and travellers of adventures, and poets of ideas, and all men of money, I go in search of arrowheads when the proper season comes round again. So I help myself to live worthily, and loving my life as I should." His finds he calls the perennial crop of Concord fields, which the melting snow and rain have washed bare. He even confesses: " I feel no desire to go to California or Pike's Peak, but I often think at night with inexpressible satisfaction and yearning of the *arrowheadiferous* sands of Concord. I have often spent whole afternoons, especially in the spring, pacing back and forth over a sandy field, looking for these relics of a race. This is the gold which our sands yield."

No wonder that Thoreau developed an uncanny professional skill in what practically amounted to an occupation. The high sandy places, which the Indians instinctively had picked for their wigwams as the only dry places after the early thaw, richly rewarded him. Frequently he distinguished these localities half a mile off, would go forward and pick up arrowheads. He even claims: " Indeed, I never find a remarkable Indian relic — and I find a good many — but I have first divined its existence and planned the discovery of it. Frequently I have told myself distinctly what it was to be before I found it." This almost sixth sense was the result of long cultivation. Emerson tells us that those pieces of good luck which happen only to good players happened to him, and relates an instance, which Channing also mentions. " In a walk, a companion, a citizen, said, ' I do not see where you find your Indian arrowheads.' Stooping to the ground, Henry picked one up, and presented it to him, crying, ' Here is one.' "

Evidently in a semi-serious mood he says in his *Journal:* " I have not decided whether I had better publish my experience in searching for arrowheads in three volumes, with plates and an index, or try to compress it into one." In whatever mood that remark may have been made, it was never followed up, but his collection of arrowheads and other Indian relics was kept together. At his death he turned this material over to the Boston Society of Natural History, of which he was an honorary member. Later, when the Peabody Museum of American Archæology and Ethnology was formed at Cambridge, the Society, according to the 1870 report of the Museum, " deposited with this Museum a large series of Indian implements of stone from various parts of New England, but chiefly from the neighborhood of Concord, Mass. This collection was made by the late Henry D. Thoreau, of Concord. There are over one hundred specimens of axes, pestles, gouges, mortars, chisels, spear points, ornaments, etc., and a larger number of arrow-points of very varied patterns and materials. The entire collection comprises about nine hundred pieces."

Thoreau was greatly interested in the Indian's manufacture of arrowheads. He doubted that they had one arrowhead-maker for many families, as for instance white men one blacksmith. He found the marks of too many forges, so to speak, and inferred that each family, with infinite patience and skill, chipped its own. So much stress did he lay upon this matter that shortly before his death he enjoined a young man travelling to the region of the Rocky Mountains to investigate the point carefully, as such information would be worth a trip in itself. The same interest he manifested in the manufacture of the other weapons and tools of the aborigines, such as axes, pestles, and mortars, and he admired the vital energy and patience necessary to rub industriously stone upon stone for a long time until the workman had fashioned the intended instrument.

Naturally Thoreau would not have devoted so much time and attention to Indian relics if he had not attached great importance especially to the stone arrowheads of an extinct race. As he expresses it so forcefully: " Such are our antiquities. These were our predecessors. Why, then, make so great ado about the Roman and the Greek, and neglect the Indian? We [need] not wander off with boys in our imagination to Juan Fernandez, to wonder at footprints in the sand there. Here is a print still more significant at our doors, the print of a race that has preceded us, and this is the little symbol that Nature has transmitted to us. Yes, *this* arrowheaded character is probably more ancient than any other, and to my mind it has not been deciphered. Men should not go to New Zealand to write or think of Greece and Rome, nor more to New England. New earths, new themes expect us. Celebrate not the Garden of Eden, but your own."

Each of the arrowheads yields Thoreau a thought that brings him nearer to the maker than his very bones would. The latter might be hidden in some crypt or grave or under a pyramid with no indication of wit as in the case of the arrowhead. Instead of a disgusting mummy, a clean stone as the red man's mark is the best symbol or letter that could have been transmitted to him. Thus he himself can easily supply the artificer. And no vandals will destroy them. " Time will soon destroy the works of famous painters and sculptors, but the Indian arrowhead will balk his efforts and Eternity will have to come to his aid. They are not fossil bones, but, as it were, fossil thoughts, forever reminding me of the mind that shaped them." When he sees these signs, he knows that the subtle spirits that made them are not far off, in whatever form transmuted. The arrowheaded character hardly will be destroyed, for it promises to outlast all others. It will never cease to wing its way through the ages to eternity. It is the footprint, the mind-print of the oldest men. The arrowheads will outlast the British Museum and tell to the shepherd or savage who may be wandering over its ruins their own story. Meanwhile, it is better that nature take care of our antiquities, which are cleaner to think of than the rubbish of the Tower of London, and they are more ancient armor.

In his desire to detect the dawning of civilized life among the aborigines of America, Thoreau eagerly scanned his finds for traces of artistic work. Few they were indeed, but on that account the more eagerly welcomed and prized. A bird's-head knob ornamenting the handle of a pestle he pronounces as the first step toward a complete culture. By the exercise of fancy and taste in adding pure beauty to pure utility, the maker had begun to redeem himself from the savage state and was entering the thought-realm of civilized man. " Enough of this would have saved him from extinction," is Thoreau's enthusiastic conclusion.

An extensive acquaintance with the natives soon convinced him that they were at home in the great out-of-doors, practically never lost their bearings, and utilized whatever nature offered. Game, fish, vegetables, and fruits furnished sustenance, shelter, and clothing; and transportation was also drawn from the wilderness. The roots of the black spruce were used for sewing the birch-bark canoes, and in addition yielded a kind of pitch to render them water-tight. The bark of the leatherwood tree served as cordage, a knowledge of such qualities possibly having been discovered only after the long-continued search of many generations. The Indian's sharp vision would detect objects where nothing appeared to the unpracticed eye. As proof he cites the example of the St. Francis Indian on Moosehead Lake, who spotted the canoe of his boy far away under the mountain long before anyone else could see it.

Most of Thoreau's observations were made on his trips to Maine under the guidance of Joe Aitteon and Joe Polis. Not only was the latter clever and quick to learn, but his own information and skill especially in woodcraft were truly remarkable. He could keep a trail almost like a hound, while the experienced naturalist, to the great astonishment of Joe, often went astray. The red man could go back through the forest wherever he had been during the day; he would steer by the wind or by the limbs of the hemlocks, which were largest on the south side. Thoreau himself several years before had observed that the shoots of the young soft white pines are bent to the east. When later informed that this mark served the Indians as a guide in cloudy weather, he was highly pleased to be one of the few civilized men who probably had ever made an observation so important to the savage. He infers that much may have been known by the native which has never been detected by science.

Aboriginal influence upon the food of the white man hardly can be overestimated. The Indian cornhills still found in pastures remind us that the native taught the newcomer the use of corn and how to plant it. He also made him acquainted with various berries which we should long have hesitated to eat if he had not set the example, knowing from old experience that they were not only harmless but salutary. Thoreau himself added a few to his number of edible berries by walking behind his guide in Maine, who ate such as he had never thought of before. Whortleberries and especially his favorite huckleberries were extensively used by the hunting tribesmen. He claims that the huckleberry cake, made of Indian meal and huckleberries, was the principal cake of the aborigines over a wide area — a cake much more national and universal than anything among whites at his time.

The Indian was a man of nature — as familiar with her as constant acquaintance could develop. While the white man has the habits of the house, which is really a prison and which circumscribes him in every way, "the charm of the Indian . . . is that he stands free and unrestrained in Nature, is her inhabitant and not her guest, and wears her easily and gracefully." To such a being, nature must have made a thousand revelations which are still secrets to us, for one revelation was made to the Indian, another to the white man. Not infrequently the dweller in the forest was admitted to a rare and peculiar society with nature, a privilege that helped him to preserve his intercourse with his native gods. However, though a familiar, he is still free, not carrying the familiarity as far as the gardener, but moving independently in untamed nature.

Impatient with the knowledge of civilization and of irrelevant things, the lover of nature thought that he had much to learn of the Indian, nothing of the missionary. He was satisfied that his excursions into the wilds of Maine in company with the intelligent native also initiated him into some of the secrets of nature; his journey with Joe Polis in 1857 made his world larger and extended his range, because he had made an excursion, even if short, into the world of the Indian, which begins where the white man leaves off, for only now he realized that the Indian's earthly life is as far from us as heaven is. The knowledge that intelligence flows in other channels than he knew, redeemed to him portions of what had seemed brutish before and increased his own capacity.

The knowledge of nature acquired by the native is practically never shared with civilized man. When among the members of his own race, the Indian is social and communicative. The tribal instinct and dread of solitude is so strong that he is loath to settle on land removed from members of his organization even if he has to utilize poorer land for the sake of nearness. And within his own circle he has few secrets. But outside of it he stoutly maintains his stolidity. Even Joe Polis after an agreement with his employer that they would tell each other what they knew, at times proved reticent so that Thoreau might just as well have been thumping at the bottom of the canoe he was carrying. As Emerson so aptly said in his funeral address, he well knew that asking questions of Indians is like catechizing beavers and rabbits. Thoreau regretted such reserve on the part of the aborigines as it had a tendency to lock their secrets within them. If they had been willing to become laboring men among the whites, many of these secrets might have been given to the world.

Means of communication adapted to his mode of life the native did not lack. His language, unaltered and unchanged from the time of the discovery of America, is a tongue mainly dealing with concrete things. As such it is wonderfully copious, much more so than that of civilized man, who stands in much less intimate relation with nature. Our scientific names convey only a very partial information; for instance, the term *arbor vitae* is but a word, indicating a classification; but the Indian, so well acquainted with its wood, its bark, its leaves, has twenty words for the tree and its various parts. And so in regard to other plants, to flowers, to animals and all animate and inanimate things; his intimacy is reflected in his language. On the other hand, living and dealing largely with the concrete, the savage was often unable to convey an abstract idea adequately.

However, the Indian's capacity for improvement was such that Thoreau marvelled at his ability to turn from a savage warrior to a skilful diplomat negotiating a just treaty. Though his interest in the native never made him blind to the atrocities, the indiscriminate slaughter, the torture and burning at the stake, and the cannibalism practiced by some tribes, all of which lowered them below the level of a beast, he nevertheless believed that even then the Indians were not essentially worse than white men in war. At conferences these savages conduct themselves with perfect dignity and decorum, and deal with each other with as much consideration as the most enlightened states and enter into the most formal agreements, all of which reveals a genius for diplomacy equal to that of the white man.

In spite of his love for the native of the wilderness and his appreciation of the many fine qualities of these children of nature, the man steeped in the culture of centuries did not overrate them. As a matter of fact, the civilizations developed by the kinsfolk farther south draw more approving comment when in one of the notebooks he exclaims: " What a vast difference between the savage and a civilized people. At first it appears but a slight difference in degree — and the savage excelling in many physical qualities — we underrate the comparative general superiority of the civilized man." He invites us to contrast the relics of the so-called American family, at most rude earthen mounds, pottery and stone implements, with the architectural remains, such as pyramids, temples, grottoes, bas-reliefs and arabesques, and. the roads, aqueducts, and fortifications of the Toltecs of Mexico. So profound was Thoreau's interest in this native civilization of Mexico and Peru that he had planned to devote at least partly the opening chapter, entitled Ante-Columbian History, of his proposed book on the Indians to this interesting subject.

Certain inherited character traits of the improvident son of the forest began to irk and irritate the methodical naturalist. Economical as he himself was in his dispositions, he noted even in Joe Polis a carelessness hardly to be excused in one dependent upon foresight for his comfort. Boots left standing under the eaves of the tent were apt to be half full of water in the morning, and the whites had to see that the powder was kept dry, while more than one box of matches was spoilt by being left outside during the night. Skilled as the natives were in nature's ways, yet they were sometimes slow to become proficient in the use of white man's tools. Thoreau was not a little disappointed that his guide, of whom he speaks very highly as a rule, became so excited at the sight of a moose that he could hardly load his gun properly.

He even claims that like the hunter the Indian makes a wrong use of nature. He soon became nauseated and disgusted with moose-hunting. " What a coarse and imperfect use Indians and hunters make of Nature! " he exclaims. " No wonder that their race is so soon exterminated. I already, and for weeks afterwards, felt my nature the coarser for this part of my woodland experience, and was reminded that our life should be lived as tenderly and daintily as one would pluck a flower." Necessary as the wilderness may be as a resource and a background, the raw material of all our civilization, to him there could be no comparison to the smooth but still varied landscape of civilization and the simple, almost barren landscape, and it was a real relief for him to get back to Concord. " The partially cultivated country it is which chiefly has inspired, and will continue to inspire, the strains of poets, such as compose the mass of any literature. Our woods are sylvan, and their inhabitants woodmen and rustics,— that is *selvaggia,* and the inhabitants are salvages. A civilized man, using the word in the ordinary sense, with his ideas and associations, must at length pine there, like a cultivated plant, which clasps its fibres about a crude and undissolved mass of peat."

Whenever the remnants of the natives came to Concord or elsewhere crossed his path, Thoreau eagerly observed their actions and movements. These wandering groups were especially interested in basket making, and on arriving in a strange neighborhood tried to ascertain at once where the black ash grew. They quickly went about their work and exhibited and offered the baskets for sale, making a house to house canvass. Their naïve suppositions the sophisticated white found either amusing or pitiable. They labored under the assumption that entering business like white men would bring wealth, and that through mere basket making riches would flow to them as a matter of course. Such an unfortunate man seems to think that his part is merely manufacturing the article, the duty of the white man to buy it. He forgets that going into trade means not only making baskets, but selling them; it is not only a problem of production, but of profitable distribution. If astonished and indignant at the sales resistance of the whites, it is his place to learn the principles of business.

Fatalist that Thoreau professes to be in regard to the destiny of individuals, he also holds that this same fate undoubtedly has made the Indian what he is, and by giving him certain qualities, fate likewise decrees his extinction. Retaining his habits wonderfully, he is still the same man that the discoverers found. The history of the red man is essentially a history of fixed habits of stagnation, while that of the white man is a history of improvement. The white man's brow is clear and distinct; it is eleven o'clock in the forenoon with him; with the Indian it is four o'clock in the morning, and a slight haze or mist always covers his brow. The red men seem like a race which has exhausted the secrets of nature, tanned with age. The constitution of his mind is the very opposite of that of the white man, and he is acquainted with a different side of nature. He measures his life by winters, not summers; his year is governed not by the sun, but by the moon, and the moons are measured not by days, but by nights. Thus he has taken hold of the dark side of nature; the white man, the bright side. But Thoreau evidently forgets that the ancient Germanic tribes similarly reckoned time, and nobody ever pointed to that fact as a sign of decay and degeneration of a virile people.

That the Indian has sadly fallen from his former dignified state is symbolically illustrated when little Indian boys with bow and arrow cried: " Put up a cent." The white man has driven off the game of the hunter race and substituted a cent in its place. The Indian's hold on the bow has indeed become feeble. And in that elastic piece of wood with its feathered dart, so sure to be unstrung by contact with civilization, he sees the type, the coat of arms for the savage. When on his trip to Maine in 1846 he passed the Indian Island near Oldtown, he observed a short, shabby, washer-woman-looking Indian, with the wobegone look of the girl that cried for spilt milk, landing on the Oldtown side near a grocery. Drawing up his canoe, the Indian took out a bundle of skins in one hand, an empty keg or half-barrel in the other, and scrambled up the bank with them. This picture he considered appropriate to preface the history of the Indian's extinction. As he found at Oldtown very little land cultivated, but an abundance of weeds, indigenous and naturalized — indeed, more introduced weeds than useful vegetables — he notes that the Indian is said to cultivate the vices rather than the virtues of the white man. They have become degraded beings without character and without honor. The Indians he had engaged as guides for one of his Maine trips missed their appointment on account of a drunken frolic and shamelessly advanced sickness as the cause of their delay. To him the degraded savage, comparable to the sinister and slouching fellow picking up strings and paper in the streets of a city, is singularly out of place in his native woods, the fitting abode of nature's nobleman.

Though Thoreau would have the Indian remain an Indian and preserve his original state as a source of inspiration to civilization, as will appear later, he knew only too well that the irresistible march of civilization with its blightening influence would wipe out the native American. He reviews the melancholy history of almost total extinction in New England: the white man comes and frightens the Indian's game; the honey-bee hums through the Massachusetts woods, sips the wild flowers round the Indian's wigwam, and with prophetic warning stings the red child's hand, forerunner of that industrious tribe that was to come and pluck the wild-flower of his race up by the root. This sturdy, intelligent and calculating race first buys the Indian's moccasins and baskets, then his hunting-grounds, and at length he forgets where he is buried and plows up his bones.

In Thoreau's day only a few representatives of the race were to be seen: perhaps a solitary, pure-blooded Indian stepping into a railroad car with his gun; or an Indian squaw gaining a precarious living by making baskets or picking berries, and being subjected to insults by the school children at that. Her melancholy face is indicative of her history and destiny; stepping after her people such a lone woman seems to wear the shroud of her race, and perform the last offices of her departed kindred. A daughter of the soil and one of the nobility of the land, she is not yet absorbed into the elements again. The white man Thoreau considers an imported weed, like burdock and mullein, which displace the ground-nut. However, he and not the native will survive.

At least a few of the natives should be preserved in their original state. When on his trip to Maine Thoreau saw on Indian Island near Oldtown as the only trim-looking building a church, he explains, " that is not Abenaki, that was Rome's doings. Good Canadian it may be, but it is poor Indian. These were once a powerful tribe. Politics is all the rage with them now. I even thought that a row of wigwams, with a dance of powwows, and a prisoner tortured at the stake, would be more respectable than this." At another place he asks: " Why should not we, who have renounced the king's authority, have our national preserves, where no villages need be destroyed, in which the bear and panther, and some even of the hunter race, may still exist, and not be ' civilized off the face of the earth,' — our forests, not to hold the king's game merely, but to hold and preserve the king himself also, the lord of creation, — not for idle sport or food, but for inspiration and our own true recreation? " He confesses in his *Journal* that he has no little sympathy with the Indians and hunter men. To him they seem to be a distinct and equally respectable people, born to wander and to hunt, and not to be inoculated with the twilight civilization of the white man.

However much sympathy one may accord the native, there can, of course, be no question as to the ultimate result, according to the clear-sighted Thoreau. As a race of hunters he can never withstand the inroads of a race of husbandmen. Even if the hunter were brave enough to resist, his game is timid and has already fled. The rifle alone would never exterminate it, but the plow is a more fatal weapon; it wins the country inch by inch and holds all it gets. No sense of justice will ever restrain the farmer from plowing up the land which is only hunted over by his neighbors. The bounds of the hunting field are not accurately marked, and it is property not held by the hunter so much as by the game which roams it, never well secured by warranty deeds. The farmer will year by year encroach upon the forest as fast as his seed corn allows it.

Fate sternly commands the Indian: " Forsake the hunter's life and enter into the agricultural, the second state of man. Root yourselves a little deeper in the soil, if you would continue to be the occupants of the country." What detained the Cherokees so long were the 2923 plows which that people possessed. And if they had only grasped their handles more firmly, they would never have been driven beyond the Mississippi. Thus for the Indian there is no safety but the plow. If he would not be pushed into the Pacific, he must seize hold of a plow-tail and let go his bow and arrow, his fish-spear and rifle. This is the only Christianity that will save him. There is, of course, another alternative: " The Indian, perchance, has not made up his mind to do some things which the white man has consented to do; he has not, in all respects, stooped so low; and hence, though he too loves food and warmth, he draws his tattered blanket around him and follows his fathers, rather than barter his birthright. He dies, and no doubt his Genius judges well for him. But he is not worsted in the fight; he is not destroyed. He only migrates beyond the Pacific to more spacious and happier hunting-grounds."

The influence of the Indian in Thoreau's life is so deep and thoroughgoing as to color his whole existence. Native terms became such an integral part of his vocabulary that he customarily spoke of the musquash and the Musketaquid instead of the muskrat and the Concord River. The reticence and the stoicism of the native ingrained themselves in the very fiber of his being as he moved about the ancient hunting-grounds of the vanished tribes, pondering the destiny, and gathering the sacred remains of the former possessors of the soil.

But his interest in the native was not merely historic and sentimental, for aboriginal life in its practical aspects fascinated him even more. When Penobscot Indians visited Concord, Thoreau noticed how slight a shelter is absolutely necessary, for they lived " in tents of their cotton cloth, while the snow was nearly a foot deep around them, and I thought that they would be glad to have it deeper to keep out the wind." How much better off did not the savage seem as the owner of his own shelter when compared with the civilized man who often has to rent his. The savage could construct a serviceable and easily moved lodge in a day or two, while the white laborer, even if unencumbered with a family, had to spend from ten to fifteen years or about half his adult life to acquire his dwelling. Such a disparity seemed to Thoreau nothing less than preposterous. For the lot of the degraded white, as for instance the Irish, appeared every whit as wretched as that of the poorest savage. Why then should he spend the greater part of his life for necessaries which the Indian obtained almost without labor? Somehow modern life, with all its inventions and industries that should make man's tasks the easier, exacts too high a price for what it gives in return. As the more experienced and wiser savage that he really is, civilized man should live simply and wisely, so that his maintenance become a pastime instead of a hardship.

Economy, one of the master ideas of his life, Thoreau saw exemplified in the native's adaptation to his environment. It was that same idea he put into practice by proving that the work of six weeks in a year would be sufficient to meet all his expenses of living. And the experiment described in *Walden, or Life in the Woods,* is nothing else but the embodiment of economy on the part of civilized man. True, Thoreau withdrew to the shanty at Walden Pond in order to " transact some private business," namely to write a book, but the real and deeper motive was to drive life into a corner, and to reduce it to its lowest terms. He wanted to front only the essentials of life, and to learn what it had to teach. And that could be done best in the great out-of-doors and in an environment that furnished both the means of livelihood and the opportunity to live in all the faculties of the soul. It was such fullness of life which Thoreau admired among the Indians, and at Walden he sought to practice a similar adaptation to his own environment, an experience which left him wiser, and which has given our frenzied and extravagant age a lesson it might well take to heart.

CHAPTER XVI

THE ROMANCE OF JOAQUIN MILLER

The life of Joaquin Miller (1841–1913) is inextricably interwoven, both in fact and fiction, with the native Americans. At least once he enthusiastically wrote that all he was or ever hoped to be he owed to them. Their influence made itself felt early in his life. His Quaker father and his gentle mother were on the best of terms with the Indians of the Miami Reservation and the river valleys of Ohio and Indiana. They sold to them maple sugar and chickens, and at one time only reluctantly accepted half of what a good old savage thrust upon them in compensation for sheep presumably killed by Indian dogs. Thus they were the very opposites of the numerous white men who hovered about in order to separate the good Indian from his good money.

It was a memorable day when Miller's father brought home a book borrowed from the Indian agent, which dealt with the bold explorations of Captain Frémont and his daring guide Kit Carson. Fired by the accounts, the family decided to move west, especially as General Joe Lane, Miller's former pupil, had been appointed governor of Oregon. The report that Dr. Marcus C. Whitman had been butchered by Indians under the leadership of the cruel and foolish Catholic half-breed Canada Joe cast only a temporary shadow upon the journey to the promised land. The Millers started in March 1852, and on May 15 crossed the Missouri ten miles above St. Joseph. Indians lined the bank, decent, tall and fine fellows who marvelled at the continuous stream of white people flowing west. The proud and stern men scorned all presents, but the Indian women, extraordinarily fond of the white children, refused nothing, although they did not beg as at a later date. Soon the party began to experience the dangers incidental to cholera, tornadoes, and hostile Indians. West of the Divide there occurred a brush with a wild band of mounted Indians, and the eleven-year-old boy saw their chief, a splendid warrior in long black hair and gaudy dress, fall mortally wounded from his horse. Finally, after seven months and five days, the eventful journey of three thousand miles ended in the celebrated Willamette Valley of Oregon, and the Miller family was ready for the pioneer experiences of the Pacific slope.

For the enterprising boy these experiences took on a more adventurous character when at the age of fourteen he ran away from home and made his own way among the rough element in northern California. According to his friend and biographer Harr Wagner there is no doubt that he led a wild, free life among the Indians, the miners, and the settlers of the Shasta region from 1855 to 1859. Naturally this life tended to become more romantic and unconventional as the boy grew up. Though the facts of this period cannot be fully ascertained, he took a part in the campaign of Judge R. P. Gibson against hostile Modocs who had risen when the pollution of the rivers by the numerous miners deprived them of their customary fish diet. In the headlong assault upon Castle Rocks June 15, 1855, Miller was severely wounded by an arrow, and nursed back to health by an Indian woman he later called Sutatot. In spite of his claim that their relations were purely platonic, there is reason to believe that she became his first wife and bore him a daughter known as Calli Shasta. The lovers later seem to have drifted apart, for, after some years as prisoner among the Modocs, this Shasta woman escaped through the efforts of a white scout named Brock and married him.

Somehow Miller was also involved in the horrible Pit River massacre in the spring of 1856. If not informed beforehand of the plans, he at least seems to have viewed the scene of slaughter soon after, and narrowly escaped the vengeance of the troops. After less exciting events, the boy came close to feeling the hangman's rope around his neck. According to documentary evidence, on July 16, 1859, he was so reckless as to steal a horse and so unfortunate as to be caught by a posse and lodged in the Shasta City jail. In the middle of the night an Indian girl is said to have sawed through the bars and liberated him. Possibly as a result of these dangerous experiences Miller seems to have forsaken this wild life and thereafter engaged in more peaceful pursuits. However, it is an established fact that in 1864 as judge at Canyon City, Oregon, he gathered a group of civilian volunteers to assist a small detachment of regular soldiers to recover stolen horses from the Indians of eastern Oregon, a quest that proved unsuccessful.

It is interesting to note the reflection of the stormy career of this picturesque figure of the Western frontier in his prose and poetry, provided we always remember that the difference between romance and fact is never sharply defined. In the introduction to the *Bear* edition of his poems, one of the more trustworthy accounts of a rather uncertain record, Miller early speaks of two Indian children quite at home around Mt. Shasta, who play such a large part in that medley of fact and fiction published in 1881 under the title of *The Shadows of Shasta*. There he describes, at least partly in story form, the desperate attempt to save the two children from the degradation that a transfer from their cool mountain home to a California reservation beside a malaria-breeding alkali lake would inevitably have brought about. He denounces such transfers in the strongest terms and claims that the freedom of the native alone will save him, for the real Indian in the mountains is " a free man yet; not a beggar, not a thief, but the brightest, bravest, truest man alive," and that " the only really religious, unquestioning and absolutely devout Christians I have ever met in America are the Indians."

To reconcile the various and often contradictory statements of Miller's Indian experiences and other contemporary activities is an impossible task. It is probable that the semi-autobiographic introduction to the *Bear* edition, 1909, *Memorie and Rime,* 1884, *The Shadows of Shasta,* 1881, and the extensive *Life Among the Modocs,* 1873, furnish facts in a declining scale, the less recent works curiously enough being predominantly fanciful. The contents of the more factual narratives may properly engage our attention first, to be climaxed with an analysis of the romantic deviations of his most famous tale.

Early in 1855 Miller seems to have met near Mt. Shasta a romantic person often called " The Prince," but who later is revealed as a plain American with the common name of James

Thompson. According to the memoir prefixed to the *Bear* edition, this " Prince " had great plans, which he slowly unfolded to Miller, making him almost believe these plans for the salvation of the perishing savages were his own. In brief, the idea was to make the mountain sacred to the Indians; to persuade the United States to proclaim it a city of refuge, a sanctuary, and to create a sort of Indian republic. But when later news arrived that a body of Modocs had taken up a position in Castle Rocks, cut off all communication with the north, captured the mule mail train, killed not only men, but also women and children, the " Prince " found it convenient to go south, and Miller, then only fourteen years old, took up his abode with friendly Indians and Joseph De Bloney or Mountain Joe, a Swiss horse trader. During the attack upon the mountain fortress by his adventurous companion and by Judge Gibson and his band of scouts, Miller was present and fell at Gibson's side. He felt no real pain, he says, as one would think, with an arrow thrust through the side of his neck and face till the point stuck away out at the back of his neck, but he was stunned. It seemed to him as if his head had been crushed, and he remembered putting up his hand to feel his head. This was, perhaps, on account of the arrow having pierced so nearly the base of the brain. He did not remember anything else that day, and very little else the next year. The battle is said to have taken place on the 15th day of June 1855, but his accounts vary in important particulars, for in *Memorie and Rime* the leader in this battle is Mountain Joe, the Swiss adventurer, who with a company of men punished unfriendly Indians for burning his camp. An Indian woman prisoner is said to have adopted the boy to take the place of a lost son, and Miller claims that she was truly a mother to him.

Rejoining his red brethren at the foot of Mt. Shasta after a brief experience in teaching school, incomprehensible in view of his convalescent state, Miller narrowly escaped a tragedy in the spring of 1856. For when the Modocs rose up one night and massacred eighteen men, every man in Pitt River Valley, he alone was spared; and spared only because he was *Los bobo,* the fool. Then he engaged in more battles and received two more wounds. His mind was as the mind of a child, he claims, and his memory is uncertain here. Uncertain it evidently must have been, for in *Memorie and Rime* he claims to have spent part of the winter previous in a beautiful little valley given him by the Indian chief Blackbird and even to have been instrumental in saving the starving Indians through the providential finding of a large herd of elk. " But, alas, for my dream of lasting rest and peace with these wild people of Mount Shasta! As the birds of spring began to sing a bit, and the snow to soften about our lofty camp, a messenger came stealing tiptoe over from the Pit River Valley. And lo! the Indians had risen, starved and desperate, and murdered every white man there. And I knew I should be accused of this." Drawn into the Pit River war, he escaped with a bullet through the right arm.

During this time and the following years seems to have taken place the attempt of Joseph De Bloney and Miller to carry out the idea of " The Prince " of establishing an Indian republic at Mt. Shasta. We are told that the fourteen-year-old boy early in 1855 had met this scion of a famous Swiss family who was reputed to have crossed the plains with Frémont, that daring explorer whose adventures had aroused the Millers from their midwestern abode. " His ambition was to unite the Indians about the base of Mount Shasta and establish a sort of Indian republic, the prime and principal object of which was to set these Indians entirely apart from the approach of the white man, draw an impassable line, in fact, behind which the Indian would be secure in his lands, his simple life, his integrity, and his purity. Some of the many tribes were friendly; some were hostile. It was a hard undertaking at best, perilous, almost as much as a man's life was worth, to attempt to befriend an Indian in those stormy days on the border, when every gold-hunter crowding the hills in quest of precious metals counted it his privilege, if not his duty, to shoot an Indian on sight. An Indian sympathizer was more hated in those days, is still, than ever was an Abolitionist . . . De Bloney gradually gathered about twenty-five men around him in the mountains, took up homes, situated his men around him, planted, dug gold, did what he could to civilize the people and subdue the savages. . . . But he had tough elements to deal with. The most savage men were the white men. The Indians, the friendly ones, were the tamest of his people."

By and by De Bloney matured his plans and "armed his Indians in defense against the brutal and aggressive white men." It is not unlikely that the Pit River massacre had at least the sympathy of Miller and his associates. Following it, the young renegade took part in several raids to secure ammunition for the infant republic. On one of these raids to Shasta City his horse was shot under him and he himself dreadfully bruised by the fall. His two Indian companions tried to save him from the pursuing whites by placing him on a stolen horse, but on account of his serious wound had to abandon him to some Indians by the road, where he was captured. Since he was only seventeen and small for his size, "really not big enough to hang," he was fortunate in being only placed in the Shasta City jail, "and my part in the wild attempt to found an Indian republic was rewarded with a prompt endictment for stealing horses." After lying in that hot and terrible pen for some time, more dead than alive, he was rescued by the Indians on July 4, 1859. In our discussion of *Life Among the Modocs* and *The Tale of the Tall Alcalde* we shall become acquainted with the more romantic details of this stirring episode.

When De Bloney lost heart and sank into drunkenness, his young associate took over the direction of affairs, but his last venture proved to be even more disastrous than the former. "I never saw De Bloney after this final failure. I would not be taken again prisoner, and so an officer in pursuit was shot from his horse. We separated in the Sierras, and sought separate ways in life." At least one other direct contact with the Indians he reports later. Following more peaceful pursuits, he went into the mountains of Oregon, and in an emergency led the whites against hostile Shoshone Indians. From then on his experiences with the savages seem to have been in the realm of the imagination, though it is practically certain that the account given thus far contains also a large admixture of fiction.

As might be expected, Miller alludes to the Indians in a number of his poems, although only a few deal exclusively with this subject. Of these *The Tale of the Tall Alcalde,* depicting his romantic experiences with the chief's daughter of Mt. Shasta, may properly be woven into that extraordinary prose poem *Life Among the Modocs* dealing with his renegade life among the natives. Though it cannot be said that the aborigines occupy a prominent place in his poetry, there are casual references to them in his portrayal of Western life, generally but not altogether complimentary. He points out that the tawny Piute will dispute no boundary with the Men of Forty-nine, and he mentions with evident satisfaction how the Comanches who had left behind fair woman's hair upon the blood-soaked hearth in a blazing home were pursued and cornered by the rangers who await only daylight to destroy the Ishmaelites of all the earth. The prowling savage lurks in the desert to shoot from behind the tired traveller, and the tasselled brave sweeping by on his horse gives a warning yell to the pioneer pointing his covered wagon Oregonward. The land they once owned is rapidly slipping from the grasp of the tribes, with only the mountains as a refuge, and the tall savage spearman striking the salmon in the waters of the Oregon will soon give way to his more efficient white competitor.

To the bravery and self-control of the Indians, including the small children, Miller pays eloquent tribute. In *The Song of Creation* he asserts that no one ever heard one poor brown Indian baby cry, not even during those long hot marches with mothers starving. As he himself lay desperately wounded at Castle Rocks and a baby crept up to him, his urgent desire that its cry bring help was not gratified; attacked by the terrible lion the baby remained silent, only the crunch of its bones filling the air. But the situation is by no means always as serious, for in *The Great Emerald Land* of Oregon the native is thrilled by the beauty of the sunrise; throwing back his beaded strouds and stretching his hand above the scene, he cries out that the sun is bathing in a silvery sea of clouds.

Of the poems utilizing native material two deal with the love of the dusky maiden. In the stirring *Kit Carson's Ride* the famous trapper and Indian fighter, though the red Comanches are hot on the trail, revels in the unrestrained love of his stolen brown bride. Throughout the dangers of the buffalo stampede and the prairie fire her eyes are full of longing, pity, and at last despair when the flames begin to envelop her, but just in the nick of time he snatches her from the staggering beast and bears her to safety. Equally as grim is the situation in *The Sioux Chief's Daughter,* where the maiden prefers her tall Idaho lover to a wrinkled and mighty chief. In order to settle the issue, the wily maiden proposes a swimming race across the river for a bough of autumn berries, the winner bringing her the fruit to be rewarded with her love. When her tall fleet lover is slowed up by the knife of the disappointed chief, she resolutely kills the treacherous savage and vows to nurse as the real victor the wounded brave.

According to a note by Miller, *The Last Taschastas* is based upon the fortunes of Tc'hastas (a corruption of the word for chaste) or King John of the Rouge Indians of Oregon, whose story is glorious with great deeds in defense of his people. A devoted daughter is said to have followed his fortunes in all his battles. When finally overpowered and sent to Fort Alcatraz in the Golden Gate, he and his son Moses gained a temporary victory aboard ship, but being desperately wounded, they surrendered; the chief died a prisoner, but the son escaped and was never recaptured. In the poem Miller tries to picture the daughter and her people in a midnight camp before the breaking out of the war. The Indians, hunted and oppressed by the whites, are driven to desperate resistance. We see a bereft widow, wrinkled and brown as a bag of leather, a brave chipping a flint into an arrowhead and his squaw molding balls of lead, with others getting ready for battle. At the council the chiefs, described as thin and wiry, wise as brief and brief as bold, fierce, fiery, bronzed and battered, begin their lament. In particular the war chief complains that the white man's plowshare grinds his father's bones for bread in a land where for ages the Indians have laid their bravest and dearest dead. To that plowshare clung the flesh of his own children, while his mother's tangled hair trailed along in the furrow. When the dejected old man sits down, Loua Ellah, the Spotted Lily (she who was taller than the tasselled corn, far sweeter than the kiss of morning, but as sad as some sweet morning star), arises and sounds the battle cry. In that battle the Indians lose, and the chief is to be exiled beyond the shores of the Pacific. When the rude captain urges the old chief and his beautiful daughter into the boat, the fierce warrior bitterly arraigns the whites, and just as the daughter pushes off the frail craft, he snatches from his panther skin a poisoned arrow and shoots. Fatally wounded the captain falls, while the grand and grim warrior with his child, defying the shouts and the shots of his oppressors, escapes to the west. In Miller's eyes the last act is a fit although entirely inadequate retribution that overtakes the white oppressor for driving the owner of the soil into the Pacific.

While in Europe during 1872 and 1873, Miller was aroused by the stubborn resistance the Modocs offered to their removal to a new reservation, during which they killed two peace commissioners, an act that naturally excited public indignation. Though he had at least once fought against them, he now became their advocate and defender in what proved to be his longest work. Prentice Mulford had a share in it, as also a stranger who is allowed to mystify his readers for many pages, for in the introduction to the *Bear* edition Miller admits that the Prince, on a visit to Paris from Nicaragua at the time, helped him to recall their life among the Modocs, adding such romance of his own as he chose. The resultant book, by far the finest and best of Miller's prose productions, he published in 1873 in France and England as *Life Among the Modocs,* later also issued under the titles *Unwritten History; Paquita, My Own Story;* and *My Life Among the Indians.*

In spite of the author's assertion that he will " endeavor to make this sketch of my life among the Indians . . . true in every particular," the *Life Among the Modocs* contains much more poetry than truth. He wishes to make it clear that he speaks of the native as he was, not as he is, for in one little spot in America he saw him as he was centuries ago in every part of it perhaps — " 'the gentle savage,' the worst and the best of men, the tamest and the fiercest of beings." On account of his unexcelled opportunity to study the Indian in his native habitat, his descriptions he regards as of the highest value. And throughout the book the author explains or actually defends the conduct of the natives as the result of white injustice and brutality.

Miller confines his praise of the Indians mainly to those whom the mountain environment had made nature's noblemen, for others are characterized as low, shiftless, indolent, and cowardly. Among the former he spent months, recuperating from his wounds and sharing their interesting life which was affected by the changing seasons of the year that influenced even their very moods. During the long evenings their passionate and poetic souls found expression in the revelation of the future, and therefore " no wonder they die so bravely, and care so little for this life, when they are so certain of the next." Sympathizing with the boy, they took him into their inner life and told him of their traditions. Before this he had become acquainted with natives willing to mix with the whites, " but the real Indian, the brave, simple, silent and thoughtful Indian who retreats from the white man when he can, and fights him when he must, I had never before seen or read a line about. I had never even heard of him. Few have. Perhaps ten years from now the red man, as I found him there in the forest of his fathers, shall not be found anywhere on earth." And as they sometimes showed him the Indian question from an Indian point of view, the thought came to him that they should be permitted to remain there; that the region should become a great national park peopled by the Indian only, untraversed and untouched by the Saxon.

When the wandering boy strayed beyond this Indian paradise and fell in with a romantic gambler called " the Prince," the decorations of a painting in a saloon concretely showed him the attitude of the miners. " An Indian scalp or two hung from a corner of this painting. The long matted hair hung streaming down over the ears of the bear and his red open mouth. A few sheaves of arrows in quivers were hung against the wall, with here and there a tomahawk, a scalping knife, boomerang and war-club, at the back of the ' bar-keep.' " Further experience brought home to his mind the injustice the native is subjected to, often culminating in brutal murders of members of a helpless race. Not that he would excuse the sins of the red men, but their depredations are magnified, " while a hundred Indians are killed in cold blood by the settlers, and the affair is never heard of outside the county where it occurs." As proof of the pacific attitude of the natives he points to the fact that his Quaker father during forty years among the Indians was never molested, not even to the extent of an uncivil word.

At this point there enters into Miller's life the little Paquita, whom the Prince had adopted when the Indian wigwams were burnt. She developed into a neat, modest, sensitive girl, intelligent, beautiful, and industrious, altogether a lovely creature. After various hair-raising adventures the strange group made its way to Mt. Shasta with somewhat more conventional activities. Occasionally the author finds time to insert his observations and comments, as when he claims, " Indians in the aggregate forget less than any other people. They remember the least kindness perfectly well all through life, and a deep wrong is as difficult to forget. The reason is, I should say, because the Indian does not meet with a great deal of kindness as he goes through life. His mind and memory are hardly overtaxed, I think, in remembering good deeds from the white man." The lives of these Shasta Indians were rather monotonous, " listless, dull, and almost melancholy," but brightened by the stories told at night, and by the periodical feasts. In course of time the white renegade almost thoroughly became an Indian, Miller admits. His sympathies always had been with them, and now his whole heart and soul entered into the wild life of the forest. In extravagant terms he praises his red friends as the first of the land, noted for physique, valor, savage defiance of the white man, and a thirst for knowledge. Their code of morals consisted chiefly of a contempt of death, belief in immortality, sincerity, and temperance in all things. Their children, fortyfold more civil than the children of the whites, seldom needed correction. In their profound veneration for the Good Spirit, the natives never ascended Mt. Shasta above the timberline, which they looked upon as the dwelling place of the Great Spirit.

Meanwhile a romance between the fourteen-year-old boy and the Indian maiden had sprung up. It is true, the Prince himself had been attracted to the lovely creature, " tall and lithe, and graceful as a mountain lily swayed by the breath of morning." But that noble, generous, and self-denying knight cavalierly said goodbye, leaving in addition all his gold with his rival, and with the way thus cleared, late in the fall the chief, who now suddenly assumes the rôle of her father, made the marriage feast. The ideal existence with the romantic maiden was soon marred by the depredations of hostile Indians, who although properly chastised by the forces of Mountin Joe in an encounter on June 26, 1855, were so inconsiderate as to seriously wound the bridegroom with an arrow. After his convalescence and a trip to San Francisco he returned to his Paquita and could now devote his time to a bold and ambitious enterprise, nothing less than the establishment of a sort of Indian republic, " a wheel within a wheel," with the grand old cone of Mt. Shasta for the head or center.

Details of the grandiose plan to unite the Shastas, the Pit River Indians, and the Modocs in a confederacy under the name of the United Tribes and to obtain from the government all the lands near the mountain, according to the present account appear to have sprung from the brain of the young boy, though elsewhere others are mentioned as the moving force. A real reservation this would have been, the Indians to remain in the land of their fathers without interference or outside assistance, unmolested in their rites, their customs, and their religion. Such a scheme the Modocs, their hands still red from the murder of an old trader, enthusiastically embraced, but this proposal the governmental authorities greeted with contemptuous silence. Indignantly Miller claims that only by a war could he have attracted attention to his plan to establish " a park, a place, one place in all the world, where men lived in a state of nature, and when all the other tribes had passed away or melted into the civilization and life of the white man, here would be a people untouched, unchanged, to instruct and interest the traveller, the moralist, all men."

The patience of the boy-chief does not seem to have been equal to his flights of imagination, for in the following months and years he appears in divers places and situations when according to other accounts he should have been elsewhere. He even forgot himself so far as to lead a party of white men against unsuspecting natives, and "hundreds of them lay heaped together about the lodges, where they fell by rifle, pistol, and knife," the white butchers scalping everyone, and one of the ruffians even cutting off their ears and stringing them about his horse's neck. After two of these later deeply regretted battles or massacres, Miller returned to his own Indians, with Paquita still friendly as before. Casting his lot now wholly and entirely with the natives, he endeavored by stealing horses, arms, and ammunition to strengthen his mountain republic. One more aberration he chalks up against himself, for in the neighborhood of Canyon City, Oregon, he led the settlers and miners in a long and disastrous campaign against the Indians. After some more brushes and wounds he again returned to his Modocs, but even as their "nominal war-chief" refrained from taking part in a skirmish with soldiers, in which the conduct of his braves was anything but encouraging. But his efforts to treat with officers proving unproductive, he continued his thieving and raiding practices, which finally led to his arrest and incarceration at Shasta City.

Despairing of help the renegade one night was attracted by the call of the night bird, and his dusky Paquita slipped a knife to him, and the two by hacking their knives together for the nights of a week succeeded in sawing a way out, and thus with the help of "the true and faithful little savage, the heroine, the red star of my stormy life," he escaped on horseback. But in crossing the river she was fatally wounded by the pursuers, and the "Indian maiden, pure as a vestal virgin, brave as was Lucretia, beautiful as any picture, lay dying in my arms." Nature herself seemed to be in a poetic mood. "The lovely July night was soft and sultry. The great white moon rose up and rolled along the heavens, and sifted through the boughs that lifted above and reached from the hanging cliff, and fell in lines and spangles across the face and form of my dead." And then he breaks out into a magnificent lament, as the child of nature, the sunbeam of the forest, the star that had seen so little of light, lay cold and lifeless wrapped in darkness, his own life widening and widening away till it touched and took in the shores of death. After burning her body, he gathered white stones and laid them in a circle around the embers.

In his poem *The Tale of the Tall Alcalde,* which he himself says must not be taken literally, Miller tells a somewhat different story of this peerless, dark-eyed Indian girl, here called Winnema, with eyes like those of a rabbit and a manner just as mild. Though the child of a savage war chief, she did not harm the lowliest worm. And what to him was more important, her love, deeper than the sea and stronger than the tidal wave, clung in all its strength to him. The affection was reciprocal, for the blue-eyed boy loved her with the holiest love, and when the dark forebodings were followed by strife between the white man and the red, childlike he chose the weaker side. In the terrific fight the mighty chief crashed like a broken gate of brass and pride, even in death clutching the earth so as to hold his hunting-ground still in his trust. The tragedy is complete, for he the red man's friend alone survived, and was shut up in an adobe prison. When after a long illness his senses returned, he looked into the eyes of her who by sacrificing her honor to the lust of the keeper had gained access and nursed him back to health. Freedom soon followed, but when after that fearful midnight ride they had escaped the pursuers, and he with a lover's ecstasy tried to press his wife to his bosom, she repelled all his advances, and after baring the stain of her soul, plunged a dagger into her bursting heart. On the funeral pyre she had prepared with her own hands he tenderly laid her body, in order that according to her wish she might, wrapped in a fiery shining shroud, ascend to God a wreathing cloud.

We need not follow in detail the further adventures of the hero. Intent upon bloody revenge, the kind entertainment at the hands of an old settler and his wife caused him to abandon the plan to lead his allies against green and yellow fields and peaceful farmhouses. But time and events proved that he had been wrong in not seizing Yreka and waging aggressive warfare till the government had come to terms and recognized the rights of his people. As a consequence, he himself was wounded, and his allies were defeated, scattered, and subdued, and the plans for the little republic utterly overthrown. And though the chief Warrottetot presented him with the beautiful Now-aw-aw valley, the disappointed leader left in despair. When after an absence of ten years the wanderer returned, nearly all of the old friends were gone, among them the great chief of the Shastas, whose ashes rest not far from the beautiful valley once his own.

But among the survivors is one who bears a close relationship to him: Calli Shasta, on her mother's side the last and best blood of a once great tribe flowing in her veins and with her fatherhood a little secret. If Miller fails in life, then " she is not mine; but if I win a name worth having, then that name shall be hers." Evidently she is the offspring of his union with Paquita (what a transformation of the motherly Sutatot!), whose memory moves him to implore fate to touch the little girl gently, for she is so alone, she is the last of the children of Shasta.

Thus came to an end the author's life among the Modocs, for which he professes no regrets; in fact, he snaps his fingers at the world and is proud of that period of his life. This he declares to be the only white spot in his character, the only effort of his life to look back to with exultation, and the only thing he has ever done or endeavored to do that entitles him to rank among the men of a great country. Eloquently he defends the cause of the native whom only Penn and the Mormons consistently treated peaceably and fairly since the savage first lifted his hands in welcome to Columbus. Whenever he shall return to Mt. Shasta, he will seek out the spot where the last man fell, with his own hands rear a monument of stones, and name the place Thermopylae. Yea, he vows to be the red man's advocate even in the life beyond, for " when I die I shall take this book in my hand and hold it up in the Day of Judgment, as a sworn indictment against the rulers of my country for the destruction of this people."

Miller's *Life Among the Modocs* has been pronounced by the late Stuart P. Sherman the most original and the most poetical of all his books in prose, and, on the whole, perhaps the most interesting book that he ever produced. It is true, around a small autobiographical core there are thick layers of fiction and pure romance, and even what purport to be sober statements of fact supported by emphatic assurances must be interpreted in the light of records with which they are often hopelessly at variance. But this does not detract from the value of a work noted for the charm of sentimental and idyllic forest life, and the touch of romantic and humanitarian idealism, all hallowed by the poetic imagination of a seer and prophet, albeit a visionary one. Although the Poet of the Sierras does not altogether absolve the native from guilt, yet his stand in defense of the red man is one of the most courageous and sweeping anywhere to be found in the annals of American literature.

CHAPTER XVII

THE MISSION INDIANS AS VIEWED BY A WOMAN

The fortunes and final dispersal of the so-called "Mission Indians" of California form the theme of an exceedingly interesting romance by Helen Hunt Jackson (1832–1885). Since its publication in 1884, *Ramona* has steadily maintained its popularity, and not a few will agree with A. W. Turgée in characterizing it as "unquestionably the best novel yet produced by an American woman." Its melancholy if sentimental interest is bound up with the characters which as types of the decaying Indian and Mexican civilization are swept away by the relentlessly onrushing wave of Anglo-Saxon civilization.

Helen Hunt Jackson conceived the story as a vehicle of her propaganda to relieve the miserable plight of the Mission Indians in California. From the slave and the unfranchised woman her warm-hearted interest in the underdog had turned to the aborigines in their hopeless struggle for survival. Undoubtedly her travels in the Far West had prepared her for the production of the story by which she is best known; but it was not till she had heard Standing Bear and Bright Eyes lecture in the East on the wrongs suffered by the Poncas that she began to direct almost her whole attention to the Indian question. Impulsively she threw herself into the work of studying the material, and spent three months at the Astor Library in preparation of her *Century of Dishonor,* 1881, a sketch of the dealings of the United States with some of the Indian tribes, which consists in reality of a passionate and somewhat one-sided arraignment of the federal government for wrongs inflicted upon her wards. This rather detailed study of several of the tribes is based upon facts, and while the guilt of our government and many of her citizens is undoubtedly great and unquestioned, yet the work lacks that breadth of vision and unprejudiced and dispassionate treatment which the subject deserves. It bears all the earmarks of propaganda in a noble cause, but hardly adds to Mrs. Jackson's fame, even though in her enthusiasm for reform she did not disregard literary execution as is sometimes charged.

The genuine interest shown in the aborigines brought Mrs. Jackson two years later an appointment as one of the United States commissioners to report on the condition and needs of the California Mission Indians. In order to gather the necessary information, she visited all or most of these tribes in the spring of 1883, and the excellent report of the commission was largely drawn up by her. As was natural under the circumstances, she also studied the history of these early Spanish missions with considerable enthusiasm, and was impressed by their picturesque romance. The literary result of these travels and studies appeared as *Ramona* in 1884, one year before her death.

When face to face with the grim reaper, Mrs. Jackson insisted that her work on behalf of the unfortunate aborigines alone really mattered. Into the following letter she poured her inmost feeling on the subject: " I feel that my work is done, and I am heartily, honestly, and cheerfully ready to go. You have never fully realized how for the last four years my whole heart has been full of the Indian cause — how I felt, as the Quakers say, ' a concern ' to work for it [Mr. Jackson was a Quaker]. My ' Century of Dishonor ' and ' Ramona ' are the only things I have done of which I am glad now. The rest is of no moment. They will live and they will bear fruit. They already have. The change in public feeling on the Indian question in the last three years is marvellous; an Indian Right's Association in every large city in the land. . . . Every word of the Indian history in ' Ramona ' is literally true, and it is being reënacted here every day." She had meant to prepare a child's story on the same theme, but doubted whether she could have made it so telling a stroke. Only four days before her death she wrote a letter to President Grover Cleveland, thanking him for what he already had done for the Indians, and urging him to read her *Century of Dishonor*. She closes with this poignant sentence: " I am dying happier for the belief I have that it is your hand that is destined to strike the first steady blow toward lifting this burden of infamy from our country, and righting the wrongs of the Indian race."

Ramona is the story of a pure-hearted half-breed Indian girl won by the Indian Alessandro Assis, whom the influx of ruthless American settlers drives into temporary insanity and a tragic death at the hands of a ruffian. The Mexican culture of California crumbles before the onslaught of the newcomers, and its downfall buries the scattered remains of the Mission Indians. Instead of a gold-digger's paradise and a prospector's El Dorado, California appears as " the Indian's lost heritage and the Spaniard's desolated home," trampled into the dust by the heartless advance of a new order of things.

The author did not succeed in making the work an indignant protest against the treatment of the red man and a flaming appeal in his behalf, as she had intended. For the purely Indian material is overshadowed by the romance of the personal fortunes of Ramona and Alessandro, which pushes into the background the fate of the race; so when the reader lays down the book, the story of the two individuals remains in his mind, a story told with a skill that grips and carries along our elemental nature to the very end.

In reality the Indian material does not bulk large. Ramona is a half-breed, the daughter of an Indian squaw and the Scotchman Angus Phail. But her training has been entirely under Mexican supervision, and her Indian instincts appear only when her mode of life approaches the primitive. Her married life with Alessandro is distinguished from that of her fellow-villagers mainly by her refinement acquired under white tutelage. In no sense does she revert to the Indian. And after the lamented death of her husband she soon finds happiness in the home and in the arms of her Mexican foster-brother Filipe, her earlier connection with the Indian fading from view.

Likewise, though naturally in a lesser degree, the full-blooded Alessandro, pure-minded, open-hearted, and generous-souled, with his passionate heart and repressed nature, is more of a Mexican than an Indian. His father Pablos, a headman of the Mission Indians, was vitally influenced by the Spanish culture of the

Franciscan fathers. Alessandro himself has superimposed upon his primitive nature the delicacy and refinement which contact with civilization is apt to give. Under the distressing circumstances of the forceful ejection from Temecula and the ruthless seizure of land at San Pasquale his proud and naturally suspicious nature reasserts itself. But his is evidently not the reasoning mind of the trader and diplomat, but that of the shy wild beast eager to escape to the untroubled solitude of the wilderness; a mind too weak to cope with the mounting difficulties and overthrown by the force of events except for a few lucid intervals which are too brief to repair the damage wrought.

As for the Indians, so highly praised as generous and honest people, they are on the whole a wretched lot, miserable, half-starved creatures, grown even more incapable under the paternalistic care of their spiritual fathers. Their tragedy is a continuation of that decay of the missions which had set in with the despoiling under the Secularization Act long before the coming of the energetic and relentless Anglo-Saxon. Gone were those early and happy days of the Franciscans, a gradual but dark foreboding of greater changes still to come. The picture of the Indians' loss of home and possessions at Temecula and their being cast adrift is a heart-rending and pitiful one; and equally so their dispossession of the lands and homes at San Pasquale. Their former somewhat incompetent protectors are compelled to withdraw before a stronger and more efficient civilization. Though in our study there appears only the harshness of the newcomers as a unit, sympathy and a sense of justice are not absent in the case of individuals. But all must conform to the new standards or be swept away by men impatient of obstacles in the march of progress.

CHAPTER XVIII

TRAGEDY STALKS AMONG THE CLIFF DWELLERS

The intriguing story of the cliff dwellers of the Southwest long before the advent of the white man is interestingly told by the ethnologist Adolf F. Bandelier (1840–1914) in his novel *The Delight Makers*, 1890, which of late has experienced increasing popularity. The author was in a position to master completely the basic material of the novel, for he spent eight years in exploration among the Pueblo Indians of New Mexico. While the plot of the book is his own, many of the scenes described he witnessed among the present-day Pueblos, who according to available evidence are on the same level of culture as their remote ancestors and at heart nearly the same Indians. By clothing the sober facts of exploration in the garb of romance, Bandelier hoped to make the truth about the cliff dwellers more accessible and perhaps more acceptable to the public in general. In this he succeeded to a measurable degree.

The center of the scene is the romantic and secluded gorge or canyon twenty miles west of Santa Fé, called in the Queres dialect Tyuonyi, and in Spanish El Rito de los Frijoles. This narrow valley half a mile wide and six miles long, with its high northern rim cliffs of yellowish and white pumice adaptable to human habitations, as well as its southern rim-timbered mesa, Bandelier describes with the exactness of an ethnologist and the sharpness of a photographer. Throughout the book he practically never leaves the solid ground of archeologic and ethnologic facts, vouched for by the most competent authorities. As might be expected from a scientist, the descriptions of scenes and primitive life bulk large, and to the general reader may appear too detailed and too long. But then, English literature has its Bulwer-Lytton with his *Last Days of Pompeii*.

The main actors of the moving drama are the Queres of the picturesque Tyuonyi valley, while their Tehua enemies to the north and the roving Navajos to the south also play prominent parts. The title *Delight Makers* is a translation of Koshare, a semi-religious and social brotherhood among ancient and modern Pueblo tribes whose chief function was that of merry-making at public performances held in connection with the prayers for the indispensable rain. Their religious, social, and especially political influence affects the action of the story at many points. The fathers of the two lovers Okoya and Mitsha are Delight Makers, and one of them, Tyope, the father of the girl, represents the villain of the story. For he accuses his former wife Shotaye and Okoya's mother Say of sorcery and witchcraft, which among the Indians were considered the superlative of depravity. The details of the demonic art with its black corn and owl's feathers Bandelier describes with considerable skill. Rare psychological insight into the mental and emotional life of the women practicing the black art is likewise revealed, coupled with excellent accounts of the frequent meetings and accusations of witchcraft. However, in spite of his malicious cunning the capable Tyope does not succeed in fastening the guilt upon Say and the woman whose energetic actions had ousted her husband from the common dwelling.

Through the villain's desperate attempt to reach his objectives by additional means Bandelier lays bare the political and foreign relations of the cliff dwellers. At a nocturnal meeting with a young Navajo named Nacaytzusle, once domiciled with the Queres but rejected by Mitsha as a lover, Tyope bargains for the assassination not only of his former wife but of the head war chief Topanashka, who stands in the way of his own ambitions. Treachery among the suspicious redskins, however, is two-edged, and the wily contriver barely escapes with his life the net spread by the jilted Navajo and his companions. Unsuccessful in these his machinations, he next tries to pit clan against clan in an attempt to split the tribe and assume command of the disgruntled party. The long and illuminating council meeting dealing with questions of irrigation and the division of land, at last broken up by the charge of witchcraft, reveals to the reader the very heart of tribal organization and the deep-seated clan jealousies.

Descriptions of Indian cunning and warfare fill a not incon-

TRAGEDY STALKS AMONG THE CLIFF DWELLERS

siderable portion of the book. Hostile action and bloody conflicts with the northern enemies are clearly indicated when the suspected and despised Shotaye on her botanical expedition on the northern rim meets the Tehua warrior Cayamo on his way south to gain a Navajo scalp. Events begin to move fast when later a pre-arranged meeting takes place, and the successful young brave leaves with the resolute woman's promise to join him at the cave dwellings of his people just as soon as a favorable opportunity offers itself. Previously the exceedingly interesting episode of the mountain lion capturing a turkey not only shows uncommon powers of observation on the part of the author, but it also foreshadows what is to follow that ominous meeting witnessed by Topanashka, war chief of the Queres. We see him foolhardily even though cautiously examine the trail of the disappearing Tehua, and we watch with breathless interest his every movement as the peculiar behavior of the crows and other indications point to the fact that something extraordinary is on foot. In the description of the wounding of the war chief by his Navajo enemy just when he decides to return home and the death throes of the unfortunate warrior Bandelier has painted a picture so faithful and realistic that it deserves to be exhibited to the admiring eyes of the student of aboriginal life.

"A sharp humming twang, a hissing sound, and a thud followed in lightning-like succession. Topanashka bends over, and at the same time tumbles forward on his face. There he lies, the left cheek and shoulder on the ground. The left arm, with which he has sought to support the body, has slipped; and it now lies fully extended partly below the head, the prostrate head. The chest is heaving painfully, as if under extraordinary pressure. Face and neck are colouring; the lips part; the throat makes a convulsive effort to swallow. The eyes are starting; they denote suffocation and terrible pain. The legs twitch; they seem struggling to come to the rescue of the body's upper half.

From the back of the old man there protrudes an arrowshaft. It has pierced it close to the spine, between it and the right shoulder-blade, penetrating into the lungs, where it now stabs and smarts.

From a distant tree-top there sounds the hoarse 'kuawk, kuawk' of the crow. Otherwise all is still.

The wounded man coughs; with the cough blood comes to his lips, — light red blood. The thighs begin to struggle as if formication was going on in the muscles. It is an impotent movement, and yet is done consciously; for the trunk of the body, which was beginning more and more to yield, now begins to turn clumsily backward; the left hand clutches the soil; the arm is trying to heave, to lift. But the weight is too heavy, the shaft inside too firmly and too deeply rooted. Nevertheless the hips succeed in rising; the trunk follows; then it tumbles over on the back, contracts with a moan of pain and suffering, and lies there trembling with spasmodic shivers.

Topanashka has made this superhuman effort for a purpose. He feels that his wound is severe, that his strength is gone; his senses are darkened and his thoughts confused. Still there is a spark of life left, and that spark demands that he should attempt to see whence came the arrow that so terribly lacerates his breast. But as he has fallen over heavily, the point of the arrow has been pressed deeper. Flint — an arrow-head of flint with notched edges — tears; the muscles do not close about the intruder. The blood flows into the chest; it fills the lungs; he suffocates. Yet all consciousness has not vanished, although pain and oppression overwhelm the physical instruments of consciousness, and deprive the will of its connection with its tools. The will longs to see him who has destroyed its abode, but it no longer controls the shattered tissues; the nerves shiver like the broken springs of clockwork ere they come to a stand-still forever. The eye still distinguishes light occasionally, but it cannot see any longer.

Weaker and weaker become the breathings. On both sides of the mouth a fold begins to form over the blood that has curdled and dried; new fillets stream to the lips from within. The legs still twitch convulsively.

Now a stream of blood gushes from the open mouth; wave after wave rushes up with such swiftness that bubbles and froth form between the lips and remain there. A chill pervades the whole body; it is the last nervous tremor; the lower jaw hangs

TRAGEDY STALKS AMONG THE CLIFF DWELLERS 257

down, showing with fearful distinctness the folds, the ghastly folds, of death.

All is still. Through the tops of the pines comes a humming sound like a chant, a last lay to the brave and dutiful man. Still, stark, and stiff he lies in his gore. His career is ended; his soul has gone to rest.

And thus all remained quiet for a short time. Then the grass was waved and shaken in the direction to which the old man had turned his back in the last hapless moment. The grass seemed to grow, to suddenly rise; and a figure appeared which had been lying flat behind a projecting rocky ledge. As this figure straightened itself, bunches of grass dropped from its back to the ground. It was the figure of a man.

But it is not the Tehua Indian who stands there motionless, with bow half drawn and an arrow in readiness, who gazes over to the corpse to see whether it is really a corpse, or whether it will need a second shaft to despatch it forever. The man is of middle height, raw-boned and spare. Shaggy hair bristles from under the strands that surround his head like a turban. He wears nothing but a kilt of deerskin; from his shoulders hangs a quiver; a flint knife depends from the belt. This man is no village Indian, notwithstanding that dark paint on his body. It is one of the hereditary foes of the sedentary aborigines, — a Navajo!

He is eying the dead body suspiciously. If it is surely dead the second arrow may be saved. Those glassy eyes; that sallow face; and the fold, the ghastly fold that runs on both sides of the mouth, of that mouth filled with blood now clotting, — they show that life is gone.

Still the savage keeps his bow well in hand, as with head and neck extended he steals forward slowly, mistrustfully approaching his victim. When he is close to the body his eyes sparkle with delight and pride, and his face gleams with the triumph of some hellish spirit.

He touches the corpse. It is warm, but surely lifeless. He grasps at the wrap; it is of no value to him, although made of cotton. Beneath, however, there must be something that attracts his attention, for he quickly tears off the scanty dress and fumbles about the chest of the victim. A horrible grin of delight distorts his features, already hideously begrimed, for he has found the little bag and takes from it the fetich of the dead man. That fetich is a prize, for with it the magic power that was subservient to the victim while alive now becomes the victor's. He handles the amulet carefully, almost tenderly, breathes on it, and puts it back into the bag. Then he detaches his stone knife, grasps it with the right hand, and with the left clutches the gray hair of the dead man and with a sudden jerk pulls the head up. Then he begins to cut the scalp with his shaggy knife-blade of flint."

Contrary to Navajo custom which demanded only a lock, the cunning warrior takes the old man's scalp in order to mislead the Queres and to fasten the guilt on the Tehuas. After the discovery of the body by members of the war chief's tribe and its cremation in a ceremonious manner, the Queres under the leadership of Tyope are ready and eager to take the warpath against their enemies to the north.

The two chapters which describe how the long smoldering enmity of the two peoples breaks out in a devouring flame really mark the climax of the novel. Betrayed by the embittered Shotaye, who willingly supplies the suspicious Tehua leaders with all the necessary information, the plans of the Queres completely miscarry. They themselves fall before the surprise attack of the intended victims who swiftly move toward bloody and ruthless execution. Tyope, when suddenly confronted by his former spouse, believing her to be an apparition from the other world, is completely unnerved and almost paralyzed. Utterly crushed, he relinquishes the reins of command into the hands of the medicine man and drifts, but to Shotaye's furious disappointment succeeds in escaping with the retreating Queres. The bloody encounter in the woods with its occasional fierce rushes and the Indian tactics of hide-and-seek, as well as the warrior psychology animating the whole action, is faithfully and vividly portrayed.

In order to emphasize the ferocious passions of a primitive race the author paints one more bloody picture. For during the absence of the Queres war party the Navajos have surprised and massacred the people of the village. While a few find safety in precipitous flight, scores upon scores die a horrible death.

At this point our interest might properly end were it not for the fact that the author has yet to reveal the fortunes of Okoya and Mitsha, whose courtship he had described in great detail before. To all appearances they have utterly vanished. Consequently Zashue and Hayoue, father and uncle of Okoya, begin a heartbreaking search for their dear ones, rewarded after many and various experiences when they find them at the harvest festival in the pueblo of the Tanos tribe. So at last we see the lovers united.

The love story intended to bind together the various parts of *The Delight Makers* is not of a high order, although to interest the white reader, Bandelier exaggerates the Indian type of lovemaking. There is too little of suspense, with the final outcome in plain view. And after the stirring forest battle between the Queres and the Tehuas it drags the novel to a weak anti-climax. Though not without some merit in throwing further light upon the topography of the Southwest and the fortunes of the various tribes, the last part of the novel when looked at from the standpoint of art must be considered an egregious blunder.

Within the framework of the story Bandelier has reconstructed the civilization of an ancient people. Before us he unfolds the daily life of a city hemmed in by the narrow canyon walls beyond which lurking enemies are apt to bring swift destruction. The blood relationships as represented by the clans with their conflicting ambitions and bickerings play a large part in the economic and social life of the cliff dwellers. Rites and ceremonies directed by the medicine men are indispensable means of winning the favor of "Those Above," so necessary for the abundant rain and protection on the warpath. Superstitions and beliefs especially in fetiches tend to make life a burden and a terror to those under their influence.

On the whole, Bandelier has succeeded remarkably well in recreating a civilization that flourished so long ago. In only a few points did the insufficient knowledge of his time lead him into grave errors. For instance, it is now known that the Navajos as a warring tribe made their first appearance several centuries after the time of the story. But aside from a few inevitable blunders, Bandelier's work in contradistinction to most literary productions takes high rank as an accurate portrayal of Indian life.

Ancient Pueblo society with its multifarious activities assumes form and substance in the various actors, practically all of them drawn from life with no attempt at idealization. Topanashka, the aged war chief, noble, fearless, and dignified, as a true Indian commands respect. In striking contrast to him the unscrupulous and ruthless Tyope embodies the native Machiavelli. However, his diabolical designs are fully matched by his former wife Shotaye, expert in the art of healing and crafty machinations. Another feature is not neglected. For the lighter vein of Indian life, commonly but wrongly considered non-existent, crops out in not a few passages, notably in those dealing with the Delight Makers and Hayoue, the Don Juan of Tyuonyi, who mixes amorous adventures with his sceptical disposition toward the claims of supernatural forces. The lovers, though sympathetically drawn and not without interest, represent only a thin thread, and when compared with the main actors lead a somewhat feeble existence, as might be expected of young and immature people in a primitive and warlike environment. They are evidently only the means to an end, the convenient bait that is to attract the reader to what the author considers more important and valuable material.

> We are the Ancient People;
>   Our father is the Sun;
> Our mother, the Earth, where the mountains tower
>   And the rivers seaward run;
> The stars are the children of the sky,
>   The red men, of the plain;
> And ages over us both had rolled
>   Before you crossed the main; —
> For we are the Ancient People,
> Born with the wind and rain.

Thus does Miss Edna Dean Proctor (1829–1923) open *The Song of the Ancient People,* 1893, in which the inmost thoughts and feelings of the Moqui-Zuñi tribes of our Southwest are revealed. In his preface John Fiske pronounces the poem a contribution of great and permanent value, while F. H. Cushing bears witness to the author's strict fidelity of statement and her true reflection of the spirit and feeling as well as the lore of an ancient people. Such tribute of both historian and ethnologist as to the correctness of a literary contribution is as rare as it is well deserved. For *The Song of the Ancient People* is also noble poetry, to which Whittier listened with rapt attention and keen pleasure. Within twenty short pages it unrolls a picture of the customs and manners, the folk-lore, the mythology and religion of the Hopi and Zuñi, those intensely interesting Pueblo Indians of the Southwest.

Much of the excellent work is quotable, but a few lines here and there will suffice to reveal some of the most beautiful passages. The Pueblos pride themselves upon their knowledge, gathered painfully through the centuries:

> For ours is the lore of a dateless past,
>   And we have power thereby,—
> Power which our vanished fathers sought
>   Through toil and watch and pain,
> Till the spirits of wood and wave and air
>   To grant us help were fain.

Just before, the singer had mentioned

> Why the Rainbow, A-mi-to-lan-ne
>   From the Medicine lilies drew
> Orange and rose and violet
>   Before the fall of the dew,—
> The dews that guard the Cornmaids,
>   And the fields keep fair to view;
> But the Rainbow is false and cruel,
>   For it ends the gentle showers,
> And the opening leaves and the tender buds
>   Like the ruthless worm devours,
> And still its stolen tints are won
>   From the blanching, withering flowers.

In the course of the poem there appears a figure similar to Hiawatha, Po'-shai-an-k'ya, the master,

> Whose help we never lose,
> Who bade us turn from hate and guile
> And ever the noblest choose,
> And said that whoso smites a man
> His own heart doth bruise.

Of him the author says that

> His voice was sweet as the summer wind,
> But his robe was poor and old,
> And, scorned of men, he journeyed far
> To the city the mists enfold, —
> Far to the land where his treasured lore
> And secret rites were told;
> And there with a chosen few he dwelt
> And made their darkness day,
> Till lo! while his words yet thrilled their hearts,
> Unseen, as the summer wind departs,
> He vanished in mist away! —

With his passing there comes the note of sorrow and gloom, the lament of those ancient people as at sunset they sit on the mesa top and contemplate what the white man has brought:

> The cry of the owl comes mournful up
> From the dusky glen below, —
> That boding cry when death is nigh
> And days that are dim with woe; —
> Sit, and think that but ruins mark
> The realm that erst was ours,
> The countless cities wrapped in dust
> Which once were stately powers,
> And that over our race, as over the plain,
> The gathering darkness lowers;
> And see how great from the Sunrise-land
> *You* come with every boon,
> We know that ours is the waning,
> And yours is the waxing moon!
> Know that our grief and yearning prayers,
> As reeds in the blast, are vain,
> And with arrows of keenest anguish
> Our tortured hearts are slain.

However, since the earth has been created for both white and red men, the plea is made that they should be brothers before

TRAGEDY STALKS AMONG THE CLIFF DWELLERS 263

death takes them. Only a few of the original possessors of the soil now remain to express their hopeless woe, and these few have nothing left except the graves beneath and the waiting sky above. Even from the lowest hill, the white man's pastures may be seen, and

> Our deep canals are furrows faint
>   On the wide and desert plain;
> Of the grandeur of our temple-walls
>   But mounds of earth remain,
> And over our altars and our graves
>   Your towns rise proud and high!
> The bison is gone, and the antelope
>   And the mountain sheep will follow,
> And all our lands your restless bands
>   Will search from height to hollow;
> And the world we knew and the life we lived
>   Will pass as the shadows fly
> When the morning wind blows fresh and free
>   And daylight floods the sky.
> Alas for us who once were lords
>   Of stream and peak and plain! —
> By ages done, by Star and Sun,
>   We will not brook disdain!
> No! though your strength were thousand-fold
>   From farthest main to main;
> For we are the Ancient People,
>   Born with the wind and rain!

Thus ends *The Song of the Ancient People* with a note of disdainful pride swelling the despairing cry and lament of a vanishing race. It is a true lyric over which broods the pathos and gloom of fate and defeat.

CHAPTER XIX

THE STRUGGLE FOR THE BISON PASTURES OF THE PLAINS

John Gneisenau Neihardt (1881–   ), "poet laureate of Nebraska," has spent the better part of his life in producing a series of works dealing with what he calls the great American epic period, beginning in 1822 and ending in 1890. His early surroundings tended to inspire him for such a task. Born in Illinois, he soon gravitated westward, and made Nebraska his home. After trying such diverse occupations as those of farmhand, hodcarrier, marble polisher, office boy, stenographer, teacher, and journalist, he turned to writing about the West. The Indian naturally attracted his attention early, especially as for three years he was an assistant in the office of an Indian trader among the Omahas in Bancroft, Nebraska, handling land leases, collections, and doing work of a similar nature. As a result of his intimate acquaintance with the Omaha Indians he wrote *The Lonesome Trail,* a collection of short stories dealing with various phases of Indian life.

The narratives included in the volume of 1907, more recently issued with some changes under the title *Indian Tales and Others,* were received in some quarters with considerable favor. According to Julius T. House, Neihardt's biographer, "Dr. Susan La Flesche Picotte, a highly educated Omaha woman, daughter of Iron Eye, last head chief of the Omahas, said concerning Neihardt's Indian stories, that everything a white person from Cooper to Remington had written about the Indians angered her except ' The Lonesome Trail.' She averred that Neihardt alone had discovered the real Indian, and expressed amazement that any white man could so get into the consciousness of the Indians as to make their general attitude and even their idioms comprehensible to the white race." As a matter of fact, the stories are rather uneven in composition and value. *The Alien,* unquestion-

THE STRUGGLE FOR THE BISON PASTURES 265

ably of outstanding merit and by far the best of the group, deals but slightly with the Indian element, for it focuses the interest not so much upon the half-breed as upon the unbreakable tie that binds wild life. The semi-civilized native appears unattractive and unsuited for imaginative treatment. Neihardt himself says that " the typical Reservation Indian is primarily a stomach and secondarily nothing in particular. Let him fill his belly and he is easily handled." [1] Most of the tales reveal a knowledge of a side of Indian life seldom touched upon in literature and of little interest to the white reader, so strange and distant are the thought and emotional life of the aborigines. A few, like *The Fading of the Shadow Flower,* are noted for descriptive power, but on the whole, Neihardt's work in the short story is not such as to hold the attention of the student for long. His strength evidently lies elsewhere.

For Neihardt's reputation must stand or fall with the series of poems comprising the Epic Cycle of the West, which he conceives as part of the story of Aryan migration, " one phase of the whole race life from the beginning; indeed, the final link in that long chain of the heroic periods stretching from the region of the Euphrates eastward into India and westward to our Pacific Coast." He believes that the epic of the typical heroic period of America remained to be written. Longfellow's *Hiawatha* he dismisses as " not concerned with our race, and but little with the real American Indian, for that matter." And *Evangeline* he finds typical neither in matter nor manner. " Nor is it likely ever to be written on a theme concerned with the original Colonies, for the reason that in the Colonies society was never cut loose from its roots." The precious saga stuff which according to Neihardt forms the material of the true American Epos was developed between the Missouri River and the Pacific Ocean in approximately the first four decades of the 19th century. These years of the flourishing fur trade west of the Missouri River are represented in *The Song of the Three Friends* and *The Song of Hugh*

[1] All quotations from Neihardt's works are by permission of The MacMillan Company, publishers of *Indian Tales and Others* and of *Collected Poems* of John G. Neihardt.

Glass. Also a part of the Epic Cycle of the West, which is to preserve the great race-mood of courage, is *The Song of the Indian Wars,* to be followed later by works dealing with the period of exploration and migration. Not unnaturally, a great many students of American history and civilization decline to accept the limitations as to time and place imposed by Neihardt.

The Song of the Three Friends comes first. Will Carpenter, Mike Fink, and Frank Talbeau, representing Saxon, Celtic, and Norman blood respectively, accompany Major Henry in 1822 to the Northwest and go into winter quarters at the mouth of the Yellowstone. When the visit of a party of Bloods presents an opportunity for profitable trade at the Musselshell, the three comrades are in the group which proceeds to the village of the Indians. While in winter quarters there, Fink becomes infatuated with a half-breed girl, whose young and unwise mother had for a time preferred the company of a member of the Lewis and Clark expedition to that of her husband chief. But the affections of the maiden are unfortunately bestowed upon Carpenter, and the inevitable quarrel temporarily ends with Fink's discomfiture in the fight and the rival's enjoyment of the dusky bride. A double tragedy follows, for at the ceremonious reconciliation Fink shoots a few inches too low, and instead of the whisky cup perforates the brain of the erstwhile rival. But when his drink-loosened tongue has revealed the " accident " as a design, Talbeau at the opportune moment deprives the desperado of gun, powder horn, water flask, and sun-dried bison meat, and thus stripped of all means of subsistence he is sent forth into the thirst- and hunger-haunted expanse to a horrible death, his distant and widowed bride probably forever remaining ignorant of the fate that had overtaken him.

Though the story of the three friends is primarily one of the white trapper and trader, not a few noteworthy descriptions dealing with the natives occur. The stampeding of the horses and their capture by the Assiniboines has a realistic touch when

> Now outlined sharply on the sky-rim there
> The victors pause and taunt their helpless foes
> With buttocks patted and with thumbs at nose
> And jeers scarce harkened for the wind's guffaw.

THE STRUGGLE FOR THE BISON PASTURES

Later the dozen volunteer trappers blithely follow the Indian party to the mouth of the Musselshell, their slim craft carrying

> scarlet cloth and beads,
> Some antiquated muskets, powder, ball,
> Traps, knives, and little casks of alcohol
> To lubricate the rusty wheels of trade.

Fink's party upon reaching the Musselshell is received in true Indian fashion, and all seems well. But " the net is cast," for there was the Long Knife's girl, " a miracle of shapely maidenhood." Neihardt describes as sentimental love what would seem merely the beastly lust of the hardened Fink, who woos the maid in the traditional Indian manner by gifts to her father. The chief's daughter, however, ignores him, and sets her little pot of steaming meat at the feet of Carpenter. Soon the wife of the chief pitches for her son-in-law the nuptial lodge where he enjoys his new-found bliss until in the spring the light-hearted voyagers return home, with the new bride left behind and the enactment of the final tragedy later.

Indian life with its ups and downs, its drudging squaws, its ever present curs, and the not infrequent alarms is well described. It is at times dreariness itself, as the people sit fur-robed about the smoky fires that sting their eyes to streaming, when a freak gust flings the sharp reek back with flaws of powdered snow; and again life is filled with zest and an eager enthusiasm when the hunt and the battle invite the plains Indian to pursuits dear to his soul.

Although *The Song of Hugh Glass* is likewise only incidentally concerned with Indian life, it nevertheless gives us revealing glimpses into the soul of the native. Based upon the experience of a famous trapper accompanying General Ashley up the Missouri in 1823, the tale relates the fortunes of old Hugh Glass who in a brush with the Rickaree Indians or Rees had saved young Jamie. The two, Graybeard and Goldhair, now become intimate friends, and somewhat later the boy arrives just in time to rescue the grizzly hunter from what seemed the fatal embraces of a bear. Since it appears wasteful that eighty men should be delayed by the death struggles of one, only Jamie and Jules Le Bon remain to witness his end and bury him. The grave is dug and all in readiness, but the death throes of the sturdy old trapper are unduly prolonged. Influenced by the suggestions of Le Bon, Jamie at last shares his pretended fears of the hostile Rees, and both decamp, the boy taking the rifle and the traitor appropriating the hunting knife, flint, and blanket, considered needless gear for a dying man.

However, the old hunter gradually recovers, to find himself deserted and stripped of the means of subsistence. We follow with sympathetic interest that terrible crawl of the wounded man in his attempt to reach civilization and to taste sweet revenge. On his pilgrimage of blended hope, despair, and hate he views the passing Rees whom the plundering Sioux have forced to the west. It is a motley procession that passes in review, Elk Tongue, the famous chieftain, a gnarled old man with a face like a flinty arrowhead, a sift of winter in his hair, and the bleakness of brown winter in his look, riding aloof and lonely in front. Neihardt gives a vivid description of the various types composing the band, with an indication of the mental state. of each. But as so often, the limitations of the couplet account for not a few curious and oddly expressed observations. The procession moves on, and as evening draws near, Hugh Glass in venturing forth sees a forsaken and tottering squaw slowly plodding up the trail. Momentarily he is tempted to knock her in the head and to appropriate her precious burden, the flint and steel, the kettle and the knife. But upon reflection he sees in her the mother of the race, and allows her to pass unscathed. Later he reaches the abandoned camp ground of the Indians, and with a trader's knife he picked up succeeds in killing one of the camp-curs that had remained behind, and with the help of the discovered fire prepares a delicious meal.

We need not follow in detail his further adventures in search of civilization and later of the elusive Jamie, whom far to the north in the village of the Piegans retributive justice has overtaken through the explosion of the stolen rifle. Blind and almost sick to death with remorse, he craves forgiveness when the presence of Hugh at last dawns upon him, and the story ends with the mov-

THE STRUGGLE FOR THE BISON PASTURES

ing reconciliation of the estranged friends among their Indian hosts.

Of the three parts of the cycle, *The Song of the Indian Wars* is by far the longest and for our purposes the most important. In the words of Neihardt, it " deals with the last great fight for the bison pastures of the Plains between the westering white men and the prairie tribes — the struggle for the right of way between the Missouri River and the Pacific Ocean." Since the period is of such crucial importance in the process of our national development, the author felt the obligation to be accurate, and endeavored neither to fictionize the material nor to sentimentalize the characters. He not only utilized printed sources, but also gathered a wealth of material from an impressive number of veterans who were themselves a part of what the author has to tell. And finally, his own intimate association with the Omaha tribe, a Siouan people, helped to give him a better insight into Indian psychology.

If one can speak of a unifying idea which binds the various episodes of the poem somewhat loosely together, it is the manifest destiny of the ancient and compelling Aryan urge that relentlessly sweeps all before it:

> The driving breed, the takers of the world,
> The makers and the bringers of the law.

Opposed to them are the possessors of the soil

> — and they were also men —
> Who saw the end of sacred things and dear
> In all this wild beginning; saw with fear
> Ancestral pastures gutted by the plow,
> The bison harried ceaselessly, and how
> They dwindled moon by moon; with pious dread
> Beheld the holy places of the dead
> The mock of aliens.

In consternation the natives view how ruthless hordes of white men conjure iron trails, and faces pale with greed and tongues forked to split the truth turn toward the sunset, taking whatsoever pleases them. The red men foresee the threatening disaster, when Doom shall ride the arrows of the lightning and prevail. Even if whole tribes shall have to take the spirit trail, they decide to retreat only with many wounds in front and scalps to prove to their ghostly kin how well they fought their forlorn fight.

After this brief but effective introduction Neihardt in a lengthy part entitled " Red Cloud " shows that redoubtable warrior strenuously opposing the plan of the peace commissioners to extend the iron trail through the hunting-ground of the Indians. Old and honored Spotted Tail's advice to concede the whites the Powder River road is scornfully rejected as the braves apply their hate

> To scraping dogwood switches smooth and straight
> For battle-arrows; and the teeth that bit
> The gnarly shaft, put venom into it
> Against the day the snarling shaft should bite.

Sitting Bull, long regarded the prime mover of Indian hostility, seconds Red Cloud's heroic resolve. Him Neihardt describes as a bull-torsoed, squat-necked, bow-legged man of penetrating gaze and with the reputation of a mountebank, full of vanity and craft,

> A battle-shirking intimate of squaws,
> A trivial contriver of applause,
> A user of the sacred for the base.

But, on the other hand, particular instances of his personal bravery are also recounted, mention is made of his reputed gift of talking with the dead, and we ourselves witness how his moving eloquence whips the hearers into a frenzy of hate.

The author then shows us how the storm-clouds gradually gather around Fort Phil Kearney, which the advancing white hordes had erected as a means of protection. With a great deal of skill Neihardt portrays the farthest frontier with its frequent brushes and bloody encounters. The wagon train bringing in logs is saved only in the nick of time by Fetterman with his forty troopers. Once again that daring and impetuous officer rescues the log train, but in direct and reckless disregard of orders he pursues the enemy too far and is surrounded. A fierce but unequal fight ensues on terrain suitable for Indian strategy where that little band of eighty-one dwindles as one after another is picked off. At last the white chief rolls from his saddle, vainly tugging at a shaft that has sprouted from his belly.

> Then a yell
> Of many bowmen mocked him as he fell,
> His wreathing body feathered like a goose.

They all perish to the last dog on that barren hill beside the Peno, simply "rubbed out."

Like so many other Western men, Neihardt does not credit the government with any understanding of or ability to handle the situation. Condescendingly he speaks of "Omniscience in a swivel chair, unmenaced half a continent away" muddling things. After an unusually severe winter there rises at last a camp at the Piney, with Piney Island filled with men and mules to cut lumber. Now Captain Powell and his thirty-two men serve as a protective shield against the attacking tribes. The description of the desperate fight around the wagon boxes arranged by the troopers and wood-cutters as a rampart is one of the finest in the song. Those brave men in their preparations for beating off the attack do not forget the possibility of defeat and grimly prepare as a last resort to shoot themselves so as to evade torture. Wave upon wave of the charging savages breaks before the thunder-spew of death and pain from the breech-fed Springfields, which pour a steady stream of lead into the living tempest that would also light the fire so often disastrous to the otherwise invincible soldier. White discipline, weapons, and strategy prevail and the twenty-nine, "knee-deep in standing arrows," joyously greet their relief-bringing comrades from the fort.

If it were not for the almost interminable descriptions of the changing seasons and the landscape especially at the beginning, the thrilling episode entitled "Beecher's Island" would be one of the most enjoyable ones of the poem. "A strange trail cleft the bison world," and Indian raid after raid had to be fought off. Soon after the Civil War Colonel Forsyth and Beecher, in following a trail, camp where a gravel bar had split the shank-deep Rickaree in two and formed an island. True to expectations, the Indians attack early in the morning, but incomprehensible as it may seem, allow the troop sufficient time to cross over to the island, which in the course of the next days becomes a slaughter pen. The assault of Roman Nose, naked on his horse except for a war-bonnet and followed by the thundering stampede of his braves, with the flaring out of the Flame of Many Roofs before the fire of the Spencers, is well described, although the whole lacks verisimilitude. The condition of the troop is a pitiable one, cooped up for nine days while a grizzly old trapper and his companion pierce the ring and bring help from Wallace eighty miles away — meanwhile men and horses dying, and wolves and buzzards eagerly waiting to feed on the carcasses. For once Neihardt forgets his customary long descriptions and with a few words paints a graphic picture:

> The slow sun sank.
> The empty prairie gloomed. The horses stank.
> The kiotes sang. The starry dark was cold.

At times the author injects not a little of humor into the situation, grim though it be. As the wounded Forsyth tumbles from the lifted blanket when one of the carriers in trying to avoid the fire of the Indians lets his corner slip, even his ordinarily kind nature does not prevent him from speaking out, " but what he said the angels didn't write." The injured doctor, singing or moaning as the west was getting sober-toned, choked a little and forgot the tune. But finally on the ninth day as the colonel, pretending to read, vainly strives " to regiment the herds of dancing letters into marching words," the long-looked-for relief from Wallace arrives.

In the next canto, " The Yellow God," gold irresistibly draws the whites to the Black Hills, and we are at last privileged to meet among the troop commanders protecting them Yellow Hair, far-famed General Custer, with the tale of his exploits on every lip. Here also appears Crazy Horse, described at great length as one of the heroes of the Song, who defies the command to appear at the agency. During the winter raid of his village he proves himself at least equal to Reynolds in cunning, and actually succeeds in rescuing the driven-off herd. After a long description of the sundance in preparation for war, Neihardt shows us the Seventh

THE STRUGGLE FOR THE BISON PASTURES 273

marching with Custer in command. Many are the forebodings of doom as the men playing with that magic name speak of " Custer's daring and of Custer's luck." That same resolute but reckless spirit of the fated man dominates when he takes leave with his column six hundred strong.

In the canto entitled " High Noon on the Little Horn " the reader naturally expects the central part of the poem, for here the author describes the fateful twenty-fifth of June 1876, when Custer was wiped out. The beginning is unpromising, for it is made up of a conversation of two fishermen and the trivial imaginings of the boy Hohay among the grasshoppers and his fight with the weeds. Twice the boy views from his windy rise the mile-long Indian village on the Little Big Horn, the second time in commotion at the approach of Major Reno's troopers. Panic grips the town till the booming voice of Gall,

> His naked body and his massive face
> Serene as hewn from time-forgotten rock,

rallies the warriors to meet the halting troop at the river bend. Without difficulty they smash the Ree scouts, who are said to have started for home without farewells.

The Custer partisan then describes in detail what he brands the cowardly retreat of Reno, who was the first to turn —

> 'Twas like a bison hunt, the Sioux have said,
> When few bulls battle and the fat cows run
> Less fleet than slaughter

as the troopers threshed through the stream and up the steep slopes closely pursued by their relentless foes. When the Indians notice the approach of additional columns from the east, panic spreads until Crazy Horse,

> That lean, swift fighting spirit of the Sioux,
> His wizard eyes, the haggard face and thin,
> Transfigured by a burning from within
> Despite the sweat-streaked paint and battle grime,

collects thousands to meet the advancing Custer. From an observation post a few details preceding the bloody conflict are described, but then " the scene went out in rumbling dust." This silence, just at the point where elaboration had become a duty, is one of the most disappointing parts of the poem — a thousand times rather omit the puerile speculations of Hohay than cut out the very heart of the central portion.

Next we watch with Neihardt Major Reno's inactivity and the attempted advance of Captain Wier, Godfrey, and French in support of Custer pressed back by the avalanche of enemies when the cowardly Reno remains in his position. Surrounded by alert foes, the beleaguered troops watch in the town below the demon exultation of the victors, and petulant with dread talk of Custer,

> grumbling at a name
> Already shaping on the lips of Fame
> To be a deathless bugle-singing soon.

The next day the very sun seemed Sioux, but toward evening, preceded by what seemed a treacherous silence, the league-long village of the Sioux goes up in smoke, and the Indians, women, children, warriors and all, are discovered fleeing toward the sheltering Big Horn Mountains at the approach of General Terry.

In the part entitled " The Twilight " Neihardt shows how retribution, or, if you will, irreparable wrong descends upon the race of the Sioux who are hunted down like wild beasts. He recites the story of the constant harrying on the part of the troops that leads to the disintegration of the Indian bands of Dull Knife, Sitting Bull, and Gall. Disasters come thick and fast; and in course of time Spotted Tail, an emissary with his cheeks full and his belly round, convinces Crazy Horse of the hopelessness of the situation, who agrees to bring his people in. And so

> with the crow
> And kiote to applaud his pomp of woe,
> The last great Sioux rode down to his defeat.

In scenes of poignant grief the author pictures him brooding over the care-free and happy life of the native once roaming the plains.

The tale approaches its close as the news of Nez Percé Joseph and his exploits induces Crazy Horse to vanish from his assigned camp during the night. Found in the camp of Spotted Tail, he is persuaded by assurances of safety to go to Robinson where the

THE STRUGGLE FOR THE BISON PASTURES

soldier chief would talk to him. There stark tragedy awaits him, best described in Neihardt's own lines, which occasionally border on the sentimental. Detecting the treachery that would confine him behind bars, the chief resolutely whips out his butcher-knife

> And, leaping door-ward, charged upon the world
> To meet the end. A frightened soldier hurled
> His weight behind a jabbing belly-thrust,
> And Crazy Horse plunged headlong in the dust,
> A wreathing heap.

Recovering consciousness, he is hardly able to pant his parting speech:

> I had my village and my pony herds
> On Powder where the land was all my own.
> I only wanted to be left alone.
> I did not want to fight. The Gray Fox sent
> His soldiers. We were poorer when they went;
> Our babies died, for many lodges burned
> And it was cold. We hoped again and turned
> Our faces westward. It was just the same
> Out yonder on the Rosebud. Gray Fox came.
> The dust his soldiers made was high and long.
> I fought him and I whipped him. Was it wrong
> To drive him back? That country was my own.
> I only wanted to be let alone.
> I did not want to see my people die.
> They say I murdered Long Hair and they lie.
> His soldiers came to kill us and they died.

Choking and shivering, the once strong chief in his death agony calls for his father and mother, whom the callous soldiers prevent from comforting him.

> But when at length the lyric voice was dumb
> And Crazy Horse was nothing but a name,
> There was a little withered woman came
> Behind a bent old man. Their eyes were dim.
> They sat beside the boy and fondled him,
> Remembering the little names he knew
> Before the great dream took him and he grew
> To be so mighty. And the woman pressed
> A hand that men had feared against her breast
> And swayed and sang a little sleepy song.

And when after a night of lament the morning came,

> The last great Sioux rode silently away.
> Before the pony-drag on which he lay
> An old man tottered. Bowed above the bier,
> A little wrinkled woman kept the rear
> With not a sound and nothing in her eyes.

The great chief's burial place on a crumbling summit of the Badlands, forgotten save for the voices of the owl and the day-long sorrow of the crows, fittingly symbolizes the melancholy and unwept end of the native's tribal existence.

The Song of the Indian Wars deals with an arresting and important subject, in the composition of which immense masses of interesting and potentially rich materials were at the author's disposal. Neihardt brought to the task a discriminating knowledge of Indian character and of the scenes of the conflict, as anyone with a first-hand acquaintance of the plains tribes and of the various localities will testify. It also must be admitted that in describing the undulating plains and the broken character of the Western country he conveys an air of reality and actuality. The bold and telling strokes of the painter's brush depicting spirited action as well as the more subdued tones revealing the native soul should likewise be counted among the excellencies of the work. And not a few of the portraits of leading actors in the moving drama are exceptionally well done, especially in regard to external characterization.

But, on the other hand, as a work of art *The Song of the Indian Wars* labors under a number of rather serious disadvantages. Somehow the rimes of the heroic couplet impose limitations that might have made the adoption of a different verse form seem advisable. The unusual terms in their strained positions tend to lessen the enjoyment of the reader, who is often surprised and bewildered at the strange turns the lines take. Apart from that, the author seems to delight in ransacking the dim recesses of the vocabulary and bringing to light curious and archaic forms.

More serious, because it violates the very spirit of the poem, is the introduction of the classical element, entirely foreign to the subject matter and the mood of a North American epic. However much it may do credit to Neihardt's learning, its omission would have been vastly preferable, for the red man is decidedly not a Greek or Roman, and his world and his ideas are not those of classical antiquity. Another serious blemish is the many and strange personifications of a fanciful and introspective nature foreign to the healthy imagination of the great out-of-doors. Less inherently objectionable as mere personal idiosyncrasies, but still artistically indefensible, are the curiously figurative, lengthy, and monotonous descriptions especially of time, of the weather, and of the scenery. For instance, only part of such a description tells us how

> Suddenly a gale
> That blustered rainless up the Bozeman Trail
> Was bringing June again; but not the dear
> Deep-bosomed mother of a hemisphere
> That other regions cherish. Flat of breast,
> More passionate than loving, up the West
> A stern June strode, lean suckler of the lean,
> Her rag-and-tatter robe of faded green
> Blown dustily about her.

The rather lengthy work could have been measurably shortened and improved by a suitable economy of expression.

Probably the most serious defect of the poem is its lack of unity and of emphasis. Aside from the cold-blooded Aryan urge to conquer, there is no real central idea welding the loosely strung episodes into one harmonious whole. The work appears to be a recital of historical events, with presumably high points following each other on the same unrelieved plane. Closely connected with this is the lack of any decided stand for or against the two contending and clashing races. Half approving the course and the necessity of events, and yet not unsympathetic toward the natives, the author never emerges from an ambiguous vacillation. The same deadly level of Indian chiefs is spread before our eyes: Red Cloud, Sitting Bull, Roman Nose, Gall, and Crazy Horse, all play their parts, but none really assumes the rôle of an overshadowing hero, though possibly Crazy Horse comes nearest to it. Disavowing sentimentalization, yet in the dying speech of Crazy Horse and in the pathetic figures of his aged father and mother Neihardt has overstepped the limits he himself set. Closely akin to the lack of emphasis in drawing native characters is the fact that the figure of General Custer never assumes heroic proportions, but as the story goes on, becomes more and more vague and nebulous, as already Miss Hazard has pointed out. A shortcoming of major importance appears in that Custer's last stand is obscured by a cloud of dust, though ordinarily the author is not averse to lifting the curtain and describing an action at great length. And this from an outspoken Custer partisan! What the reader justifiably expects to be a focal point of the poem is regrettably absent, while less important and even trivial passages are elaborated without any need or justification.

That shortcomings such as these should mar *The Song of the Indian Wars,* as also the two frontier poems commented upon, is all the more regrettable in view of the fact that the work has the basic elements of true greatness. With a comprehensive knowledge of both setting and character plus considerable descriptive ability Neihardt had it within his power to weld the rich materials into a work of surpassing art. If only he had disciplined his imagination sufficiently to reject the extraneous and the bizarre, and instead unified and stressed the pertinent and the striking, the struggle for the bison pastures of the West would give unalloyed joy to the discriminating reader.

CHAPTER XX

TRAVELLING THE WHITE MAN'S ROAD

One of the most systematic as well as sympathetic treatments of the American native and his problem is found in the works of Hamlin Garland (1860–   ), the great realist of the West, particularly in *The Captain of the Gray Horse Troop,* 1902, and in *The Book of the American Indian,* 1923. His auto-biographical *A Daughter of the Middle Border,* 1921, and *Companions on the Trail,* 1931, serve as a valuable record of his life among the Indians and his attitude toward the red man. For Garland in his characteristic way bases his observations upon a first-hand acquaintance especially with the plains tribes. In addition, the book contains some minor portraits of aboriginal characters. Unforgettable among them is Slohan, chief of Sitting Bull's bodyguard, who serves as the type of inconsolable parent heartbroken over the death of his granddaughter. *The Book of the American Indian,* which also contains the epic *The Silent Eaters,* a story of Sitting Bull's life and death, depicts in a number of short stories the Indian's troubled attempt to walk the white man's road. The perplexities of the reservation problem and its final solution are systematically treated in *The Captain of the Gray Horse Troop,* in which Garland proposes to transform the Indian, without doing violence to the soul of the native, into a useful member of civilized society.

The Silent Eaters is Garland's epic of the Indian race, told in a sympathetic manner by one of Sitting Bull's partisans. According to the account given in *A Daughter of the Middle Border* and *Companions on the Trail,* the author secured most of his material at the Standing Rock Reservation in North Dakota from persons closely associated with the great Sioux Chief. Among them were the half-breed Primeau and the French-Canadian Carignan, who had taught school near the chief's camp and often entertained him. Even more detailed and intimate glimpses were given by Slohan, the annalist of the tribe and the leader of the " Silent Eaters," Sitting Bull's bodyguard, which derived its name from the fact that the members met in private feasts and talked quietly without songs or dancing, while all the others in the tribe made merry. In the epic he appears as Shato, father of the narrator, and is drawn upon for many of the details of the story. Another valuable contributor was a warrior called Looking Stag, who had known the chief. Close observation of the Indian tribes and a sympathetic insight into their psychology on the part of Garland supplied the rest.

As novelist of the great Northwest the author felt that justice demanded that he portray in addition to the pioneer also the Sioux and the Algonquin as part of the history of the border and fully as significant. The prose poem *The Silent Eaters* has as its central figure the great typical Sioux warrior and statesman, who makes out a strong case for the native. In spite of strong temptations to be diffuse, Garland with admirable self-control has achieved complete unity. Only once, and then with a reminder that the story is not of himself, does the narrator venture to insert a few lines of direct personal interest. The whole is well told in a simple and unadorned yet impressive manner, by means of the short, direct, and pregnant sentences one might expect from an Indian schooled for years in the polished East.

As the narrator the author has chosen Iapi, son of the chief of the " Silent Eaters," who confides his inmost thoughts to the sympathetic listener. The tragedy begins way back in 1854 when the Uncapappas are summoned to a conference by the great war chief of the whites. This council of the Sioux could not have been held under more favorable conditions among the prairie tribes, with the grass new and sweet, the buffalo fat, the horses swift, and each day a feast, even the aged smiling like children. " In those days the plains were black with buffalo and the valleys speckled with red deer and elk, and no lodge had fear of hunger or frost. In winter we occupied tepees of thick warm fur with the edges fully banked with snow and we were not often cold. We had plenty of buckskin to wear and no one went unsatisfied. You would look long to find a people as happy as we were, because we lived as the Great Spirit had taught us to do, with no thought of change." [1]

The warning note sounded by The Hawk against the white givers of dubious gifts is reenforced and deepened by the twenty-two-year-old *Ta-Tank-io-Tanka,* the Sitting Bull whose sentiments and determination earn him the title and position of Chief Soldier of Treaties or in our parlance Secretary of War. Garland has the hero pictured as brave, tactful, and wise, with the welfare of his tribe at heart, and personal aggrandizement far from his mind. As the four head chiefs pass on, he is elevated to the headship of the whole band and determines the policy of the tribe, ever refusing to cede the ancestral lands for the proffers of friendship and gifts.

In keeping with his noble character, peaceful yet courageous, and protected by a band of trusted warriors, Sitting Bull treads the thorny path which greed and aggression force him upon. The Black Hills controversy about the yellow gold leads to the tragedy of the Battle of the Big Horn, when in defense of children and home the braves strike down Custer's attacking columns. Dark days follow. But the surrender of Ogallallahs and Cheyennes to superior white forces and the defections among his own people do not weaken the determination of the great chief; skilfully he evades General Miles and succeeds in subsisting in the bleak north near the Canadian border.

"I shall never forget that dreadful winter. It seems now like one continuous whirling storm of snow filled with wailing. We were cold and hungry all the time, and the white soldiers were ever on our trail. Many died and the cries of women never ceased. It was as if the Great Spirit had forgotten us."

When the soldiers press him too hard, Sitting Bull crosses the dividing line to Canada; but though this affords temporary respite, it furnishes no protection from hunger and cold, which drive the sufferers almost to despair. We can sympathize with the chief's desire not to sell the ancestral lands and mode of living for the blankets and food of the white man. "If the Great Spirit had de-

---

[1] All quotations from Garland's works are by the kind permission of the author.

sired me to be a white man, he would have made me so in the first place. He put in your heart certain wishes and plans, in my heart he put other and different desires. Each man is good in His sight. It is not necessary for eagles to become crows."

But both Garland and the great Sioux are compelled to bow before the force of circumstances. At last the necessity of abject misery leaves no choice, and the proud chief, guided by the soldiers, goes south to the Standing Rock Reservation where many of his kin already have found shelter under the wings of the whites. The restricted life of the reservation, with the Indian's vast hunting-ground appropriated by his enemies, is shown to be distasteful and repugnant to the roamer and lord of the unmeasured expanse. " I do not wish to be shut up in a corral. It is bad for the young men to be fed by the agent. It makes them lazy and drunken. All the agency Indians I have ever seen are worthless. They are neither red warriors nor white farmers. They are neither wolf nor dog."

When on his return from Washington Iapi recognizes in a sad and ashamed teamster his father, the leader of the " Silent Eaters," he makes the significant observation: " I could not but perceive that we were both more admirable as red warriors than as imitation Saxon farmers." The old chief is ignored in order that his power as a dangerous reactionary may be broken; the lands are signed away by others. The situation is indeed tragic: the natives are physically, mentally, and spiritually submerged by the rising tide of an alien race. Their customs and habits are sinking beneath the white man's civilization as dances, prayers, and ceremonies are discouraged or forbidden. No wonder that this forced transformation brings about a distressing situation, the injustice of which the author takes pains to emphasize.

In the words of an impartial Commissioner of Indian Affairs: " Suddenly and almost without warning they were called upon to give up all their ancient pursuits and without previous training settle down to agriculture in a land largely unfitted for such uses. The freedom of the chase was exchanged for the idleness of the camp. The boundless range abandoned for the circumscribed reservation, and abundance of plenty supplanted by limited and decreasing subsistence and supplies. Under these circumstances it is not in human nature not to be discontented and restless, even turbulent and violent."

In this intolerable winter night of tragic dejection, and the proud and inflexible race resigned to die, there rises the star of prophecy in the rumor of the Messiah in the West. Had the natives remained true to the ways of the fathers, misfortunes would not have befallen them. Even now the message is hopeful: " If all the red people unite, casting away all that is of the white man, praying and purifying themselves, then will the old world come back — the old happy world of the buffalo, and all the dead ones of our race will return, a mighty host, driving the buffalo before them." The so-called " ghost dance " begins, four days long, a weird, thrilling song assailing the sky:

> " The whole world of the dead is returning.
> Our nation is coming, is coming, is coming.
> The eagle has brought us the message,
> Bearing the word of the Father —
> The word and the wish of the Father.
> Over the glad new earth they are coming,
> Our dead come driving the elk and the deer.
> See them hurrying the herds of the bison.
> This the Father has promised,
> This the Father has given."

In great, probably too great, detail Garland describes the " Messiah craze " with its effect especially upon the less intelligent and more emotional members of the tribe who had been weakened by the loss of dear ones. The chief remains sceptical as none of his trusted warriors fall hypnotized into the trance and visit the spirit world, though he gives suitable answers to the miracle-believing whites who look upon the visions as mere nonsense.

To the unsympathetic agent the head of his people, however, proposes to find out the truth of the rumor, exhibiting a trait by which the author exalts him far above the scheming tormentors. Even before this, he had broken the peace pipe, " for if the new religion is true, then there is no more war. If it is not true, then he wishes to die as a warrior dies, fighting." As the agent refuses to go to the bottom of the rumor, the chief himself decides to investigate, but before he can leave, the Indian police arrest him. The " Silent Eaters " hurry to his assistance, killing one of the policemen, but the chief is shot, and when the fight ends, " eight of the ' Silent Eaters ' lay dead beside their chief, and with them fell four renegades who went to their tragic end under a mistaken call of duty — to be forever execrated for slaying their chief at the white man's command."

Thus the tragic epic comes to a close with the death of the last great Sioux chief, whom the leader of his bodyguard lauds in extravagant terms as a noble and mighty man. In the words of the son, the singer of the saga: " He epitomized the epic, tragic story of my kind. His life spanned the gulf between the days of our freedom and the death of every custom native to us. He saw the invader come and he watched the buffalo disappear. Within the half century of his conscious life he witnessed greater changes and comprehended more of my tribe's tragic history than any other red man."

As might be expected from a partisan of Sitting Bull, his character appears almost flawless like that of a hero working and dying in behalf of his people. And yet, there is perhaps little inherently improbable in such a portrait. However, the life of the natives before the interference of the white man is described as too idyllic, and though there may be considerable truth in the claim that the plains Indian was the most perfect adaptation to his environment, nevertheless strife and war between the tribes are too much minimized. It must of course not be forgotten that the whole is dominated by the contrast of a native's retrospect of his unhindered roaming of the prairies and the present life of enforced labor within the bounds of the reservation. With the doom of impending tragedy constantly overhanging the people, no happy note of pleasure is ever sounded: all is sadness and gloom.

It is a well known fact that Hamlin Garland is a sympathizer of the red man, who never held the settler's view of the Indian as a wild beast to be ruthlessly exterminated. In beautiful and simple language adapted to the subject he lets the poignant story be told as felt in the inmost soul of the native who knew that his own road inevitably led to destruction. If the reader should complain that the narrative is not so romantic and thrilling as he may have been accustomed to from his youth, let him remember that Garland is a realist who desires to complete the history of the border, and that truth and moderation alone can paint the picture worthy of a great and magnificent subject, the passing of a once powerful race.

The most significant of Garland's short stories dealing with the native are also found in *The Book of the American Indian*. He believes that " we have had plenty of the ' wily redskin ' kind of thing," as he told Major Stouch on the Cheyenne Reservation. " I am going to tell of the red man as you and Seger have known him, as a man of the polished stone age trying to adapt himself to steam and electricity."

Since he had no patience with the writers who regarded the Indian as a wild beast, Garland based his interpretation on the opinions of sympathetic men who by their long experience had proved the red man's fine qualities. The fourteen stories give us glimpses of various tribes whose members are confronted with new conditions to which they react in their own individual way. Generally speaking, they reveal the Indian as a human being and neighbor who is finding it hard to forsake his own ways and to travel the white man's trail, but whose problem can be solved by justice, sympathy, and tact on the part of his more advanced white brother.

Not a few of the narratives are at least semi-historical, faithful delineations of life and character, for, even if partly imaginary, they grew out of a careful study of real people and real conditions. With only a few touches of the humorous and the sentimental, they reveal the Indian's soul in his more serious and even tragic moods. Fierce and uncontrollable anger and likewise uncontrollable grief after having slain his aspiring cousin seize the Teton chief in *The Remorse of Waumdisapa,* while in *The Storm Child* the kindness of a white hunter in rescuing the small Teton boy during a snowstorm brings from a widowed mother an offer of marriage. A human and supernatural element is present in *The River's Warning,* in which the Cheyenne Big Elk tells of a planned raid of the agency in his younger days, first delayed by the kindness of the Quaker agent, and then brought to naught by the river's rising as foreshadowed in a dream, which touches the "deepest chord in the red man's soul — the chord which vibrates when the Great Spirit speaks to him in dreams." *The Blood Lust*, throbbing with passion, shows how the Cheyenne Little Robe, who on his horse-stealing raid into Mexican territory had lost his only daughter, takes bloody revenge on a whole town, and then beside the heaps of ashes sleeps at last peacefully.

The Indian's inherent distrust of the cattleman is clearly brought out in *Lone Wolf's Old Guard*, where the grizzled warriors threaten to fight the drawing of the line and the building of the fence until the army steps in. In all of Garland's writings there is found on the part of the red man a wholesome respect for the soldier and a partial acknowledgment of his justice.

But the author only too well knows that the onward march of the white man is irresistible, and that the roamer of the plains must either bow or break. The chief significantly called Drifting Crane in the tale named after him, who uses "none of the absurd figures of rhetoric which romancers invariably put into the mouth of the Indians," meets the just but inflexible oldest settler of the Jim Valley, Henry Wilson, who stands upon his right to stay by virtue of Uncle Sam's decrees. "Each man was a type; each was wrong, and each was right. The Indian as true and noble from the barbaric point of view as the white man. He was a warrior and hunter; made so by circumstances over which he had no control. The settler represented the unflagging energy and fearless heart of the American pioneer. Narrow-minded, partly brutalized by hard labor and a lonely life, yet an admirable figure for all that. As he looked into the Indian's face he seemed to grow in height. He felt behind him all the weight of the millions of westward moving settlers; he stood the representative of an unborn state." At last the despairing Indian as one of the rear guard of retreating barbarism bows to the irresistible logic of the pioneer who points out that force on the part of the native will be of no avail. Even more tragic with its poignant grief is *The Story of Howling Wolf*, whose chief character in spite of his meek effort to travel the white man's road falls a victim to what Garland condemns as the " cruel, leering racial hate of the border man, to whom the red man is big game," and dies a most outrageous death.

Only reluctantly does the native allow his offspring to be exposed to the culture of the white man, and at times parental resentment prevents all educational efforts. The Navajo in *Big Moggasen* refuses to depart from the way of his fathers and send his children to school even at the price of not receiving help. Among the brown people of the mesa a similar spirit of independence prevails; for in *The Iron Khiva* the two boys singled out to go from the missionary school to a strange institution by their suicide prevent such a plan.

The atmosphere in *Wahiah — A Spartan Mother* Garland has skilfully surcharged with danger and grief, though in the end common sense triumphs over the instinctive repugnance of the Indian toward seeing his children whipped. The recalcitrant boy is transformed by a sound thrashing into an obedient child by the just but firm schoolmaster Seger, assisted in the end by a Spartan mother who destroys her son's symbols of freedom, his bow and arrows, although her heart is almost breaking. Beautiful in its simplicity and for its sympathy with primitive life is *The New Medicine House,* in which the author proves that an Indian doctor's psychology and contact with home are better medicine than the scientific treatment in the school hospital.

However, Garland's most systematic fictional study of the red man trying to walk the white man's road under difficult circumstances is found in *The Captain of the Gray Horse Troop,* 1902, a powerful novel and quite generally accepted by reviewers as a truthful presentation of life on an Indian reservation in the nineties. The book proved popular on its appearance, and was heartily praised by President Roosevelt, who, in full sympathy with Garland's position, put some of his suggestions into practice.

The novel is partly based upon an " outbreak " of the Northern Cheyennes fomented by rapacious cattlemen, types of whom Garland met on his way to the Lame Deer Agency in Montana in order to study the problem at the source. To him " the violence of their antagonism, their shameless greed of the red man's land revealed . . . for once and for all the fomenting spirit of each of the Indian Wars which had accompanied the exterminating, century-long march of our invading race. In a single sentence these men expressed the ruthless creed of the land-seeker. 'We intend to wipe these red sons-of-dogs from the face of the earth.'"

At the agency Garland succeeded with the help of Major George Stouch and other sympathetic officers to win the confidence of White Bull, Two Moon, Porcupine, American Horse, and other principal Cheyenne warriors. An Indian policeman called Wolf Voice, who one summer had served as guide to Frederick Remington, the great painter of Indians, also was of incalculable value in obtaining the source material for the study based upon the little war. Various trips to Indian reservations, especially into the Indian Territory, were of considerable help in creating the atmosphere.

The scene of the story is laid at old Fort Smith near Pinon City in Montana among the Tetongs (Sioux), westernmost representatives of a once powerful race of hunters. The rascally Sennett is supplanted as agent by Major George Curtis, who fears from the beginning that the settlers will prove the chief cause of friction. They are backed by a powerful Senator Brisbane, who had come to the state early and succeeded in grasping and holding the natural resources of the great territory. " It mattered nothing to him and his kind that a race of men already lived upon this land and were prepared to die in defence of it. By adroit juggling, he and his corporation put the unsuspecting settler forward to receive the first shock of the battle, and, when trouble came, loudly called upon the government to send its troops in support of the pioneers."

In keeping with Garland's opinion, these so-called pioneers were in the eyes of the army officer by no interpretation martyrs in the cause of civilization, but either poor or degenerate whites with not the slightest interest in their primitive red neighbor, or greedy cattlemen who expected to fatten their stock under the protection of the military. His attitude in defending the rights of the aborigines is only partly appreciated by the daughter of the powerful Senator, who writes Curtis: " I feel the force of what you say, but the course of civilization lies across the lands of the 'small peoples.' It is sorrowful, of course, but they must go, like the wolves and the rattlesnakes." The politician himself hardly considers them human beings, but a greasy lot of vermin, worthless from every point of view, whose rights cannot stand in the way of civilization.

But these powerful forces fail in ousting Curtis, who at Washington defends the fragment of a proud and free people sitting in wonder before the coming of an infinite flood of alien races, helpless to stay it and appalled by the breadth and power of the stream which swept them away. He is ably supported by the flinty chairman of the Committee on Indian Affairs, who, refusing to consider the red man in the light of a reptile, looks upon him as one who has certain rights under our treaties. With such masterly defense, all attacks fail.

Like Garland, Curtis has a high opinion of the outstanding characters among the natives, such as Crawling Elk, the annalist and story-teller of the tribe, who in addition to his historical knowledge and his lore of the mysterious universe has a mind thronging with poetical images: " In the eyes of God, I am persuaded there is no wide difference between old Crawling Elk and Herbert Spencer. The circle of Spencer's knowledge is wider, but it is as far from including the infinite as the redman's story of creation."

Another opinion, probably not less sympathetic to the author, finds expression in the painter Lawson, who, like the Senator's daughter Elsie considering the natives good artistic material, looks upon the old life as a beautiful adaptation of organism to environment. He minimizes their wars, which to him appear as small affairs, hardly more than skirmishes, with even insignificant forays given considerable importance in their winter counts. They assumed serious proportions only when the coming of the white man crowded one tribe into another tribe's territory. But he dissents from Garland when he characterizes as futile the efforts of the humanitarian agent to make the red race a woof of our national life without producing grotesque caricatures of American farmers, since the red man as a social being, from time immemorial accustomed to a communal life, is too much dependent upon his tribe to conform to the isolated, dreary, lonesome life of the Western farmer.

The avowed principles of the Major, who in reality is only the mouthpiece of the author, receive their supreme test when he surprises a crew of woodchoppers in the act of burning alive an old Indian tied to a tree, and when a sheepherder disappears, presumably killed by the outraged natives. The campaign against the agent and his wards grows bitter, and the accusers threaten to stop at nothing in their desire to kill and slay. So much is certain, the murderer must be found out if peace is to be restored. At the council meeting the chief, knowing full well the consequences for the whole tribe if the man is not given up, orders the killer to stand forth.

" A low mutter and a jostling caused every glance to center upon one side of the circle, and then, decked in war-paint, gay with beads and feathers and carrying a rifle, Cut Finger stepped silently and haughtily into the circle and stood motionless as a statue, his tall figure erect and rigid as an oak.

A moaning sound swept over the assembly, and every eye was fixed on the young man. ' Ahee! Ahee! ' the women wailed, in astonishment and fear; two or three began a low, sad chant, and death seemed to stretch a black wing over the council. By his weapons, by his war-paint, by his bared head decked with eagle plumes, and by the haughty lift of his face, Cut Finger proclaimed louder than words, ' I am the man who killed the herder! '

Standing so, he began to sing a stern song:

> ' I alone killed him — the white man.
> He was a thief and I killed him.
> No one helped me; I alone fired the shot.
> He will drive his sheep no more on Tetong lands,
> This dog of a herder.
> He lies there in the short grass.
> It was I, Cut Finger, who did it.'

As his chant died away he turned. ' I go to the hills to fight and die like a man.' And before the old men could stay him he had vanished among the young horsemen of the outer circle, and a moment later the loud drumming of his pony's hoofs could be heard as he rode away."

Later, however, he peacefully submits to arrest and incarceration at Pinon City. But the precautionary measures of the agent prove to be of no avail when in the ensuing riot the unfortunate man is shot and dragged to death by the mob. This outrage produces a reaction, with the better citizens regaining control, while in the subsequent campaign the bad element is defeated, and the settlers have to leave. A new day is beginning to dawn for the Indians, which according to the author will lead to the solution of the Indian problem.

Under this new disposition, all are set to work building fences, digging ditches, plowing and planting. Even the old, hard as it is, follow where Swift Eagle, the agent, leads, though the white man's road is long and runs into strange country. To satisfy the communal spirit and the social longings, mimic war parties against the weeds are organized and festivals celebrate the peaceful achievements. Curtis and Elsie, whom he has won over and now claims as his bride, view the transformation and evolution of a race from hunting to harvesting. Since the game has vanished, its members must put the rifle away and take up the hoe; as every wild thing must pass before the ever-thickening flood of white plowmen pressing upon the land, the original possessors of the soil likewise must enter the road of peace and happiness by turning to agriculture. Thus only — and this is Garland's solution of the problem — can they save themselves in the inevitable march of civilization by becoming a part of it.

Strange as it may appear to some modern readers, *The Captain of the Gray Horse Troop* has been Garland's best seller, close to a hundred thousand copies having found their way into the hands of the public. The late Brander Matthews thought it "a rattling good story," and Theodore Roosevelt was delighted with it, the part assigned the army officers especially striking his fancy. The advocate of the "big stick" in international affairs readily admitted the essential justice of the red man's case over against the greed of the cattleman and the settler. Here as elsewhere the author takes the cruelty and dirt and sloth of camp life for granted, subjects he thought sufficiently emphasized by other writers. His main concern is to present the native's point of view, the tender and humorous side of Indian life finding adequate expression beside the heroic and patriotic endeavors of a proud and sensitive race.

There is of course no question that the stories of *Main Travelled Roads* are better known than the tales and the tragic epic of *The Book of the American Indian*. Likewise it is only natural that at present *A Son of the Middle Border* and *A Daughter of the Middle Border* should interest more readers than *The Captain of the Gray Horse Troop*. The former deal with the hopes, joys, and sorrows of pioneer families and their offspring in the conquest of a new continent, while the latter concern themselves with an alien world and a vanishing race ruthlessly trodden under foot by the advancing march of white civilization.

If it appears to some that the picture of the native is too flattering, and that his qualities are painted with too bright colors, let them remember that a troublesome conscience brushes aside the wrongs inflicted upon a weaker and less resourceful opponent, and endows with a halo of glory the achievements of kinsfolk even if unscrupulous in the choice of weapons. Hamlin Garland has not only sung in a sympathetic manner and in a dignified way the farewell lament of a brave race, and impressed individual representatives upon our mind, but he has also indicated the method by which its few remnants may be built into the structure of a mighty state reared upon the ruins of mere tribal organization.

CHAPTER XXI

CONCLUSION

In distinct contrast to English literature, the American Indian is an integral part of the writings produced within the boundaries of what is now the United States of America. It is true, the English also took cognizance of him, but with them he was a rather strange, shadowy figure, often a mere toy of the imagination. But here he is a native plant springing from the soil, not an exotic product or the result of a philosophic theory. This does not mean that Rousseau's and Chateaubriand's dream of nature's nobleman living the perfect life in the American wilderness was without influence on our literature, especially in the heyday of romanticism. But these forces were much less potent than in Europe and even at their height were constantly modified by the realities close at hand. The traveller and the missionary, the soldier and the frontiersman all could give first-hand accounts of the inhabitants of the prairie and the forest, which were naturally reflected in the delineation of the red man. The portrait was apt to be more realistic than a painter three thousand miles away from the scene would produce.

At first, close contact with the savage on the frontier often made the colonial estimate of the only good Indian as a dead Indian a universal border sentiment. In imaginative literature as well as in history the aspect of the Puritan is grim and forbidding, and the conflict between the two races assumes an unparalleled ruthlessness on the dark and bloody ground of Kentucky. Later, a wistful regret over the native's passing from the eastern part of the country and the apparent injustice of his treatment caused brighter colors to predominate. Especially was this the case during the first four decades of the 19th century, when the border atrocities progressively began to fade from the public mind, while the native under conditions of comparative freedom in what was then the West still retained many of his admirable qualities. If anywhere, the noble savage of Rousseau's creation would find his natural habitat in the expansive valley of the Mississippi, an illusion that vanished with the first advance of the pioneer. Generally speaking, the colorful pageant as reflected in literature moves from the East and the South to the West, though we should always remember that some authors, like Irving and Cooper, are interested in both Eastern and Western tribes.

The character of the Indian is variously described and interpreted, mainly as a result of the purpose of the author and the circumstances under which he became acquainted with the native. The early travellers and explorers meeting the lord of the wide expanse were apt to dwell upon the picturesqueness of his character and life. The missionary sought out the nobler qualities of a being he desired to win for his God, and in return was not seldom rewarded by viewing the more amiable traits of one who recognized in him a benefactor. The military man and the settler, on the other hand, ordinarily disputed with the savage the ownership of the soil, and it was but natural that they should easily have detected in him the demonic characteristics of a cunning and ferocious enemy. It is apparent that all these attitudes and estimates, sometimes in bewildering combination, are reflected in American literature.

Within certain limits, the summary of the red man's character given by Francis Parkman in his *Conspiracy of Pontiac* is an admirable one. There he points to the native as the embodiment of the most contradictory qualities: independence and hero worship, love and hate, self-control and passionate action, bravery, generosity, and honor, as well as treachery, envy, and revenge are all shown mingled in one personality, fired with a desire for glory and imbued with the spirit to resist all change. But in spite of its apparent brilliance, the summary is somewhat superficial in that it does not probe the depths of aboriginal character and sins by its omission of important if less obvious traits the native displayed when not under the scrutiny of white men. It should be kept in mind that Parkman as the historian of the clash of French and English interests and cultures on American soil not unnaturally was impressed by the darker side of aboriginal character which such a conflict inevitably revealed.

It is also true that in surveying the whole field of literature dealing with the Indian one cannot but be impressed by the large part the struggle for the possession of the soil has played. A great number of authors center their efforts around the heroic figure of some chief valiantly fighting for his people, generally the last of his line. So we have King Philip, Conanchet, Pontiac, Logan, Tecumseh, Sitting Bull and a host of others, with a culture hero occasionally thrown in. Practically everywhere some conflict is raging, if not with the whites, then among the tribes themselves.

The more popular poems and dramas are mostly built around historical persons, while the more enduring prose fiction generally deals with imaginative characters. The drama especially with its need for action drew largely upon biographical material, no fewer than six of the extant plays, more than one fourth, dealing with Pocahontas, and both King Philip and Pontiac appearing in at least two. It is a curious and perhaps significant fact that as the figure of King Philip, the great New England chief, in the person of the superb Forrest gave Indian drama unexampled popularity for two decades, so the embodiment of Powhatan in Brougham should have sounded the death knell of the whole genre. Thus heroic and humorous figures marked the turning point of the stage Indian. King Philip is probably the most favored character, poems, dramas, and prose fiction all featuring him. Of late, however, Sitting Bull as the last bulwark of Indian resistance against the swirling tide of white domination has become an increasing favorite.

It is apparent that in not a few of the works the imagination of the white man has endowed his characters with emotions and traits alien to the red man. However necessary the interpolation of romantic ideas may have appeared for the sake of a larger audience, such a device remains an anomaly both historically and psychologically. And with few exceptions the benefit has been a doubtful one. For the author who described his characters in all their native grandeur but little influenced by white contact ordinarily achieved the greatest success. The primitive is triumphant.

The figure who under his red paint wears a white heart and exhibits white manners is a sorry spectacle, with the half-breed, embodying the worst traits of both races, the least poetic and the least attractive of all.

All the virtues and vices which could possibly be ascribed to a human being are found in the native. The clash of opinion is indeed a violent one. On the one hand, we have the creations of *Yamoyden* and Miller, on the other hand, those of Bird and Emmons. Such contrasting figures as Uncas and Le Renard Subtil are also found in one author. There is no evolution from the noble savage to the bloodthirsty fiend or vice versa, a fact readily explained if we keep in mind that personal observation or study rather than a philosophical movement produced the individual works. The naturalist, the missionary, and the philanthropist were not less influential than the soldier, the hunter, and the settler in determining what pigments should go into the picture. With not a little of interest we note how the former would preserve the native in his original state by furnishing him an asylum or a paradise safe from white intrusion. But this wistful hope of a Thoreau and the vehement plea of a Miller were met by the raucous demand for extermination voiced by the greedy and callous settler. Both embodied extremes that proved impossible of realization under the prevailing conditions of civilized American life, though conformity to the ways of civilization and its modes of support has become the only safeguard against extinction.

While on the whole Simms' estimate of the native is probably the most balanced, Cooper under the partial guidance of Heckewelder has undoubtedly been most influential in molding and fixing the world's conception of the American Indian. In spite of the varied and not wholly unjustified criticisms of his delineation, the portrait he paints is, all things considered, not far from the truth. One harbors a well-founded suspicion that Cooper's unpopularity during his controversial period may have added considerable weight to the strictures of his critics, especially with the general public. The antipathy of others can readily be traced to different motives. For instance, Mark Twain's savage attack on Cooper's Indians as belonging to an extinct tribe which never existed may be ascribed to the customary picturesque bluntness of a humorist rather than to a reasoned estimate of the whole subject. His experience with the degraded Goshoots as related in *Roughing It* seems to have colored his whole subsequent attitude. He claims that an examination of authorities revealed to him, the Indian worshipper who had " been overestimating the red man while viewing him through the mellow moonshine of romance," that the natives ordinarily are treacherous, filthy, and repulsive, only Goshoots more or less modified by circumstances. But it may be gravely doubted that this examination was either fair or thorough. Certainly the trappers and fur traders meeting an occasional degraded Western tribe were much less hasty in their generalizations and conclusions than the reckless humorist.

Perhaps less strange is the unsympathetic attitude which Lowell, the cultured frequenter of drawing rooms, assumes in *A Fable for Critics*. After the ready admission that the vainglorious novelist

> . . has drawn you one character, though, that is new,
> One wildflower he's plucked that is wet with the dew
> Of this fresh Western world. . . .

and has given life and objective existence to *one* character, he blandly announces:

> His Indians, with proper respect it be said,
> Are just Natty Bumppo, daubed over with red.

Such partiality in appraising Cooper's merits reveals nothing less than abysmal ignorance. As a matter of fact, Cooper's red man bears a closer resemblance to the native of the woods than Leatherstocking does to the typical hunter and trapper of the frontier. Lowell's jibe applies with infinitely greater force to Cooper's contemporaries and imitators, especially sentimental Massachusetts ladies who, devoid of insight into aboriginal character, drew caricatures that have deservedly sunk into oblivion. Certainly, Cooper's Indians were not then, as they are not even now, in any danger of being supplanted.

Among the many writers who labored zealously in the field of Indian poetry and fiction, but without permanently fixing their conception of the native in the mind of the reading public, some deserve at least passing mention. John Esten Cooke, James Hall, N. M. Hentz, John Neal, Catherine M. Sedgwick, and D. P. Thompson among story-tellers, and Lydia H. Sigourney among poets, drew not a little of attention and applause in their own day. In traversing the whole field of Indian literature, the student is struck by the number and diversity of attempts in delineating the red man. The hundreds of works produced by aspiring writers are an eloquent testimony of the interest and fascination of aboriginal material. During the first half of the 19th century — even down to 1870 — the field was most assiduously cultivated, though it has not been neglected since.

The most dominant tribes and all sections of the country in fact have shared the interest of the writers. The New England and Virginia Indians have not even yet lost all of their fascination. The Iroquois, as the Romans among the tribes, play their part in Street and Cooper, in the latter exhibiting somewhat diabolical characteristics, but deserving a better fate as they embodied many of the nobler traits of the aborigines. The Algonquins are favorably represented in Cooper and Longfellow, in the latter's poem the hero curiously enough appearing under the confusing Iroquoian name. The intensely interesting cliff dwellers come to life in Proctor, Bandelier, and Garland, though even a Thoreau at his early date followed the explorations in the Southwest with not a little of interest. Noteworthy is the attention the Pacific slope received from various writers. Cooper and Irving at an early date describe several tribes, and in more recent times Mrs. Jackson and Joaquin Miller have bestowed upon others minute care. As would seem natural with the passing of the last frontier within the boundaries of the United States, the Sioux, as the Romans of the plains, have been thrust into the foreground. In Irving and Cooper they already played a conspicuous part, and of late Neihardt and Garland have singled them out as the last barrier to white penetration, the educated Indian himself entering as the chief witness for the defense.

Not a few authors rightly sensed the importance of environment and setting in aboriginal portrayal, though this alone does not guarantee ultimate success, as the case of Whittier obviously proves. The beautiful descriptions of the primeval forest found in Cooper, Street, Parkman, and Simms, and the faithful portraits of the Western prairies in Neihardt, Cooper, and Garland have permanently enriched American literature. In more recent decades emphasis upon local color and detailed study and portrayal of specific tribes mark an advance over most of the older writers who were too fond of vague generalizations. The Western Indian in particular has been the main beneficiary of this scientific and truly artistic interest, as exemplified conspicuously in Bandelier and Mary Austin, whose efforts have brought to life the natives of the Southwest. The danger to be guarded against would seem to be too great an emphasis upon environment and detail, lest action and pulsating human life be smothered under the avalanche of an immovable mass.

Of late years, dire necessity and fortune alike have thrust the native into the swirl of modern industrial life beside the agricultural, assigning him a new literary rôle. Thus the colorful Osage rolling in the wealth produced by the oil gushers of Oklahoma has recently appeared in Edna Ferber's *Cimarron*. Lo and behold, the poor and shunted native on his barren soil is reaping by a curious twist of fate a golden harvest, and his high-powered cars and flashing diamonds have elevated him to the status of the socially most ambitious white. Here as elsewhere powerful forces combine to usher in a new economic, political, and social era for the child of nature, who in his adaptation to this new-found freedom will more and more cease to be an Indian and become an integral part of white civilization. As such he will no longer serve as the subject of separate literary portrayal, and the picture of the native as reflected in American literature will then at last be finished, except in so far as master artists of the future may here and there retouch the immense canvas.

SELECTED BIBLIOGRAPHY

This bibliography lists writings quoted from or used in this study. It is not intended to be exhaustive. At times editions most accessible have been listed, though ordinarily the author has consulted first editions.

ALGER, W. R. Life of Edwin Forrest. 2 vols. Phil., 1877.
Anon. The Wept of the Wish-ton-Wish, A Drama. New York, 1856.
Athenaeum (London). No. 1463–. November 10, 17, 24, December 1, 15, 29, 1855.
AUSTIN, GEORGE LOWELL. Henry Wadsworth Longfellow. Boston, 1883.
AUSTIN, MRS. MARY. The Arrowmaker. New York, 1911.

BANDELIER, ADOLF F. The Delight Makers. New York, 1890.
BARKER, J. N. The Indian Princess; or, La Belle Sauvage. Phil., 1808.
BARNES, CHARLOTTE M. S. The Forest Princess; or, Two Centuries Ago. Phil., 1848.
BARTRAM, WILLIAM. Travels through North and South Carolina, Georgia, East and West Florida, the Cherokee Country, the Extensive Territories of the Muscogulges or Creek Confederacy, and the Country of the Chactaws. Phil., 1791.
BISSELL, BENJAMIN. The American Indian in English Literature of the Eighteenth Century. Yale Studies in English, LXVIII. New Haven, 1925.
BIRD, ROBERT MONTGOMERY. Nick of the Woods, or the Jibbenainosay. Rev. ed. New York, 1853.
Blackwood's Magazine, Feb. 26, 1856, pp. 135–36.
BLEEKER, ELIZA. History of Maria Kittle. New York, 1793.
BOYNTON, HENRY W. James Fenimore Cooper. New York, 1931.
BOYNTON, PERCY H. A History of American Literature. Boston, 1923.
BROILI, OTTO. Die Hauptquellen von Longfellows Song of Hiawatha. Wuerzburg, 1898.
BROUGHAM, JOHN. Metamora; or the Last of the Pollywoags. Boston, n. d.
——, Pocahontas; or The Gentle Savage. New York, 1856.
BROWN, CHARLES B. Edgar Huntley. Intr. by D. L. Clark. New York, 1928.
BROWNELL, W. C. American Prose Masters. New York, 1909.

SELECTED BIBLIOGRAPHY

BRYANT, WILLIAM CULLEN. Poetical Works. New York, 1925.
BYERS, S. H. M. Pocahontas, a Melodrama. n. pl., n. d.

CAIRNS, W. B. A History of American Literature. New York, 1830.
Cambridge History of American Literature. Ed. by Trent, Erskine, Sherman, Van Doren. 4 vols. New York, 1917–21.
CAMPBELL, W. S. The Plains Indian in Literature and in Life. In The Trans-Mississippi West, pp. 175–94. Boulder, 1930.
CASS, LEWIS. A review of Heckewelder's On the American Indians. N. A. Review, XXII, pp. 64–92.
——, A review of William Rawle's A Vindication of Rev. Mr. Heckewelder's History of the Indian Nations. N. A. Review, XXVI, pp. 336–76.
CATLIN, GEORGE. North American Indians. 2 vols. New York, 1844.
CHANNING, WILLIAM ELLERY. Thoreau: The Poet-Naturalist. Boston, 1873.
CHINARD, GILBERT. L' Amérique et le rêve exotique dans la littérature française au XVIIe et au XVIIIe siècle. Paris, 1913.
——, L' Exotisme américain dans la littérature française au XVIe siècle. Paris, 1911.
CHURCH, THOMAS. Entertaining Passages relating to King Philip's War. Boston, 1716.
CLARK, HAYDEN H. What Made Freneau the Father of American Poetry? Studies in Philology, XXVI, pp. 1–22.
COOPER, JAMES FENIMORE. The Deerslayer. Ed. by G. L. Paine. New York, 1927.
——, Notions of the Americans. Phil., 1828.
——, Works. 32 vols. Mohawk Edition. New York, 1912–.
COOPER, SUSAN FENIMORE. Pages and Pictures from the Writings of James Fenimore Cooper, with Notes. New York, 1861.
CRAWFORD, J. M. The Kalevala. Cincinnati, 1888.
CUSTIS, G. W. P. The Indian Prophecy. Georgetown, 1828.
——; Pocahontas; or, The Settlers of Virginia. Phil., 1830.

DEERING, NATH. Carabasset; or, The Last of the Norridgewoks. Portland, 1830.
DEFFEBACH, LEWIS. Oolaita; or, The Indian Heroine. Phil., 1821.
DE MILLE, WILLIAM C. Strongheart. New York, 1909.
DICKINSON, JONATHAN. Narrative of a Shipwreck in the Gulph of Florida. 6th ed. Stanford, N. Y., 1803.
DODDRIDGE, JOSEPH. Logan: The Last of the Race of Shikellemus, Chief of the Cayuga Nation. Buffalo Creek, Va., 1823.
DUNLAP, WILLIAM. A History of the American Theater. New York, 1832.

Duyckink, E. A. and G. L. Cyclopedia of American Literature. 2 vols. Phil., 1875.

Eastburn, James W., and Robert C. Sands. Yamoyden, a Tale of the Wars of King Philip. New York, 1820.
Emmons, Richard. Tecumseh; or, The Battle of the Thames. Phil., 1836.
Erskine, John. Leading American Novelists. New York, 1910.

Fairchild, H. N. The Noble Savage. New York, 1928.
Farley, Frank E. The Dying Indian. Kittredge Anniversary Papers, pp. 256–60. Boston, 1913.
Ferber, Edna. Cimarron. Garden City, 1930.
Fiske, John. Old Virginia and her Neighbors. 2 vols. Boston, 1897.
Foust, Clement E. The Life and Dramatic Works of Robert Montgomery Bird. New York, 1919.
Francis (Child), Lydia Maria. Hobomok, a Tale of Early Times. Boston, 1824.
Freneau, Philip. Poems. Ed. by F. L. Pattee. Princeton Historical Association. Princeton, 1902–07.
Friederici, Georg. Skalpieren und aehnliche Kriegsgebraeuche in Amerika. Braunschweig, 1906.

Gardiner, W. H. A review of The Spy. N. A. Review, XV, pp. 250–82.
———, A review of The Pioneers and The Last of the Mohicans. N. A. Review, XXIII, pp. 150–97.
Garland, Hamlin. The Book of the American Indian. New York, 1923.
———, The Captain of the Gray Horse Troop. New York, 1902.
———, Companions on the Trail. New York, 1931.
———, A Daughter of the Middle Border. New York, 1921.

Hazard, Lucy L. The Frontier in American Literature. New York, 1927.
Heckewelder, John. An Account of the History, Manners, and Customs of the Indian Nations Who Once Inhabited Pennsylvania and the Neighboring States. Phil., 1819.
Henry, W. W. The Settlement of Jamestown. Richmond, 1882.
Herold, A. L. James Kirke Paulding. New York, 1926.
Higginson, Thomas W. Contemporaries. Boston, 1899.
———, Henry Wadsworth Longfellow. Boston, 1902.
Hodge, Frederick W. Handbook of American Indians North of Mexico. 2 vols. Washington, 1907–10.
Hornblow, Arthur. A History of the Theatre in America. 2 vols. Phil., 1919.
House, Julius T. John G. Neihardt, Man and Poet. Wayne, Nebr., 1920.

SELECTED BIBLIOGRAPHY 303

HUBBARD, WILLIAM. The History of the Indian Wars in New England. Ed. by S. G. Drake. 2 vols. Roxberry, 1865.
HUTTON, LAURENCE. Curiosities of the American Stage. New York, 1891.
IRVING, WASHINGTON. Works. 40 vols. Knickerbocker Edition. New York, 1897.
JACKSON, HELEN HUNT. A Century of Dishonor. New York, 1881.
———, Ramona. Boston, 1884.
Jesuit Relations and Allied Documents. Travels and Explorations of the Jesuit Missionaries in New France, 1610–1791. Intr. by R. G. Thwaites. Ed. by E. Kenton. New York, 1925.
KEISER, ALBERT. Thoreau's Manuscripts on the Indians. Journal of English and Germanic Philology, XXVII, pp. 183–99.
KENNEDY, W. SLOANE. Henry W. Longfellow. Boston, 1882.
LEISY, E. E. The American Historical Novel before 1860. Abstract of Thesis, Urbana, 1923.
LONGFELLOW, HENRY WADSWORTH. Complete Poetical Works. Boston, 1893.
———, The Song of Hiawatha. Boston, 1855.
LONGFELLOW, SAMUEL. Life of Henry Wadsworth Longfellow. 3 vols. Boston, 1891.
LOSHE, L. D. The Early American Novel. New York, 1907.
LOUNSBURY, TH. R. James Fenimore Cooper. Boston, 1883.
MACOMB, ALEXANDER. Pontiac; or, The Siege of Detroit. Boston, 1835.
MASON, JOHN. A Brief History of the Pequot War. Ed. by Thomas Prince. Boston, 1736.
MATHER, INCREASE. History of King Philip's War. Boston, 1676.
MEDINA, L. H. Nick of the Woods. New York, n. d.
MILES, G. H. De Soto, the Hero of the Mississippi. MS. Univ. of Pa.
MILLER, JOAQUIN. Life Among the Modocs: Unwritten History. Hartford, 1873.
———, Memorie and Rime. New York, 1884.
———, Poetical Works. Ed. by S. P. Sherman. New York, 1923.
———, Shadows of Shasta. Chicago, 1881.
———, Works. Bear Edition. 6 vols. San Francisco, 1909.
MORTON, MRS. Quâbi; or, The Virtues of Nature. Boston, 1790.
MOSES, MONTROSE J. Representative Plays by American Dramatists. 3 vols. New York, 1918–21.
NEIHARDT, JOHN G. Collected Poems. New York, 1926.
———, Indian Tales and Others. New York, 1926.
———, The Lonesome Trail. New York, 1906.

ORR, CHARLES. History of the Pequot War, the Contemporary Account of Mason, Underhill, Vincent, and Gardiner. Notes and Intr. by Charles Orr. Cleveland, 1897.
OWEN, R. D. Pocahontas. New York, 1837.

PAINE, G. L. The Indians of the Leatherstocking Tales. Studies in Philology, XXIII, pp. 16–32.
PALFREY, J. G. A review of Yamoyden. N. A. Review, XII, pp. 466–88.
PARKMAN, FRANCIS. A review of the Author's Revised Edition of the Works of James Fenimore Cooper, 1851. N. A. Review, LXXIV, pp. 147–61.
——, Works. 20 vols. Champlain Edition. Boston, 1897.
PARRINGTON, V. L. Main Currents in American Thought. 3 vols. New York, 1927–30.
PATTEE, F. L. A History of American Literature. New York, 1909.
——, A History of American Literature since 1870. New York, 1915.
PAULDING, JAMES KIRKE. Koningsmarke, The Long Finne. New York, 1823.
PAYNE, L. W. History of American Literature. Chicago, 1919.
PICKERING, J. A review of Correspondence between Heckewelder and Duponceau respecting the Language of the American Indians. N. A. Review, IX, pp. 186–87.
PROCTOR, EDNA DEAN. The Song of the Ancient People. Boston, 1893.

QUINN, ARTHUR H. A History of the American Drama. 3 vols. New York, 1927.
——, Representative American Plays. New York, 1925.

REED, PERLEY I. Realistic Presentation of American Characters in Native American Plays prior to 1870. Columbus, 1918.
REES, JAMES. The Dramatic Authors of America. Phil., 1845.
——, Life of Edwin Forrest. Phil., 1874.
ROGERS, ROBERT. Ponteach; or, The Savages of America. Ed. by Allan Nevins. Chicago, 1914.
ROWLANDSON, MRS. MARY. A Narrative of the Captivity and Restoration of Mrs. Mary Rowlandson. Ed. by H. S. Nourse and J. E. Thayer. Lancaster, 1903.
RUSK, R. L. The Literature of the Middle Western Frontier. 2 vols. New York, 1925.
RUSSELL, J. ALMUS. Articles in periodicals listed in American Literature, IV, p. 451.

SANBORN, B. FR. The Life of Henry David Thoreau. Boston, 1917.
——, Thoreau. Boston, 1897.

SELECTED BIBLIOGRAPHY

SCHOOLCRAFT, HENRY R. Algic Researches. Vols. 1-2. New York, 1839.
——, History, Conditions and Prospects of the Indian Tribes of the United States. 6 vols. Phil., 1851-57.
——, The Myth of Hiawatha and Other Oral Legends. Phil., 1856.
——, Oneóta, or Characteristics of the Red Race of America. New York, 1845.
SIMMS, WILLIAM GILMORE. The Cassique of Accabee. 1849.
——, The Cassique of Kiawah. New York, 1859.
——, The Wigwam and the Cabin. New York, 1882.
——, The Yemassee. Rev. ed. New York, 1866.
SMITH, CAPTAIN JOHN. Generall Historie of Virginia, New England, and the Summer Isles. London, 1624.
——, A Map of Virginia. London, 1612.
——, New England Trials. London, 1622.
——, A True Relation of Virginia. Ed. by Charles Deane. Boston, 1866.
STONE, JOHN A. Metamora. Part of MS. in Forrest Home, Philadelphia.
STREET, ALFRED B. Frontenac: or the Atotarho of the Iroquois. New York, 1849.

TANNER, JOHN. Narrative of the Captivity and Adventures of John Tanner. New York, 1830.
TEN KATE. The Indian in Literature. Smithsonian Report 1921, pp. 507-28.
THOMPSON, STITH. The Indian Legend of Hiawatha. Publications of Modern Language Association of America, XXXVII, pp. 128-40.
THOREAU, HENRY D. Extracts Relating to the Indians in eleven MS. Notebooks in the Pierpont Morgan Library in New York City.
——, The Writings of Henry David Thoreau. 20 vols. Walden Edition. Boston, 1906.
TRENT, W. P. A Brief History of American Literature. New York, 1905.
——, William Gilmore Simms. New York, 1892.
TWAIN, MARK. Fenimore Cooper's Literary Offenses. N. A. Review, CLXI, pp. 1-12.

VESTAL, STANLEY. Sitting Bull. Boston, 1932.

WAGNER, HARR. Joaquin Miller and His Other Self. San Francisco, 1929.
WALCOT, CHARLES M. Hiawatha; or, Ardent Spirits and Laughing Water. New York, 1856.
WHITTIER, JOHN GREENLEAF. Complete Poetical Works. Boston, 1895.
WINGFIELD, EDWARD MARIA. A Discourse of Virginia. Ed. by Charles Deane. Boston, 1860.

INDEX

Abenakis, 211, 230
Adventures of Captain Bonneville, The, 52, 62–64
Afloat and Ashore, 107
Ages, The, 179
Alger, William, 75, 76
Algic Researches, 191, 196, 198, 212, 216
Algonquins, 68, 122, 123, 196, 198, 280, 298
America Independent, 31
American Museum, 28
American Village, 21, 29
Arboretum, 215
Arickaras, Rickarees, Rees, 61, 62, 64, 267, 268, 273
Arrowmaker, The, 97–99
Assiniboines, 266
Astor, John Jacob, 52, 55, 63
Astoria, 52, 55, 56, 63
Atala, 152, 206
Austin, George L., 191, 192
Austin, Mary, 97–99, 299

Bancroft, George, 205
Bandelier, Adolf F., 253–260, 298, 299
Barker, J. N., 70
Barnes, Charlotte M. S., 84
Bartram, William, 40, 212
Bird, Robert M., 95, 144–153, 296
Blackfeet, 57–60, 63, 64
Blackhawk, Chief, 191
Bleeker, Ann Eliza, 33
Bonneville, Capt., 62–64
Book of the American Indian, The, 279, 285–287, 292
Borderers and Squatters, 54, 109, 114–117, 119, 120, 137, 284, 286–291, 296
Bowles, William A., 28
Braddock, Gen., 73
Brevoort, Henry, 52
Bridal of Pennacook, The, 177, 178
Brief History of the Pequot War, A, 12
Brougham, John, 85–88, 295
Brown, Charles B., 33–37
Brown, John, 209
Bryant, William Cullen, 75, 178–180

Bulwer-Lytton, 253
Burial of the Minnisink, 189
Byers, S. H. M., 88, 89

Campbell, Thomas, 29, 142, 143
Captain of the Gray Horse Troop, The, 279, 286–292
Captivities, 17–20, 33, 108
Carabasset, 90, 91
Carey, Matthew, 28, 29
Caribbeana, 22
Cartier, 213
Cass, Gen. Lewis, 104–106, 143, 215
Cassique of Accabee, The, 155
Cassique of Kiawah, The, 157–162
Catawbas, 157
Catlin, George, 143, 200
Century of Dishonor, A, 249, 250
Chainbearer, The, 101, 112, 114, 115
Champlain, 213
Channing, William E., 209, 220
Charlevoix, 41, 103, 213
Chateaubriand, 144, 293
Cherokees, 28, 154, 155, 157, 231
Cheyennes, 281, 285–288
Chippewas, Ojibways, 128, 138–142, 198, 199, 201
Chocktaws, 157
Christianity and Religion, 10, 11, 14, 15, 24, 26, 39, 40, 50, 67, 69, 74, 77, 78, 81, 89, 90–92, 97, 98, 103, 112, 113, 115, 118, 120, 128, 132, 133, 138, 140, 142, 160, 172, 176, 185, 191, 203, 204, 213, 230, 231, 235, 243, 259, 283, 286, 287, 294, 296
Church, Thomas, 16
Cimarron, 299
Clark, Gen. George R., 57–59, 103, 151, 266
Cleveland, Grover, 250
Cliff dwellers, 253–263, 287
Colden, C., 103
Comanches, 239
Companions on the Trail, 279
Conanchet, 53, 109, 110, 143, 295
Conspiracy of Pontiac, The, 294

Contrast, The, 271
Cooke, John Esten, 298
Cooper, James Fenimore, 17, 25, 95, 96, 101–143, 163, 164, 215, 216, 294, 296–299
Cooper, Susan Fenimore, 102, 144
Coosaws, 271
Crazy Horse, Chief, 272–277
Creeks, 28, 40, 54, 154
Crows, 62, 63, 190
Custer, Gen., 272–274, 278, 281
Custis, G. W. P., 73–75, 84

Daughter of the Middle Border, A, 279, 292
De Mille, William C., 97, 99, 100
De Soto, 91, 92, 93
Deane, Charles, 5, 6
Deathsong of a Cherokee Indian, The, 27–29
Deathsongs, 25–29, 42
Deering, N., 90, 91
Deerslayer, The, 108, 117–121, 124, 128
Deffebach, Lewis, 89, 90
Delawares, 25, 35, 46–51, 55, 103–106, 116–118, 122–124, 128–130, 132, 133, 212, 215
Delight Makers, The, 253–260
Dickinson, John, 19, 20
Discourse of Virginia, A, 5
Disinterred Warrior, The, 179
Doddridge, Joseph, 93, 94
Dying Indian, or the Prophecy of King Tammany, The, 25, 29
Dying Indian: Tomo-Chequi, The, 25, 29, 38

Eastburn, James W., 38
Edgar Huntley, 33–37
Eliot, John, 10, 103
Emerson, Ralph Waldo, 205, 225
Emmons, William, 94, 95, 296
Emotions, 54, 60, 62, 111, 124, 156, 157, 159, 171, 172, 177, 179, 206, 239, 295
Evangeline, 265
Expedition Through the Upper Mississippi to Itaska Lake, 212

Fable for Critics, A, 297
Farley, Prof. E., 26
Female Review, The, 33
Ferber, Edna, 299
Fielding, Henry, 46
Fiske, John, 7, 8, 261

Forest Princess, or Two Centuries Ago, The, 84
Forrest, Edwin, 73, 75–81, 144, 295
Foxes, 190
Francis (Child), Lydia Maria, 44, 45, 108
Franciscans, 252
Fredoniad: or Independence Preserved, The, 95
Freiligrath, Ferdinand, 192, 199, 204
Frémont, John C., 233
French attitude, 67–69, 112, 118, 123, 124, 130, 132, 138, 176, 177, 181–184, 187, 188, 211
Freneau, Philip, 21–32
Frontenac: or the Atotarho of the Iroquois, 181–188
Funeral Tree of the Sokokis, The, 177
Future Life, 22, 24–26, 179

Gall, Chief, 273, 274, 277
Gardiner, W. H., 104, 105
Garland, Hamlin, 279–292, 298, 299; short stories, 285–287
Generall Historie of Virginia, 1–3, 5, 7, 74
Gerstaecker, Frederick, 214
Great Emerald Land, The, 239
Grinnell, George B., 143

Half-breeds, 53, 56, 101, 206, 233, 251, 265, 266, 279, 296
Hall, James, 298
Halleck, Fitz-Greene, 75
Hamor, Ralph, 6, 7
Heckewelder, Rev. John, 103–106, 117, 118, 122, 123, 129, 131–133, 190, 192, 212, 215, 216
Hendrik, Chief, 67
Hentz, N. M., 298
Hiawatha, 197, 198
Hiawatha. See *Song of Hiawatha, The*
Hiawatha; or Ardent Spirits and Laughing Water, 96, 97
History, Conditions, and Prospects of the Indian Tribes of the United States, 196, 212, 216
History, Manners, and Customs of the Indian Nations, 103, 122, 190, 215, 216
History of King Philip's War, 17
History of Maria Kittle, 33
History of the Mission of the United Brethren, 215

INDEX

Hobomok, A Tale of Early Times, 44, 45
Holmes, Oliver Wendell, 194
Homer, 107
Hontan, Baron, 211
Hooker, Rev. Thomas, 15
Hubbard, William, 38
Humor, 11, 46, 47, 85–88, 96, 97, 164, 292
Hunt, Thomas, 11
Hunter, Mrs. John, 27, 28
Hurons, 26, 110, 113, 118–120, 123, 124, 126, 127, 129, 130–134

Idealization, 1, 8, 10, 21, 22, 34, 37–39, 52–54, 64, 76, 101, 104–107, 117, 125, 126, 132, 142, 143, 147, 152, 153, 158, 190, 202, 207, 233–248, 284, 289, 293, 294, 296, 297
Indian at the Burial Place of his Fathers, The, 179
Indian Burying Ground, The, 29, 30
Indian Convert, The, 24
Indian Girl's Lament, The, 179
Indian Hunter, The, 189
Indian Princess, or La Belle Sauvage, The, 70
Indian Prophecy, The, 73, 75
Indian Story, An, 179
Indian Student, or Force of Nature, The, 23, 24
Indian Tales and Others, 264, 265
Iroquois, 118–121, 123, 130–132, 136, 181–188, 196–198, 200, 206, 212, 298
Irving, Washington, 52–64, 294, 298

Jackson, Helen Hunt, 249–252, 298
Jeckayra, 189
Jesuit Relations, 211–213, 215
Jesuits, 90, 91, 176, 211, 213
Johnson, 11
Journal, Thoreau's, 209, 210, 218–231

Kalevala, The, 192, 193, 195, 196
King Philip, 15–17, 38–40, 42, 52, 53, 75–81, 85, 108–111, 175, 190, 295
King Philip or the Sagamore, 144
Kit Carson, 233
Kit Carson's Ride, 239
Knickerbocker's History of New York, 52
Koningsmarke, The Long Finne, 46–51

Last Days of Pompeii, The, 253

Last of the Mohicans, The, 25, 104–106 108, 121–129, 130, 138
Last Taschastas, The, 240
Lewis, Capt. M., 57, 103, 266
Life Among the Modocs, 235, 238–248
Life of Henry Wadsworth Longfellow, 192
Life of Washington, 52
Liquor, 47, 50, 111, 117, 130–132, 140, 141, 147, 165, 166, 176, 185, 229
Logan, The Last of the Race of Shikellemus, 93, 94, 295
Lonesome Trail, The, 264, 265
Longfellow, Henry Wadsworth, 19, 96, 97, 189–208, 216, 265, 298
Longfellow, Samuel, 192
Loskiel, Rev. George H., 215
Loudon, 215
Love, inter-racial, 4, 38, 39, 42, 44, 45, 49, 71–73, 84, 89, 95, 99, 100, 107–110, 125, 126, 131, 137, 155, 156, 234, 239, 244–247, 266, 267, 285
Love, intra-racial, 22, 61, 79, 96–97, 116, 117, 131, 165, 166, 177–180, 201, 202, 204, 240
Lowell, James Russell, 297

Macomb, Gen. Alexander, 69, 70
Mahicans, 122, 123
Main Travelled Roads, 292
Maine Woods, The, 209, 217–231
Map of Virginia, A, 5, 6
Mason, John, 12–15
Massasoit, 15, 75, 76, 78
Mather, Increase, 17
Matthews, Brander, 291
Medina, Louisa, 95, 144
Memorie and Rime, 235–237
Mercedes of Castile, 107, 108
Metamora; or the Last of the Pollywoags, 85
Metamora, or the Last of the Wampanoags, 17, 73, 75–81, 85, 144
Miles, George H., 91–93
Miller, Joaquin, 233–248, 296, 298
Mingoes. See Hurons and Iroquois
Mission Indians, 249–252
Modocs, 234–236, 241, 244, 245, 247
Mogg Megone, 176, 177
Mohawks, 14, 67, 111, 116, 197
Mohegans, 12, 15, 103, 104, 117, 123, 128
Mohicans, 117, 121–129
Montcalm, 122, 127

INDEX

Monument Mountain, 179
Moravians, 103, 104, 118, 132, 215, 216
Mormons, 247
Morton, Mrs., 26
Mound builders, 178, 179, 212
Mount Agiochook, 175
Murdoch, James E., 91

Narragansetts, 12, 13, 15, 17, 109, 110
Narrative of a Shipwreck in the Gulph of Florida, 19, 20
Narrative of the Captivity and Adventures of John Tanner, 19, 198
Narrative of the Captivity and Restauration of Mrs. Mary Rowlandson, 17–20
Narrative of the Indian Wars, 38
Narvaez, 8, 92
Nature, 22, 23, 31, 34, 138, 194, 199, 205, 206, 222, 223, 225–228, 245
Navajos, 254, 255, 257–259, 287
Neihardt, John G., 264–278, 298, 299
New England Trials, 1
New Spain, or Love in Mexico, 27
Nez Percéds. See Pierced Nose
Nick of the Woods (a drama), 95
Nick of the Woods, or the Jibbenainosay, 144–153
Norridgewoks, 90, 91
Notions of the Americans, 102, 133

O'Connor's Child, 29
Oak Openings, The, 101, 138–142
Oglethorpe, Gen., 32
Omahas, 61, 189, 264, 269
Oneidas, 102, 123
Oneóta, or Characteristics of the Red Race of America, 196, 212
Onondagas, 111, 113–117, 182, 197, 198
Oolaita, or the Indian Heroine, 89, 90
Ortiz, John, 8
Osages, 54, 55, 299
Ottowas, 66, 67, 93
Owen, Robert D., 82, 83

Palfrey, Dr., 41
Parkman, Francis, 126, 142, 143, 294, 299
Parsons, T. W., 194, 205
Pathfinder, The, 128, 129
Pattee, Fred L., 28, 29
Paulding, James K., 46–51
Pawnee Chief, The, 13
Pawnees, 53–55, 61, 133–138

Pends Oreilles, 63
Penn, William, 25, 50, 51, 103, 123, 247
Penobscots, 207, 231
Pentucket, 177
Pequots, 11–15, 75, 78, 123
Peruvians, 213
Pickering, J., 104
Pictures of Columbus, The, 122
Piegans, 268
Pierced Nose, 62, 63, 274
Pilgrims, 10–19, 161. See also Puritans
Pioneers, The, 103, 108, 131, 164
Piutes, 239
Pocahontas, 1–9, 70–74, 82–84, 87–89, 295
Pocahontas, a Historical Drama, 82–84
Pocahontas, a Melo-Drama, 88, 89
Pocahontas, or the Gentle Savage, 86–88
Pocahontas, or the Settlers of Virginia, 73, 74, 84
Poncas, 61, 249
Ponteach, or the Savages of America, 66–69
Pontiac, 66–70, 295
Pontiac, or the Siege of Detroit, 69, 70
Pottawattamies, 138–142
Powhatan, Chief, 2–4, 71–74, 86–89, 295
Prairie, The, 106, 108, 128, 133–138
Prairies, The, 178
Prince, Thomas, 15
Proctor, Edna Dean, 260–263, 298
Purchas, Samuel, 7
Puritan Family, The, 109
Puritans, 10–19, 39, 40, 43, 53, 108–111, 164, 173, 293

Quâbi, or the Virtues of Nature, 26, 27
Quakers, 46, 50, 146, 148, 150, 151, 233, 250, 286
Queres, 254, 255, 258, 259, 286
Quinn, Arthur H., 70, 76, 78

Raleigh, Walter, 84
Rallé, Râle, 90, 91, 176
Ramona, 249–252
Realism, 10, 11, 18–20, 24, 25, 30, 33–37, 43, 47–50, 57–62, 66, 67, 83, 90, 94, 97–100, 126, 130–132, 143–153, 162, 163, 171, 180, 207–232, 279, 285, 291, 293, 296
Redskins, The, 101, 112, 115–117
Rees, James, 85
Reid, Mayne, 253

INDEX

Reservations, 143, 230, 233, 235–238, 244, 265, 282–285, 287, 296
Ritson, Joseph, 27
Rogers, Robert, 66–70
Rolfe, John, 4, 71–74, 83, 84, 88, 89
Romanticism, 1, 8, 11, 21, 22, 30–32, 34, 36, 37, 40, 41, 44, 45, 52–54, 71–73, 99, 105, 108, 117, 121, 122, 133, 143, 151, 155, 156, 173, 199, 204, 207, 233–253, 293, 296, 297
Roosevelt, Theodore, 289, 291
Roughing It, 297
Rousseau, 22, 293, 294
Rowlandson, Mrs. Mary, 17–20

Sanborn, 210, 217
Sands, Robert C., 38
Sassacus, 11, 12, 14
Satanstoe, 101, 112, 113
Scalps and scalping, 35, 37, 60, 68, 79, 94, 110–113, 118–120, 124, 125, 127, 129, 130, 131, 135, 136, 138–140, 148–150, 152, 155, 157, 161, 164, 178, 182, 258
Schoolcraft, Henry R., 191, 192, 195–198, 200, 206, 207, 212, 216
Scott, Walter, 194, 206
Sedgwick, Catherine M., 108, 298
Select Collection of English Songs with their Original Airs, A, 28
Shadows of Shasta, The, 235
Shakespeare, William, 41
Shastas, 243, 244, 247
Shawnees, 145, 148
Sherman, Stuart P., 247
Shoshones, 238
Sigourney, Lydia H., 298
Silent Eaters, The, 279–285
Simms, William G., 154–174, 296, 299
Sioux, 55, 61, 89, 90, 133–138, 198, 201, 217, 268–285, 287–292
Sitting Bull, 270, 274, 277, 279–282, 283–285, 295
Sketch Book, The, 52
Sketches of American History, 22
Smith, Capt. John, 1–9, 11, 71, 74, 82–84, 86–89, 103, 212
Snowbound, 175
Son of the Middle Border,. A, 292
Song of Creation, The, 239
Song of Hiawatha, The, 19, 189–208, 216, 261, 265
Song of Hugh Glass, The, 265–269
Song of the Ancient People, The, 260–263

Song of the Indian Wars, The, 266, 269–278
Song of the Three Friends, The, 265–267
Spy, The, 104
St. Francis Indians, 211, 233
Stanley, Lord Derby, 121
Stockbridges, 122
Stone, John A., 75, 85, 144
Street, Alfred B., 181–188, 206, 298, 299
Strongheart, 97, 99, 100
Sumner, Charles, 195
Superstitions, 41–43, 54, 55, 94, 134, 141, 254, 259, 283, 284
Susquehannocks, 71–73

Tale of the Tall Alcalde, The, 238, 239, 246
Tamenund, 25, 118, 122
Tanner, John, 192, 199
Taylor, Bayard, 197
Tecumseh, Chief, 95, 139, 295
Tecumseh: or the Battle of the Thames, 94, 95
Tehuas, 255, 257–259
Ten Kate, 143, 205
Thompson, D. P., 298
Thompson, Stith, 204
Thoreau, Henry D., 209–232, 296, 298
To a Driving Cloud, 189
Toltecs, 213, 226
Tom Jones, 46
Tomo-Checki, The Creek Indian in Philadelphia, 32
Torture, 26–29, 48, 56, 64, 68, 71, 111, 120, 146, 147, 151, 172, 187, 225
Tour of the Prairies, A, 52, 53, 56
Travels in America, 57
Travels through North and South Carolina, etc., 40
True Relation, A, 3–6
Tuckerman, 133
Tuscaluza, Chief, 92
Tuscaroras, 111, 112, 130
Twain, Mark, 163, 296, 297
Tyler, Royall, 27

Uncas, 12, 13, 15, 110, 111, 122
Underhill, 12–14

Van Buren, Martin, 85
Voyages, Baron Hontan's, 211

Walcot, Charles M., 96, 97
Walden, 209, 218, 231, 232

Wampanoags, 15, 17, 78, 79, 109, 175
Warren, Henry, 210
Washington, George, 73, 132
Wayside Inn, The, 194
Webster, 70
Week on the Concord and Merrimac Rivers, A, 209, 218
Wept of the Wish-ton-Wish, The, 17, 101, 108–111
Wept of the Wish-ton-Wish, The (a drama), 95, 96
Whittier, John Greenleaf, 175–178, 261, 299
Wigwam and the Cabin, The, 155

Wild Sports in the Far West, 214
Williams, Roger, 10
Wingfield, Edward Maria, 5, 7, 89
Women, 48, 49, 97–99, 117, 118, 120, 126, 131, 135, 137, 160, 165–169, 199, 234, 236, 240, 241, 243–247, 249–252, 266–268
Wyandots, 145
Wyandotté, 101, 111, 112

Yamoyden, 17, 38–44, 206, 296
Yankee in Canada, A, 211
Yemassee, The, 157, 162–174
Yemassees, 157–174

Kirtley Library
Columbia College
8th and Rogers
Columbia, MO. 65201